Advanced Apex Programming in Salesforce

Fourth Edition

By

Dan Appleman

Desaware Publishing
San Jose, California

Editor: Marian Kicklighter

Fourth Edition

ISBN: 978-1-936754-12-0
Library of Congress Control Number: 2018909218

Printed in the United States of America*.

www.AdvancedApex.com

* Copies purchased in countries outside of the U.S. may have been printed locally using print on demand technology.

Contents

Introduction

This book is not a rehash of the Salesforce Apex language documentation.

I just wanted to get that out of the way. I know there is sometimes value in the kind of book where 90% of the content is a rephrasing of the documentation and only 10% is new and interesting – a good author can organize information to make it easier for beginners to learn. But they are frustrating for intermediate and advanced developers who have to sift endlessly through familiar content to find one or two nuggets of new material.

So I'm going to assume that you either have read, or can read, the Salesforce Apex language documentation. If you are new to Apex, you will find this book helpful – especially if you are coming to Apex from another language – but it is not a tutorial and will not replace the Apex documentation. If you have Apex programming experience, I'm confident you'll find material here that will at the very least prove thought provoking, if not occasionally mind-blowing.

This book is about design patterns, best practices, and creative solutions to the kinds of problems developers face out in the real world.

You see, language documentation is generally written by the language team (or their technical writers) – which is good, because they know the language best. But the language team members are rarely application developers – that's not their job.

White-papers and application notes are generally written by technical evangelists and consultants who often do have real-world experience, but are limited by the focus and format of the particular white paper or article. Short articles (of which I've written many) serve a purpose, but are often limited in the level of depth they can achieve.

If you want to bring together real-world experience in a format that allows for as much depth as necessary, and organizes the information in such a way that concepts build on each other to really teach the material – you need a book. You need a book written by someone who actually writes production code, both as a consultant for individual clients, and as a developer of applications for distribution.

viii

Which brings me to the story how I came to write this book.

For most of my career, I was a developer on Microsoft platforms – proficient in C and C++, Visual Basic, VB .NET and C#. I ran (and still run) the company Desaware, that published software for .NET developers (desaware.com) and now publishes my books (desawarepublishing.com). I also wrote a number of programming books, and spent quite a few years on the speaker circuit - presenting at conferences that focused on Microsoft technologies.

About eleven years ago, a Salesforce consultant I know needed an Apex trigger written, and since I was one of the few programmers she knew, she asked me to take a look. Writing that first trigger was certainly easy enough – though I suspect I'd be embarrassed by the code if I looked at it now. I found myself spending more and more time working in Apex – I found it to be both challenging and fun.

About eight years ago, I joined her and two others to establish a new company, Full Circle Insights, to develop a new Salesforce application related to marketing and sales data and analytics. As CTO, I designed and built the application – which evolved into a very large and sophisticated native AppExchange app (an app that runs entirely on the Force.com platform). In doing so, I learned a lot.

As I have always enjoyed sharing what I learn, I ended up writing this book. It contains all of the things that I wish I had known eight years ago when I first started working in Apex. Things that I learned the hard way. Things that are either not found in the documentation, or are hidden in a footnote somewhere when they should be plastered across an entire page in bold flashing neon.

Think of this as a companion to the Apex Developer Guide – a commentary if you will. The focus is on the core language and design patterns. These are the essential foundations that you need to work effectively in Apex with the various platform features such as Lightning, VisualForce, and so forth (topics that are important, and deserving of their own books, but are not covered here).

Parts of this book focus on concepts – ways of thinking that will be fairly easy to follow, even for relative beginners and those completely new to Apex. But parts of this book focus more on advanced design patterns, and to really understand them, you'll need to dig into the code, and preferably install and experiment with the samples. You may need to refer back to the language documentation. You may even find parts of the book to be too hard to follow on a first reading. In truth, the book would hardly deserve the word "Advanced" in the title if this were not the case. If you do find yourself getting stuck, skip or scan a section and then move on. You'll find it easier to digest the second time through.

By the time you're done, I think you will find it was well worth the effort.

Dan Appleman

dan@desawarepublishing.com

Note to Readers of Previous Editions

The Salesforce platform is updated three times a year. Some of the updates are minor, some more significant, and some lead to radical changes in what most would consider to be "best practices". Best practices are tricky – you can't assume that just because something is new, it represents the best way to do something.

Not only has the platform changed, but my own experience has changed – or put another way, I keep learning as well. And since this is a book born of real-world experience, those new experiences are reflected in each new edition, along with those new platform features that seem truly useful.

In preparing this edition, I went through every word of text and every line of code. Some of the changes are structural – I've tried to be more consistent in naming conventions (while remaining true to my own belief that names should be descriptive). Keep in mind that Apex is a case-insensitive language, so any casing errors that may remain will not impact the functionality of the examples. And while there are numerous changes scattered throughout the text and code, here are the areas where the changes for this edition were most significant:

All chapters: Any place where discussion of Salesforce orgs, features, or the user interface comes into play, the primary focus is now on Salesforce DX and Lightning.

Chapter 2: The section on "Controlling Program Flow" has been largely rewritten with a new example.

Chapter 3: The sections on "CPU Time Limits", "Benchmarking", "24-hour Limits" and "Other Platform Limits" are new or have been rewritten.

Chapter 5: There's a new discussion on detecting duplicate fields in dynamic SOQL queries.

Chapter 6: The trigger framework has been enhanced, with particular attention to handling record DML updates across multiple trigger handlers (a subject discussed in previous editions but not actually demonstrated).

Chapter 7: New coverage of platform events.

Chapter 9 is completely new. The previous chapters 9-12 are now chapter 10-13 and the following paragraphs refer to them by their new chapter number.

Chapter 10: Additional discussion of platform events.

Chapter 11: Revised recommendations for unit tests and managed packages.

Chapter 13: Updated for Salesforce DX

With regards to sample code, previous editions of the book provided an unmanaged package to install code as well as the zipped metadata. This edition provides neither.

Instead, when you download the sample code you'll see it includes a git repository. Each chapter has a branch in Salesforce DX format that you can check out when learning that particular chapter. Some chapters include multiple commits to mark different steps or variations of the code illustrated in the chapter.

This approach simplifies the sample code – at each commit or branch you'll see the correct code for that particular part of the book, instead of having to dig through all of the code to find which components match those for a particular chapter or part of a chapter.

Salesforce DX represents both the future and today's best practice for Apex development, so my assumption is that anyone reading this book will be either familiar with it, or ready to make that transition. If you are new to Salesforce DX, there are numerous resources available to get started including Trailhead. I also assume that you have some basic familiarity with git. If you are new to git, I encourage you to use a git UI such as SourceTree which makes it easy to checkout branches and to see the files and changes in each commit.

Finally, Salesforce.com has a habit of rebranding the platform for reasons that are beyond my comprehension. When the third edition came out, Force.com was in the processing of becoming the "Salesforce Platform". At this time, the latest rebranding is to the "Lightning Platform". For the purposes of this edition, the three terms are used interchangeably.

Sample Code

You can download the sample code for this book from the book's website at AdvancedApex.com/samplecode. It is provided as a directory containing a git repository. Each branch contains a chapter in Salesforce DX format.

Depending on the chapter, progress through the chapter is represented by commits which you can check out to obtain the source code at that point in time. The commit description will match the section in the book.

The sample code for some chapters includes a permission set named "Advanced Apex" which you can assign to the current user to quickly obtain access to fields or other elements used by the examples. In other cases, you may need to explicitly set field or tab permissions.

When switching between chapters, it will generally be easiest to create a new scratch org rather than trying to push changes directly – though in many cases checking out a new branch and pushing the source code will work.

For those who are not familiar with git, I recommend using Sourcetree (https://www.sourcetreeapp.com), which is an excellent GUI on top of git.

You will need to install the sample code to follow some of the content in this book – the book does not contain the complete listings of all the sample code.

Advanced Apex Programming in Salesforce

Fourth Edition

Part I – Thinking in Apex

What is a computer language?

Ok, I know - that's a stupid question to start with. Of course you know what a computer language is. If you didn't, you'd hardly be reading a book that claims to be an advanced programming book.

At the same time, it's a useful question for exactly that reason. Because you do know what a computer language is, you'll probably be grateful if I don't waste your time answering that question. In fact, it brings to mind a long list of questions and introductory material that are not worth discussing at all, either because you should know them, or because you can easily find them in the documentation.

So let's begin with a partial list of material that I won't try to teach you.

Beyond Syntax

When we talk about computer languages in the context of actual software development, we're really talking about three different things:

- Language syntax – the actual text of the language.
- Language semantics – what that text does when it executes.
- Language platform (or framework) – what resources are available to the language, and how the language interacts with the underlying system.

Of these, this book will almost completely ignore the first item. If you've used Apex at all, you're probably well familiar with its syntax. If you are migrating from another language, suffice to say that Apex is syntactically similar to Java or C#, with most of the constructs you would expect from a modern object-oriented language, including support for single inheritance and interfaces.

Unlike Java or C#, Apex is not case sensitive. Some professional developers are offended by this. Having years of experience in both C# and Visual Basic (which is also not case sensitive), I'll take the case insensitive language any day. In my view, having to keep track of case is pointless labor, and anyone who uses case to distinguish between two variables or language elements is committing a mortal sin. But that's just my opinion – yours may differ.

In terms of semantics, we'll largely ignore the core language semantics. Most of the language constructs: control flow structures, operators, variable declarations, and so on, work exactly as you would expect. As of API 43, it even has a Switch statement!

In fact, Apex is so similar to other languages, that at first glance you might think that it will be a quick and easy migration. And in truth, it can be an easy migration – but only if you recognize a few areas that are not only different, but different in huge, fundamental ways.

Most of this book will be dealing with the third item on the list – the interaction of the language with the platform. But the rest of this part of the book will focus on the four key concepts that you must understand in order to succeed in Apex programming:

- Execution Contexts
- Static Variables
- Bulk Patterns
- Limits

These concepts dominate every aspect of software development under Apex. Because of these concepts, Apex programming involves radically different design patterns and architectures than Java and C#, even though their syntax and even semantics are similar.

In a way, this is like learning a spoken language. You can memorize words and phrases. But you don't really know the language until you start thinking and dreaming in it. My goal in this chapter is to help you take the words and phrases that you know from the reference documentation or other languages, and learn to think in Apex.

1 – The Execution Context

The execution context is one of the key defining concepts in Apex programming. It influences every aspect of software development on the Force.com platform.

An execution context has two characteristics:

- It defines the scope and lifetime of static variables.
- It defines the context for those governor limits that are reset between execution contexts.

I'll be discussing both static variables and limits in more depth later. For now, the key facts to remember (and I assure you, once you start working in Apex, you will never forget them) are:

- Static variables are maintained throughout an execution context, and are unique to an execution context.
- Many (but not all) limits are reset between execution contexts. For example, if governor limits restrict you to 100 database queries in an execution context, each execution context can have 100 database queries. Different types of execution contexts may have different limits.
- You can know when an execution context starts. You generally can't know when it ends.

Running Apex Code

An execution context begins when one of a number of possible external events or operations happen that have the ability to start running Apex code. These include:

- A database trigger: Triggers can occur on insertion, update, deletion or undeletion of many standard Salesforce objects and all custom objects.
- Future call (asynchronous call): Future calls can be requested from Apex code. They run with extended limits.

- Queueable Apex: Similar to a future call, this is another mechanism for running code asynchronously.
- Scheduled Apex: You can implement an Apex class that can be called by the system on a scheduled basis.
- Batch Apex: You can implement a class designed to process large numbers of database records.
- Platform Events: Apex can trigger on platform events – Salesforce's enterprise messaging queue.
- Web service: You can implement a class that can be accessed via SOAP or REST from an external site or from JavaScript on a web page.
- VisualForce and Lightning components: Your VisualForce pages and Lightning components can execute Apex code in controllers to retrieve or set page properties or execute methods.
- Lightning Processes and Flows: These are declarative programming tools that can call methods in Apex classes.
- Global Apex: You can expose a global method that can be called from other Apex code.
- Anonymous Apex: Apex code can be compiled and executed dynamically from the Developer Console, Force.com IDE or through an external web-service call.

When Apex code starts executing as a result of any of these events or operations, it runs within an execution context. If the event or operation was caused by Apex code, or is part of a system process, the code will continue to run in the same execution context that caused the event or operation.

I know that sounds confusing. Let's look at some examples.

Consider the simple case of a trigger on the update of a Lead object. In the trivial case of an absolutely new organization with just one trigger, the execution context begins when your trigger code begins to run, and ends when your code exits as shown in Figure 1-1.

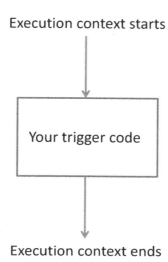

Figure 1-1 – Simple execution context

What if you have multiple triggers on lead insertion? This is not uncommon. Code in organizations tends to evolve over time, and it's very common for one developer to build a new trigger on the same event, rather than risk modifying (and breaking) trigger code written by another developer. Now you can end up with the scenario shown in Figure 1-2.

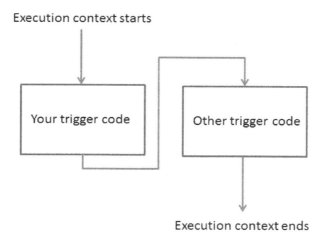

Figure 1-2 –Execution context with two triggers

As you can see, both triggers run in the same execution context. So they share the same set of limits (as long as they are in the same application – more on that later), and the same set of static variables.

This seems simple enough. But what if this particular organization has a workflow on the lead that does a field update? Now you may end up with the scenario shown in Figure 1-3.

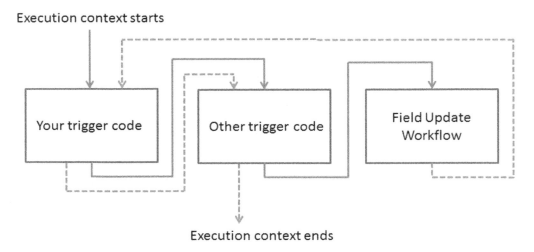

Figure 1-3 –Execution context with two triggers and a workflow

As you can see, the field update workflow not only runs in the same execution context, it can cause the triggers to execute again within the same context.

This brings up an interesting question. How can you know if your trigger is executing for the first time, or if it is executing again for the same update because of a workflow or other trigger?

This is where static variables come into play. Remember, their lifetime and scope are defined by the execution context. So, if you had a static variable defined in a class "myclass" thus:

```
public Static Boolean firstcall = false;
```

You could use the following design pattern in your trigger to determine if this was the first or subsequent call for this execution context.

```
if(!myclass.firstcall)
{
    // First call into trigger
    myclass.firstcall = true;
}
else
{
    // Subsequent call into trigger
}
```

This design pattern turns out to be extremely important, as you will see later.

Let's consider the ramifications of what you have just seen:

- You can have multiple triggers on an event, but have no control over the order in which they execute.
- Limits are shared within an Execution Context; thus you may be sharing limits with other code over which you have no control, and which may be added after yours is built and tested.
- Workflows, Flows and Lightning Processes, which can be created by non-programmers, can impact the order and execution of your Apex code in unpredictable ways, even causing your code to execute again for the same object and within the same execution context.

At this point, if you are coming to Apex from another language, you might be feeling a certain amount of shock. On other platforms, you, the developer, are largely in control of your application. User input may be unpredictable and have to be accounted for, but you know how to do that. It's not as if users can modify the underlying behavior of the application, or add code that interacts with your application. Even if you do have a plug-in model or API, those using it will be (hopefully) knowledgeable and expected to follow your specifications, guidelines and documentation.

But Salesforce.com was designed to minimize the need for custom software. The Salesforce.com logo is "no software". So there are a great many things that users can do that can impact the code that you write. Because execution contexts are shared, there are things that other developers can do that can impact the code that you write.

And by impact, I mean break.

But don't let this thought scare you. You'll quickly adjust to the idea that your finely crafted code can be broken by a junior system administrator writing a careless validation rule. It's just part of the territory – and part of what makes Apex coding a fun challenge.

My point here isn't to scare you, but to emphasize my earlier point. Apex may look like Java, but because of fundamental platform differences, it requires a different set of design patterns and different approaches for architecting applications.

2 – Static Variables

In most computer languages, a class static variable is essentially a global variable that is associated with a particular class. That means that it exists regardless of whether you've actually created an instance of the class, and that a single instance of the variable is shared by all instances of the class and, in fact, by the entire application.

So, for example, if you had the following class:

```
public class myclass {
    public static int myclassstatic;
}
```

You could access `myclass.myclassstatic` anywhere in your code and always access the same variable. Developers are accustomed to using static variables in a variety of design patterns, such as sharing data between classes, counting or maintaining lists of class instances (objects), or as a way of organizing and controlling access to general purpose global variables. Developers of multithreaded applications also know to take care to synchronize access to static variables, in order to avoid race conditions or data corruption.

That's the case with Java, C#, C++, VB .NET and virtually every block structured language.

Except for Apex.

The difference between static variables in Apex and most other languages is simple in concept, but has a huge impact on the way they are used.

Static variables in Apex have execution context scope and lifetime.

In other words, static variables can only be accessed from within the execution context in which they are created, and are deleted when the execution context completes.

Let's first consider what this means in terms of traditional static variable design patterns.

- Static variables do not persist information between execution contexts. They cannot be used to keep track of the overall execution of your application, or to cache data or objects for use while your application is running. In fact, Apex does not currently support the equivalent of application or session variables at all. Anything you wish to persist must be stored in database objects or custom settings (more on that later).

- There is no need for synchronization. A given execution context runs on a single thread, so static variables are, in effect, the equivalent of thread local storage – each thread has its own copy of these variables and there is no need to synchronize access. Which is a good thing; given that Apex has no real synchronization objects.

But if Apex eliminates some design patterns that are common in other languages, it offers some new ones that are essential for every Apex developer to understand.

Maintaining Data Across Trigger Invocations

Earlier in this chapter, you saw an example of how a static variable could be used to remember that you had already executed the code in an after-update trigger.

Here's another common design pattern.

Let's say you have a computationally intensive operation that you wish to perform in a number of different scenarios. For example, reassigning account ownership based on some rules a user has defined. You might want to do this after a field value has changed on the account, or any of its contacts or opportunities.

It's very common to move longer operations into future calls – asynchronous operations that can be queued by your code. Future calls execute at some indeterminate time in the future, but because the platform can schedule them based on server load, they are granted higher limits than other execution contexts, and are thus ideal for computationally intensive tasks.

You can only make up to fifty future calls from an execution context, and you can't make a future call from a future context. Because your code may share an execution context with other code, ideally you only want to invoke your future call once.

So in this scenario, you wish to initiate your future call from a number of different triggers or conditions. How can you keep track of whether or not you have already initiated the call? The answer: use a static variable.

But how do you use it? You can't use it as a flag to indicate that a future call is required. That's because in Apex you have no way of knowing that you are exiting an execution context. You can, however, use it as a flag to indicate that the call has already been made.

Here's a typical implementation of this design pattern:

```
public class SomeFutureOperations {

    private static Boolean futureCallCalled = false;

    public static void doFutureCall()
    {
        if(futureCallCalled || System.isFuture()) return;
        futureCallCalled = true;
        actualFutureCall();
    }

    @future
    private static void actualFutureCall()
    {
        // Actual async code here
        system.debug('actualFutureCall async operation');
    }
}
```

You'll learn more about asynchronous design patterns in Chapter 7.

Caching Data

In the previous example, you saw how a static variable can "remember" a value throughout the duration of an execution context in order to avoid one kind of limit. In this example, you'll see how they can be used to avoid another kind of limit.

Consider the case where you have one or more triggers or methods, and the execution depends in some way on the user who triggered the execution. You might be storing different field values based on the user. Or you might be prohibiting certain operations, or performing additional operations based on the user.

In this scenario, let's say you've added a custom field to the User object, call it UserIsSpecial__c, that controls these operations.

You can retrieve the current value of this field using the following code:

```
User u = [Select UserIsSpecial__c from User
        where ID = :UserInfo.getUserId()];
Boolean userIsSpecial = u.UserIsSpecial__c;
```

If you were only using this value in one place in your code, this would be fine – you could just use the query as is. But if you intend to use this value across multiple methods and triggers, this approach could result in numerous SOQL operations (SOQL being the database query language for the Force.com platform). The number of allowed SOQL calls is limited within an Execution context – so you want to minimize those calls where possible.

The solution is to cache the value the first time it is used. Rather than try to anticipate where the first use will be (which can be tricky in a complex application), it's best to centralize access of the variable by placing it in an Apex class as follows:

```
public class ThinkingInApex {

    private static Boolean isUserSpecialChecked = false;
    private static Boolean userIsSpecial = false;

    public static Boolean isUserSpecial()
    {
        if(isUserSpecialChecked) return userIsSpecial;

        User u = [Select UserIsSpecial__c from User
            where ID = :UserInfo.getUserId()];
        userIsSpecial = u.UserIsSpecial__c;
        isUserSpecialChecked = true;
```

```
        return userIsSpecial;
    }
}
```

Now, you can obtain the user information by calling ThinkingInApex.isUserSpecial() from anywhere in your code without worrying about making redundant SOQL calls.

It turns out that taking this approach has additional benefits. What if you later decide that you need other information from the user record? Say, the current user's time zone?

You could extend the previous example as follows:

```
public class ThinkingInApex {

    private static Boolean userCacheLoaded = false;
    private static Boolean userIsSpecial = false;
    private static String userTimeZone = null;

    public static Boolean isUserSpecial()
    {
        if(userCacheLoaded) return userIsSpecial;
        cacheUserInfo();
        return userIsSpecial;
    }

    public static String userTimeZone()
    {
        if(userCacheLoaded) return userTimeZone;
        cacheUserInfo();
        return userTimeZone;
    }


    private static void cacheUserInfo()
    {
```

```
    if(userCacheLoaded) return;
    User u = [Select UserIsSpecial__c, TimeZoneSidKey
            from User where ID = :UserInfo.getUserId()];
    userIsSpecial = u.UserIsSpecial__c;
    userTimeZone = u.TimeZoneSidKey;
    userCacheLoaded = true;
}}
```

With this approach, you can cache all necessary information from an object with only one SOQL call – which is very efficient. Even though the code changes needed to support more than one user field were fairly substantial, they would not have impacted existing code outside of this class. That code continues to call the isUserSpecial() function.

Generally speaking, using static class methods to centralize access to information that is (or could be) used in more than one place is a good idea. Though it has some small cost in terms of additional code, the long-term benefits of being able to make changes to the sourcing of that information, without requiring widespread changes throughout your code, are enormous.

For example: let's say that a few months after your code was deployed, you suddenly decided that it wasn't the time zone of the current user you cared about, but actually the time zone of the user's supervisor. Or that you wanted to use a specific time zone for users from certain countries. These changes could be made simply by modifying the UserTimeZone() function – you wouldn't have to make any other changes in your application.

There is, however, one caveat to this approach. You can run into trouble if you try to cache large amounts of data. You see, there is also a limit to the size of memory heap you can use in an execution context! If you need to work with larger amounts of data, you may need to requery each time you need the data instead of caching it. And if you are facing both limits – not enough heap space and not enough available SOQL operations, you may need to defer the operation into an asynchronous call where you have higher limits.

You'll read more about those kinds of tradeoffs in chapter 3, but first, there is one more static variable design pattern to consider.

Controlling Program Flow

Static variables are frequently used to modify the execution of a program.

Consider the scenario where you wish to store on the account object the name and Email of the first contact. This can come in handy when doing account-based marketing, and a useful reference point in the event that the contact is later deleted (so it makes sense to store the information in individual fields rather than a lookup to the contact – which would be set to null if the contact was later deleted).

Create two fields on the account, First_Contact_Name__c and First_Contact_Email__c.

The application will use a trigger on the contact field which will call a method in our ThinkingInApex class.

```
trigger OnContactInsert on Contact (after insert) {
    ThinkingInApex.afterInsertContact(trigger.new);
}
```

The afterInsertContact method has one parameter – the list of new contacts. It first builds a list of account IDs for those contacts that have accounts, then queries only those accounts that do not yet have the First_Contact_Name__c field set. That way, by definition, every account queried will need to be updated. Finally, the account fields are set, and they are updated.

```
public static void afterInsertContact(List<Contact> contacts)
{
    // Get all of the account IDs for the contacts
    Set<ID> accountIDs = new Set<ID>();
    for(Contact ct: contacts)
        if(ct.accountId!=null) accountIDs.add(ct.AccountId);

    // Only query those accounts for the contacts that do
    // not yet have First_Contact_Name set
    Map<ID, Account> accounts = new Map<ID, Account>(
            [Select ID, First_Contact_Email__c, First_Contact_Name__c
                from Account where ID in :accountIDs And
```

```
            First_Contact_Name__c = null ]);
    // Exit if there are no accounts to set
    if(accounts.size()==0) return;

    // We don't need to keep track of those that need to
    // be updated, as by definition all of these accounts
    // have a new first contact

    for(Contact ct: contacts)
        if(ct.accountId!=null)
        {
            Account act = accounts.get(ct.accountId);
            // Note, contact name property is not yet
            // available in the after insert trigger
            act.First_Contact_Name__c = ((ct.FirstName!=null)?ct.FirstName
                + ' ':'') + ct.LastName;
            act.First_Contact_Email__c = ct.Email;
        }
    update accounts.values();
}
```

This software works fine, at least in a development environment. But since every Salesforce org is different, and your software is almost certainly sharing the org with other applications along with workflows and processes, it may not always work in a production environment.

There are two proactive steps that should be taken in every Apex application. The first, which is probably familiar to you, is to add error handling. In this case, you might place the account update in a try catch block as shown here:

```
try
{
    update accounts.values();
} catch(Exception ex)
{
    // Code to report an error!
    system.debug('An exception occurred ' + ex.getMessage());
}
```

In this example the exception block just sends a message to the debug log, but in a real-world example there might additional diagnostics or, depending on the type of exception, a mechanism to retry the operation later. For example: in chapter 8 you'll learn approaches for handling transient (and recoverable) data locking errors.

The challenge with this code is – how do you test it?

It's easy enough to test the success case. The following test method from class TestThinkingInApex does the job:

```apex
@istest
public static void TestSetFirstContactName() {
    List<Account> accounts = new List<Account>{
        new Account(name='a1'), new Account(name='a2')};
    insert accounts;
    test.startTest();
    List<Contact> contacts = new List<Contact>{
        new Contact(LastName='c1',Email='c1@c1.com',
                    AccountId = accounts[0].id),
        new Contact(LastName='c2',Email='c2@c2.com',
                    AccountId = accounts[1].id)};
    insert contacts;
    test.StopTest();

    Map<ID,Account> actResults = new Map<ID, Account>(
        [Select ID, First_Contact_Name__c,
          First_Contact_Email__c from Account]);

    // Verify the accounts for each contact
    for(Contact ct: contacts)
    {
        Account actToTest = actResults.get(ct.accountId);
        // We only used the last name in this test
        system.assertEquals(ct.LastName,actToTest.First_Contact_Name__c);
        system.assertEquals(ct.Email, actToTest.First_Contact_Email__c);
    }
}
```

But how do you test the exception block?

One answer is to force an exception to occur, but you would only want the exception to occur when specifically requested by a test. Static variables provide an excellent way to do this.

The fakeAccountInsertException static variable in the ThinkingAboutApex class does the job.

```
@testvisible
private static Boolean fakeAccountInsertionException = false;
```

The variable is marked with the @testvisible annotation to ensure that it can only be accessed from unit tests. Not that a developer would be likely to accidentally set this variable, but there's no harm in being extra safe here.

Next, modify the code to throw an exception when the fakeAccountInsertionException variable is true. One way to do this would be to place an invalid Email address in the account's First_Contact_Email__c field during the update like this:

```
try
{
    if(fakeAccountInsertionException)
        accounts.values().get(0).First_Contact_Email__c = 'hello';
    update accounts.values();
} catch(Exception ex)
```

Next, create a new test class that is identical to the previous one except that it sets the fakeAccountInsertionException variable before inserting the contacts.

```
ThinkingInApex.fakeAccountInsertionException = true;
insert contacts;
```

Finally, change the new test class to validate the failure instead of the success condition:

```
system.assertNotEquals(ct.LastName, actToTest.First_Contact_Name__c);
system.assertNotEquals(ct.Email, actToTest.First_Contact_Email__c);
```

If you capture a debug log when running the test, you'll see a debug message much like this one:

```
USER_DEBUG [95]|DEBUG|An exception occurred Update failed. First
exception on row 0 with id 0015C00000KH1AjQAL; first error:
INVALID_EMAIL_ADDRESS, First Contact Email: invalid email address:
hello: [First_Contact_Email__c]
```

Being able to handle exceptions is a great first step. However, in the real world you never know what the side effects might be when updating an account. What's more, now that you've added a trigger to the contact, a client or customer might blame your code for problems that are completely unrelated. One of the best ways to be able to prove that your application is not involved in unrelated problems, or to check for changes in an org's behavior related to your application, is to give each application an "on/off" switch – a way to disable triggers in code.

Static variables are a key part of this design pattern as well. In this example, you can add a static variable disableContactTriggers to the ThinkingAboutApex class:

```
public static Boolean disableContactTriggers = false;
```

This time the variable is public and not decorated with the @testvisible annotation, as it is intended to be accessed by other classes and by triggers.

The static variable is placed in the class because while triggers can have static variables, those static variables cannot be accessed by other classes and triggers. Placing your static variables in classes also offers a great deal more flexibility and results in code that is easier to follow and maintain. This is just one of the reasons why you should always minimize the amount of code in a trigger, and instead implement all functionality in a class. You'll see additional reasons later in this book.

Now modify the OnContactInsert trigger as follows:

```
trigger OnContactInsert on Contact (after insert) {
    if(ThinkingInApex.disableContactTriggers) return;
    ThinkingInApex.afterInsertContact(trigger.new);
}
```

Now any time the disableContactTriggers variable is true, the trigger will exit immediately.

This design pattern can also be used to improve an application's efficiency. Let's say you have code that inserts a contact and then updates other information on the related account. You could leave the trigger in place to handle updating the First_Contact_Name__c and First_Contact_Email__c fields if necessary, but doing so results in two separate updates to the account – one caused by the trigger, and then another by your code. In this scenario you can use the disableContactTriggers static variable to shut down the contact trigger, preventing the update, and set those fields directly before updating the account. This results in having just one Account update. Given that each account update can fire multiple triggers, workflows and processes, each of which can update other objects and associated code and automation – you can see that reducing the number of object updates is a very good thing indeed.

As you have seen, the unique nature of static variables under Apex makes them an essential part of many Apex design patterns. Now let's take a look at the next key concept that fills the thoughts (and nightmares) of every Apex programmer. It's time to look at limits.

3 – Limits

You are almost certainly aware that the Salesforce platform is a pioneer in the area of cloud computing. And, if you've been exposed to any technical, marketing or investor related media, you've undoubtedly heard that cloud computing is the latest and greatest thing (next to, perhaps, big data and artificial intelligence). But cloud computing means different things to different people.

Everyone agrees on the fundamental idea of cloud computing. Instead of deploying applications and managing them on millions of client computers, run the applications on a redundant "cloud" of server machines, and access those resources through the Internet.

The advantages of such an approach are clear:

- Instead of having to update and maintain software on numerous client machines, you can do so on a relatively few server machines. This reduces the need to build up IT infrastructure and knowledge at each client site.
- Client machines typically don't use a fraction of their computing power – which wastes energy and resources. Sharing powerful server resources is much more efficient.

But the second point raises another issue. While client machines are rarely used to their full capability, that capability is there if needed. If a programming mistake or particular problem or requirement demands intensive computer resources – the drain caused by that mistake, problem or requirement is limited to that one client machine.

On the cloud, where servers are shared among many clients, how do you deal with those situations that suddenly demand a huge amount of resources?

One approach, used by cloud systems such as Amazon Web Services, is to provide users with virtual machines that have a specified limit on computational resources (memory, CPU speed, etc.). If you need more resources, you can purchase them as needed.

The Salesforce platform took a different approach as befits its different architecture. To protect the cloud from having any one bug, problem or requirement tie up too many resources, monitoring was built-in to the underlying application programming language to prevent applications from exceeding certain limits.

In a way, the choice of the word "limits" is unfortunate. After all, no programmer wants to feel limited by their tools. Yet the reality is that we are always working with limits of some sort – be it memory, or stack depth, or available language or platform features. It's just that over the past decade or two, thanks to Moore's law, the amount of computational power on the typical PC is far greater than most software developers really need. It wasn't that long ago that developers struggled to cram complex applications into 64K of memory. Some software developers do deal with limits on a regular basis – game developers are always trading off graphic quality against available hardware. Mobile developers have numerous platform limits to deal with. But even there, hardware continues to rapidly extend those limits.

So it's not that Apex limits are inherently bad. It's just that they are different and unfamiliar to most developers. Like any limits, their existence has a profound impact on architecture and design patterns. Once you become familiar with those limits, and the design patterns they require, you will find that limits are not only easy to deal with, they are part of what makes Apex programming fun. And you'll find that you have become a better programmer along the way.

I am not going to try to cover all of the limits here, or to list current limits. Limits often change between releases, so you should be referencing the platform documentation for that information. But I will discuss the limits that most often cause problems, and how you can trade off one against another.

The Nature of Limits

There is a trick when looking at limits in Apex. Don't focus on the values that you aren't supposed to exceed. Instead, consider each limit a pointer to an operation that you want to optimize throughout your code.

There are two reasons for taking this approach:

- If you focus on optimizing all of your limit related code, in many cases you will never come close to using the available limits.

- Remember that your code may not be the only code running in an execution context or organization. There may already be existing code in an organization. Some other developer may add other triggers after you are no longer around. If you are creating a package, there may be other packages installed that might be sharing some limits. If you focus on minimizing your own resource use, you are much more likely to avoid conflicts with other code.

There are many types of limits in the Salesforce platform, depending on your edition and the platform features you have purchased. For our purposes, we will only concern ourselves with the Salesforce governor limits – those that relate to Apex code. A complete and current list of limits can be found on the developer.force.com site.

Apex governor limits fall into several categories:

- Limits that apply to a single execution context, regardless of packaging.
- Limits that apply to a single execution context, where each package has its own set of limits.
- Limits that apply to a 24-hour period for an organization.

For most developers, the first two categories will actually be the same. All of the Apex code on your system will share one set of limits. There are two exceptions to this. The first, and most important, is that when creating unit tests, you have one set of limits for test initialization and validation, and another for running the test itself (the code between the StartTest and StopTest methods – you'll read more about this in chapter 11). The other exception relates to managed packages that are listed on the AppExchange by Salesforce.com ISV partners. These packages can receive their own set of governor limits within an execution context. This is important both for users – who can install packages with less worry that they will cause existing code to start failing due to Apex limits, and for package developers, who can be more confident that their packages will not fail due to limits caused by other packages or custom code on an organization.

Dealing with Limits

The type of application you are building will determine which limits concern you most. In most cases, you can, through careful design, trade off one limit against another to avoid problems. Let's take a look at the most important limits, and common ways to deal with them.

SOQL Queries

This limit was extraordinarily painful back in the days when you were limited to a small number of SOQL queries in an execution context. Now, it's unlikely that well written code will ever come close to this limit. The trick is to make sure that your code is well written:

- Always use bulk syntax (see Bulk Patterns later in this chapter).
- Use before-triggers instead of after-triggers where possible (allows modification of fields without a SOQL query and DML update).
- Cache query results if your design allows.
- Include fields from related objects in a single query.

Let's take a closer look at the last one.

Consider the scenario where you want to query a set of contacts and, as part of the functionality, make sure that if any of those contacts belongs to an account, the account has an AnnualRevenue forecast set.

Your first thought, especially if you are extending existing code, might be to build a list of the account IDs and query for those accounts thus:

```
// Query for contact info
List<Contact> cts = [SELECT ID, AccountID from Contact
                where your condition here

// Some code that operates on the contacts here....

// Get list of account IDs.
Set<ID> accountIds = new Set<ID>();
```

```
for(Contact ct: cts)
    if(ct.AccountID!=null) accountIds.add(ct.AccountID);

if(accountIds.size()>0)
{
    List<Account> accounts = [Select ID, AnnualRevenue
        from Account where ID in :accountIds];
    for(Account accountFound: accounts)
        if(accountFound.AnnualRevenue == null)
            accountFound.AnnualRevenue = 500;
    update accounts;
}
```

This is a perfectly reasonable implementation that uses two SOQL queries. It's particularly nice if you are extending code that has an existing contact query, as it minimizes impact on existing code.

But the following approach works well also:

```
// Query for contact info and annual revenue on
// account in a single query
List<Contact> cts = [SELECT ID, AccountID, Account.ID,
        Account.AnnualRevenue from Contact
            where your condition here];

// Some code that operates on the contacts here....

Map<ID, Account> accountsToUpdate = new Map<ID,Account>();

for(Contact ct: cts)
{
    if (ct.Account.AnnualRevenue == null)
    {
        ct.Account.AnnualRevenue = 500;
        accountsToUpdate.put(ct.AccountID, ct.Account);
    }
}
if(accountsToUpdate.size()>0) update accountsToUpdate.values();
```

This code is a bit trickier in that you need to pull the account objects out of the contact list in order to do the update (updating the contact list won't update any referenced objects). The code uses a map to do this instead of a list, because of the possibility that multiple contacts will reference the same account.

While you *have* to create a map to hold the updated accounts in this approach, creating a map or list to hold updated records represents a best practice for the first approach as well, as it would ensure that you only try to update those accounts that were changed, and allow you to completely avoid a database operation if no accounts were changed. You'll find an example of this in the sample code.

This second approach uses about the same amount of memory and CPU time as the first, but only requires one SOQL statement.

CPU Time Limits

The Salesforce platform monitors the CPU time used by every execution context to ensure that no one piece of code has the ability to impact the platform and possibly degrade the performance of other orgs. The amount of CPU time available depends on whether the execution context is taking place during a trigger – a synchronous execution context, or during an asynchronous execution context. Asynchronous execution contexts are allocated considerably more CPU time because the platform can schedule them more efficiently. You'll learn more about asynchronous operations later in the book.

Unlike most limits, CPU time limits are a soft limit. That means that the platform will often allow your code to exceed the CPU time limit if it only happens occasionally, and if the platform has the resources to spare. The algorithm that determines how this limit is applied is constantly evolving, so don't be surprised if your code is allowed to run for considerably longer than the expected limit.

When the limit is applied, the execution context is terminated. That means that your code just stops running, and most changes made to the database are reverted. There are exceptions: platform events that have already been inserted are not reverted. And at this time, operations performed by declarative processes may not be reverted when this limit is hit.

CPU time limits are global to all code and declarative functionality that runs during an execution context. This includes time spent in validation rules, formulas, workflows, processes, and flows, as well as your code and any code belonging to any packages that are installed in the org.

CPU time limits do not include time spent performing database operations and most queries, or time spent waiting on responses from callouts. However, some aggregate queries do consume CPU time.

While it is difficult to accurately measure the CPU time required by different operations, it is possible to do some rough benchmarking to get a general idea of how long they take. Simple operations such as assignments, simple math operations, and memory allocations typically run in under 1 microsecond. Function calls run in about 3 microseconds. Even if you assumed that other longer operations would increase your average script time to 5 microseconds, the current 10 second synchronous limit would translate into two million operations, which at first glance seems very generous indeed.

But there are some major flaws to this assumption:

- Salesforce can process records in batches of up to 200 records at a time. In an Apex trigger processing 200 records, the time for two million operations drops to 10,000 per record – still generous, but definitely a limit.
- CPU limits are shared by all triggers belonging to your code and any installed packages. If any one trigger or package uses too much CPU time, it can cause any of the others to fail.
- Some design patterns consume more CPU time than others. For example: dynamic Apex, in which fields on objects are referenced indirectly using a variable, consumes more time than static Apex, in which fields being accessed are specified in code.
- CPU time is not only consumed by Apex code. Declarative constructs such as formulas, validation rules, workflows, processes and flows use CPU time as well.

On a busy system with many customizations, CPU limits can become a real concern, especially when it comes to handling bulk operations.

It is essential that you not only optimize your Apex code, but that you also design your applications to be as efficient as possible. Even if your code works today, you'll want to ensure that future customizations have sufficient CPU time available to perform their operations.

There are a number of things you can do if you find yourself running up against CPU time limits:

- Move your code to an asynchronous operation. Asynchronous operations have, and probably will always have, larger limits than trigger execution contexts. One common design pattern is to use a custom field on an object to indicate that an operation is pending, then to query on that flag during a future operation. Another approach is to use a custom object that you create to hold all of the information needed to perform the future operation, then just query for instances of that object (deleting them after the operation is complete). You'll learn more about asynchronous design patterns in chapter 7.
- Move your code into batch Apex. This is the preferred design pattern when dealing with large data sets.
- Optimize your code. You'll see various examples of code optimization throughout the rest of this book.

Benchmarking

It has always been important to measure the performance of Apex code in order to determine where you should invest the most effort with regards to optimizing your code. With regards to CPU time limits, it is important to know how to measure not just the performance of your code, but also the performance of built-in Salesforce functionality.

Mark Twain has often been misquoted as saying: "There are lies, damned lies, and computer software benchmarks". Yes, I know – he was referring to statistics. But I'm confident that if he had lived to see computers, he would have quickly realized that when it comes to misinterpretation and manipulation of results, software benchmarks are the worst kind of statistics.

Despite this, there are a number of approaches you can use to estimate the performance of a built-in function. All of these approaches are predicated on two facts:

- The resolution of the built-in CPU time measurement system is one millisecond.
- The most accurate results can be obtained by using as much CPU time as possible without exceeding the limit.

The trick is to place the operation you want to measure inside of a loop, perform the operation multiple times, then divide the time spent by the number of iterations.

While it is possible to view CPU time usage in debug logs, the approach I'm going to show you here offers the best possible accuracy and allows you to isolate the operation that you want to measure.

All of the measurements take place inside of a test class – look for the benchmarking class in the sample code.

Each unit test profiles a single operation using two different loops. Both loops are identical except for the use of the operation being measured. The Limits.getCpuTime() function is used to retrieve amount of CPU time consumed up until that point. This value is stored at the start and end of each loop using the functions shown here:

```
private static Integer referenceStartTime;
private static Integer referenceEndTime;
private static Integer targetStartTime;
private static Integer targetEndTime;
private static void markReferenceStartTime()
{
    referenceStartTime = Limits.getCpuTime();
}
private static void markReferenceEndTime()
{
    referenceEndTime = Limits.getCpuTime();
}
```

```
private static void markTargetStartTime()
{
    targetStartTime = Limits.getCpuTime();
}
private static void markTargetEndTime()
{
    targetEndTime = Limits.getCpuTime();
}
```

The reportResults function calculates the elapsed duration of the reference and target loops, then reports the time for each operation based on the number of loops specified in the loops parameter.

```
private static void reportResults(Integer loops)
{
    if(targetEndTime==null) markTargetEndTime();
    Integer referenceDuration = referenceEndTime - referenceStartTime;
    Integer targetDuration = targetEndTime - targetStartTime;
    Integer benchmarkResults = targetDuration - referenceDuration;
    // Time in microseconds is duration * 1000 / loops
    Decimal eachItem = benchmarkResults * 1000;
    eachItem /= loops;
    eachItem.setScale(2);
    system.debug(LoggingLevel.Error,
    'Reference Duration: ' + referenceDuration +
    ' Target duration: ' + targetDuration +
    ' Benchmark Results: ' + benchmarkResults +
    'ms or ' + eachItem + ' us per operation');
}
```

Note that the logging level in the system.debug statement is set to LoggingLevel.Error. You'll see shortly why this is important.

Consider an example where you want to measure the time to perform a very simple operation – say, incrementing an integer number.

```
@istest
public static void primitiveTests()
```

```
{
    Integer v = 0;
    markReferenceStartTime();
    for(Integer x = 0; x<1000000; x++) {}
    markReferenceEndTime();
    markTargetStartTime();
    for(Integer x = 0; x<1000000; x++)
    {
        v += 5;
    }
    reportResults(1000000);
}
```

There are two loops here. The reference loop does nothing – it allows us to calculate the overhead of the loop operation itself. The second loop adds the operation being measured.

CAUTION!

You must adjust debug log levels as shown below in order for your results to be accurate!

Before running a test, it is absolutely essential that you set your debug log levels to capture the minimal amount of information. That's because debug logging consumes CPU time – lots of CPU time. So if you don't change your debug log levels you'll end up measuring the debug logging time and not the operation you're trying to benchmark.

In the developer console, select the Debug – Change Log Levels menu command. Add a new entry – in the example shown in Figure 3-1, I named it "None". Set all of the debug options to the lowest level of capture except for Apex code, which should be set to "Error". This level ensures that system.debug statements with the logging level set to "Error" will still appear in the debug logs.

Figure 3-1 – Log level setting in the developer console

Always remember to select this debug log level before doing benchmarking – the developer console will reset it to the default SFDC_DevConsole any time it is closed and then reopened, or logging resumes after being suspended.

After running a test, open the resulting log and search for the debug statement (in the developer console you can easily do this by checking the "Debug Only" filter). You'll see the elapsed CPU time for the reference and target loop, and the calculated time for each operation.

The Benchmarking sample class demonstrates a number of interesting measurements including memory allocation and the difference in field access time between dynamic and static Apex.

Let's take a closer look at a few of the examples and how they can impact your design choices.

The testNewAllocate example uses the following reference and target loops:

```
List<List<Integer>> numbers = new List<List<Integer>>();
List<Integer> emptyList = new List<Integer>();
markReferenceStartTime();
for(Integer x = 0; x<1000000; x++)
{
    numbers.add(emptyList);
}
markReferenceEndTime();
markTargetStartTime();
```

```
for(Integer x = 0; x<1000000; x++)
{
    numbers.add(new List<Integer>{x});   // Add a new list
}
```

The reference loop adds a fixed integer array into another list. The target loop dynamically creates a new array with a single integer value and adds it into the list. The only difference between the two loops is the creation and initialization of the new array, so that is what we are measuring. The result is about 3 to 4 microseconds. What this tells you is that memory allocation is fast, so designs that create many lists are acceptable – it's probably not going to be something you have to optimize for. Or put another way – knowing that certain operations are fast can be just as important as knowing which ones are slow.

Speaking of slow operations, the Schema.getGlobalDescribe function, which is used to obtain a list of all objects in an org, is a good example. The testGlobalDescribe example demonstrates a subtle variation in approaching benchmarking.

```
markReferenceStartTime();
for(Integer x = 0; x<1; x++)
{
    Map<String, Schema.SObjectType>
        describeInfo = Schema.getGlobalDescribe();
}
markReferenceEndTime();
markTargetStartTime();
for(Integer x = 0; x<1000; x++)
{
    Map<String, Schema.SObjectType>
        describeInfo = Schema.getGlobalDescribe();
}
reportResults(1000);
```

The fact that the second loop has only 1000 iterations is a good indication of how slow this function is. But the reference loop is the interesting one here – it only executes once. What's going on here?

The Schema.getGlobalDescribe function is documented as using internal caching, so it should run slowly the first time and more quickly on subsequent calls. The function is slow enough so that even a single execution is measurable – on a clean developer org you'll probably see numbers around 10 to 15 milliseconds. You can expect this number to be substantially higher on a large production org.

The results do show that subsequent calls run more quickly, but they are still in the 3-millisecond range. What this means is that even though the function uses caching internally, you definitely would not want to call it inside of a loop. And if your application uses it frequently from different places in code, you'd likely want to cache it in a static class variable to ensure that it is only called once during an execution context.

When you're dealing with loops, even a small change can make a significant difference. The TestCheckForSpam example demonstrates how a little bit of benchmarking can result in significant performance improvement. Refer to the actual sample code for the complete example – I'll only be showing highlights here.

The example uses a typical scenario where you might want to test an email field against a series of known spam domains. In an interesting twist, for this example the email field is defined dynamically – to support cases where you may wish to check a field other than the standard email field.

The main test routine creates 10,000 lead objects. No, we won't actually try to insert them – the large number of objects is intended just to help obtain accurate measurements.

The spam domains are stored in a static set variable.

```
private static Set<String> spamList = new Set<String>
    {'@yahoo.com','@gmail.com','@hotmail.com',
    '@whitehouse.gov','@test.com','@nobody.com',
    '@abc.com','@spam.com','@xyz.com','@ignoreme.com'};
```

The reference example represents an obvious way to implement this. The email field, which is passed as a parameter, is retrieved using dynamic Apex (the ld.get(emailField) term). It is checked for each entry in the spam list.

```
// Dynamic field, test against each entry
private static List<Lead> checkForSpam1(
   List<Lead> leads, String emailField)
{
   List<Lead> results = new List<Lead>();
   for(Lead ld: leads)
   {
      for(string spamDomain: spamList)
         if(ld.get(emailField)!=null &&
         ((String)ld.get(emailField)).endsWithIgnoreCase(spamDomain))
            results.add(ld);
   }
   return results;
}
```

The sample code then tests this against four other possible target loops. In each case, we're not concerned with accurately measuring the time for a particular operation, but rather with comparing overall CPU time usage of the different approaches.

The first test target assumes that the email field will usually be 'email'. So, it tests for that, and if it is 'email', uses static Apex to retrieve the field value. The loop inside the checkForSpam2 function looks like this.

```
for(Lead ld: leads)
{
   switch on emailField
   {
      when 'email' {
         for(string spamDomain: spamList)
            if(ld.email!=null &&
               ld.email.endsWithIgnoreCase(spamDomain))
                results.add(ld);
      }
      when else {
         for(string spamDomain: spamList)
            if(ld.get(emailField)!=null &&
               ((String)ld.get(emailField)).
```

```
                    endsWithIgnoreCase(spamDomain))
                    results.add(ld);
        }
    }
}
```

In my sample test run, this brought the total CPU time down from 3042 ms to 1229 ms when using the standard email field. Clearly static Apex performs significantly better than dynamic Apex. The sample code also includes functions testStaticFieldReference and testDynamicFieldReference, not shown here, that do additional benchmarking of static and dynamic fields.

Back to our spam filtering. Static field references are fast, but how do they compare with variables? What happens if you retrieve the field, store it in a temporary variable, and test it for a spam domain? This scenario is shown here in the loop from the checkForSpam3 function.

```
Boolean useStaticEmail = (emailField=='email');
for(Lead ld: leads)
{
    String email = (useStaticEmail)? ld.email:
                    (String)ld.get(emailField);
    if(email!=null)
    {
        for(string spamDomain: spamList)
            if(email.endsWithIgnoreCase(spamDomain)) results.add(ld);
    }
}
```

The temporary email variable is set using either static or dynamic Apex. That email is then used to test for spam domains. This change brought my sample time down to 969 ms – an additional 260ms.

The checkForSpam4 function tests the theory that we can save more time by converting the temporary email variable to lower case and then using the presumably more efficient endsWith method instead of endsWithIgnoreCase.

```
for(Lead ld: leads)
{
    String email = (useStaticEmail)? ld.email:
                       (String)ld.get(emailField);
    if(email!=null)
    {
        email = email.toLowerCase();
        for(string spamDomain: spamList)
            if(email.endsWith(spamDomain)) results.add(ld);
    }
}
```

In my example this resulted in a slight increase in CPU time to 1021ms. In multiple runs this approach was always slower than the checkForSpam3 function, proving that either the endsWithIgnoreCase method is as fast or faster than the endsWith method, or if slower, it still doesn't offset the cost doing of a string conversion and assignment.

The checkForSpam5 function takes a slightly different approach. Why compare each element in the spam list individually? Why not just convert the email to lower case and test if it's in the set using the set's contains method? This approach is shown here:

```
for(Lead ld: leads)
{
    String email = (useStaticEmail)? ld.email:
                       (String)ld.get(emailField);
    if(email!=null)
    {
        if(spamList.contains(email.toLowerCase())) results.add(ld);
    }
}
```

In my tests this consumed 117ms of CPU time.

Think about it. The "obvious" straightforward approach came in at 3042 ms. But with some thought, benchmarking, and design, we brought it down to 117ms. That's 25 times faster!

If you've been wondering why I've spent so much time covering benchmarking, I hope this answers your question. Understanding how Apex performs will allow you to create and choose design patterns that perform well, and the potential improvement is often dramatic.

One last comment about benchmarking. Everything you've seen here is subject to change. As the Apex compiler improves, there will likely be more optimizations that can distort the results of benchmarks. If you see a block of code whose CPU time usage does not vary with the number of iterations, that may be the cause – in which case it may be necessary to modify your code to prevent the optimization – possibly by adding some extra variable assignments.

It is important to run your benchmarks multiple times – the numbers will vary based on server load, time of day, and other factors that will forever remain mysteries.

Other Limits

Here is a brief list of some of the other key limits and some common tradeoffs you can use with each one.

DML Limits

There is a limit to the number of DML (Database) operations you can perform within an execution context.

- Combine DML operations on each object type into a single bulk DML operation.
- If your program flow calls for DML operations at different places in your code, don't perform the DML operation right away. Instead, store a reference to the object in a list, set or Map. Then perform a DML operation on all objects at once as the last part of your operation. You'll see examples of this approach in chapter 6.

Heap Size

The size of the heap is limited during an execution context.

- When performing SOQL queries, only include fields you actually need in the query. In particular, avoid querying for long text and rich text fields.
- Instead of storing objects in a static variable, store Object IDs, then requery when needed.

SOQL queries support a loop query syntax that is confusing to many developers who interpret it as a mechanism to bypass limits on the number of records that can be processed in an execution context. In fact, it's a way to avoid heap limits when processing large numbers of records.

Imagine that you need to loop through 8000 lead records. You could query them all into a list, and loop through the list like this:

```
List<Lead> leads = [Select ID, Company, LastName,
    Description from Lead];
for(Lead ld: leads) perform operation here
```

This approach loads all of the records into memory, which can potentially exceed your maximum heap size.

You can use a SOQL loop to load lists of 200 items at a time thus:

```
for(List<Lead> leads:
    [Select ID, Company, LastName, Description from Lead])
    {
        for(Lead ld: leads) perform operation here;
    }
```

The system automatically returns the results in lists of 200 records, maintaining a query locator so that the operation still counts as a single query. The Salesforce platform is largely standardized on working with batches of 200 by default. Assuming your code is bulk safe – a topic we'll cover later, you should be able to perform almost any operation including database updates within the SOQL loop and still make optimal use of your available limits.

Note that both of these approaches ultimately query the same number of records – so using a SOQL for loop does not reduce the number of records that count against your query limits.

If you're doing a very simple operation on the data and don't need to perform any DML updates, you can create a SOQL loop that iterates using a single element instead of a list as shown here:

```
for(Lead ld: [Select ID, Company, LastName,
              Description from Lead])
    perform operation here;
```

Given that in most cases you'll be iterating over data in order to perform some operation on the records, you should use a list as the iteration element instead of a single element unless you have some overriding reason not to.

Callouts

Apex code can call out to external web services. There is a limit to the number of callouts in an execution context.

- Don't try using callouts in a trigger context – it's not supported.

API Limits

You can implement API entry points in Apex that allow outside applications to call in to your code. Each API request generates its own execution context. The number of allowed API requests is limited for each organization over a 24-hour period.

- Always support bulk operations for every API call. This can reduce the number of incoming calls.
- Specify a limit to the amount of data in each call, or set an "out" parameter to specify that additional data is available in cases where you can't serve up all the data requested. This will allow you to dynamically adjust the tradeoff between the limit on the number of API calls and the limit on data that can be transferred on each call.

Email Limits

You are limited in the number of external Email you can send, both in terms of number of Emails and number of recipients.

- When sending Email to internal users with Apex code, specify the destination using their UserID, not their Email address. These Emails are not subject to limits.

24-hour Limits

There are a number of limits that deal with a maximum number of operations that can occur within a 24-hour period. The most important of these is the asynchronous operation limit, which is currently the larger of 250,000 or 200 times the number of licenses in the org. This applies to batch Apex, future methods, queueable Apex and scheduled Apex.

From a developer perspective this simply means that if you can group multiple operations into a single asynchronous operation, you should do so. You'll see some design patterns that support this in chapter 7.

Other Platform Limits

The Apex language reference and the Salesforce Developer Limits and Allocations documents are your best friends when it comes to understanding limits. If you are ISV creating managed packages for the AppExchange, there are special limits that apply to you. Don't fret – it most cases you get additional resources to work with (just not CPU time). Be sure to review these documents and check the latest release notes for changes.

Thinking of Limits

This part of the book is all about thinking in Apex. There's a tendency, when coming to Apex from other languages, to think of it as a familiar language, where limits are just one of those quirky things to consider when programming, just as every other platform has its little quirks. Then one day, when you run up against those limits, they suddenly become an annoying obstacle, and you find yourself cursing

Salesforce for building them into the system and getting in your way, even though you intellectually understand why they are there. That was certainly my experience when starting out.

My hope, with this book, is to change the way you look at limits. To accept (if not embrace them) as a fundamental part of the platform, and one that has as great an impact on software design and architecture as any other language or platform feature. Once you start seeing limits as a top-level factor to incorporate into your design and architecture from day one, you'll find that in most cases limits become easy to deal with. You'll be able to choose effective tradeoffs between various limits during project design, and even build your code to detect when it is approaching limits during execution, and automatically defer operations as necessary into future or batch Apex calls.

In no time, limits will become just another minor issue to deal with. You'll be writing good code from the start and will only rarely find yourself needing to go back and resolve limit issues.

4 – Bulk Patterns

One of the first things that every Apex programmer learns is that Apex programming has certain bulk patterns. Everyone knows that triggers can receive up to 200 objects at once. Everyone knows that SOQL queries and DML statements should not be inside of loops. The documentation on the importance of bulk patterns is clear, and not easy to miss.

Yet despite this, there's a trap that almost every beginning Apex programmer falls into, especially those coming from another language. They design and create code that is intended to work on one object at a time, and then figure out ways to "bulkify" it afterwards. In my own consulting work, I've been astonished how often I've run into triggers that are sure to fail the instant anyone does a bulk upload or update.

In this chapter, we'll walk through a number of bulk patterns and scenarios. But before we start, here's the most important thing for you to remember and follow.

**All of your Apex code should be designed to
handle bulk operations.
All of it – no exceptions.**

If you're an experienced Apex programmer, you're probably thinking: "wait a minute – there are times when bulk coding really isn't necessary. Lightning and VisualForce controllers often work on single objects. Queries that return one object either by design or a LIMIT=1 qualifier don't need bulk patterns. What are you thinking?"

Hear me out.

Bulk patterns and single object patterns, as you will see, are very different. It's true that sometimes bulkifying code is a simple matter of storing values in a collection that will be used for a bulk DML or query later. But if you design with bulk data in mind, you can often come up with far more efficient solutions.

In other words, you will end up with better code if you design your code with bulk patterns from the start, than if you write it for single objects and try to convert it later. You'll also spend less time, as you won't have to rewrite and redesign your code.

In Apex, bulk patterns are far more common than single object patterns. So common that there is actually little reason to learn the single object patterns at all. If you use bulk patterns everywhere, you'll maintain a higher level of code consistency (which will improve the maintainability of your code), and reduce your learning curve. If you commit to using bulk patterns everywhere from the beginning, it will encourage (even force) you to learn them – instead of falling back on the single object patterns that you already know from other platforms.

Most books or articles at this point would demonstrate a variety of patterns using simple examples. However, as it is my hope to help you learn to think in Apex, and since this is a book intended for advanced developers (or those who wish to become advanced developers), let's take a journey through a more complex example.

Note – I strongly recommend that you install the sample code and be prepared to examine it and experiment with it. Some of the code in this chapter is more advanced than you would see in a typical book or article.

Remember that individual commits corresponding to different steps in the solution can be checked out to see the sample code in its various stages of development as this chapter progresses.

An Interesting Challenge

In Salesforce, every sales opportunity (defined by the Opportunity object) can have one or more contacts associated with it. This association is defined using an OpportunityContactRole object, which includes a ContactID, OpportunityID and IsPrimary field. The IsPrimary field determines if this is the primary contact for the opportunity, of which there can only be one.

Consider the business case where you wish to guarantee that your opportunity always has a primary contact. If it doesn't, you want to assign one.

This may sound simple, but it's actually quite a challenge.

- The only time Salesforce automatically assigns a primary contact is when you create an opportunity from the contact page.
- When you create an opportunity during lead conversion, Salesforce does create an OpportunityContactRole for the contact on the opportunity, but it may or may not be primary (depending on whether you are using the Lightning or classic UI, and other factors).
- You could use UI techniques to make sure users only create opportunities from the contact page, but that won't help with opportunities created though external tools (API, data import, Apex, etc.)

This is exactly the kind of problem that often lands in the hands of an Apex developer. Your first thoughts might include using a trigger on the OpportunityContactRole object and performing any necessary validation when one is created or deleted. However, Salesforce does not support triggers on the OpportunityContactRole object.

So there is no perfect solution to the problem.

That means it's necessary to go back and figure out what the sales or marketing team really needs (which isn't always what they ask for).

Let's assume that, for our scenario, after extensive discussion with all of the stakeholders, it is determined that a good solution would be to make sure that a primary contact is assigned before the opportunity stage can be changed. This actually makes a certain amount of business sense, as it allows the sales team to create opportunities, but ensures that a primary contact is assigned before the opportunity moves to the next stage in the sales cycle.

To make life easier on the sales team, they want you to add some logic to automatically assign an existing contact as the primary contact based on the following logic:

- Contacts are often associated with multiple opportunities. Whichever contact is a primary contact on the most opportunities should be chosen as primary.

- If there is a tie on the above criteria, whichever contact is associated with the most opportunities (primary or not) should be chosen as primary.
- If there is a tie, choose an arbitrary contact to be primary.
- If there are no related contacts on an opportunity, create a task for the opportunity owner (if a task doesn't already exist).

This is based on the idea that the contact who is involved in the most opportunities would be the most likely contact on new opportunities.

Those are the requirements. You may be tempted to start coding right away, but doing so will likely lead you astray. Not only is there some serious design work to be done, but as is often the case with Apex, there is some testing to do as well.

Building to Tests

Testing in Apex is a very complex subject that I'll be covering in depth later. But it's worth bringing up here for a number of reasons:

- It's not exactly clear at this point how to implement the requirements we've defined. However, as you will see, implementing tests for those requirements is quite straightforward.
- Bulk patterns apply to unit tests as well as other Apex code modules. You need bulk tests to test bulk code. So test code is as good a place to start demonstrating bulk patterns as anywhere.
- You'll be seeing several different solutions to this challenge. Having a unit test in place makes it easy to compare the performance and resource use of the various implementations.

The Force.com platform is unusual in that it requires unit tests in order to deploy code to production. Since tests are required, there is no reason not to write them first if the requirements are reasonably clear. In fact, some developers subscribe to test-driven development methodologies that require you to create tests before implementation code.

For the time being, let's limit ourselves to a couple of simple tests that validate functionality. The goal is to obtain a simple yes/no answer – does the code work?

Other goals, such as obtaining code coverage, handling invalid input, and so forth, are secondary – those are subjects we'll cover in Chapter 11.

The basic flow of the tests is simple:

- Create one or more contacts.
- Create one or more opportunities.
- Create non-primary contact roles to associate those contacts with the opportunities.
- Update the stage for one or more of the opportunities.
- Verify that each updated opportunity has a primary contact.

As you can see, the basic functional test is much simpler than the scenario we need to implement. This isn't always the case.

This flow leaves some questions open. How many contacts should be created? How many opportunities? How do we handle opportunities whose stages are not being updated?

One common design pattern is to create utility functions that can be shared by multiple test classes or methods. In this example, there are two utility functions. The first one, TestBulkPatterns.initTestObjects, sets up the test scenario based on some parameters. The newOpportunities parameter references a list that is initialized by this function with the new opportunities. The numberOfOpportunities parameter specifies the number of new opportunities to create. The numberOfOtherOpportunties parameter specifies the number of additional opportunities to create – opportunities that will be associated with the contacts, but will not be updated by the test code. The contactRolesPerOp parameter specifies the number of contacts to be associated with each opportunity. The numberOfContacts parameter specifies the number of contacts to distribute among the opportunities, and is required to be larger or equal to contactRolesPerOp.

```
// Prepare the specified number of opportunities,
// with contact roles on each.
// The contact roles are distributed evenly among
// the number of contacts specified.
public static void initTestObjects(
```

```
      List<Opportunity> newOpportunities,
      Integer numberOfOpportunities,
      Integer numberOfOtherOpportunities,
      Integer contactRolesPerOp, Integer numberOfContacts)
{
   if(numberOfContacts < contactRolesPerOp)
      numberOfContacts = contactRolesPerOp;

   List<Contact>cts = new List<Contact>();
   for(Integer x=0;x<numberOfContacts;x++)
   {
      cts.add(new Contact(LastName = 'cttest_' + String.valueOf(x)));
   }

   insert cts;
```

The code for creating contacts and opportunities shows a common test pattern to create a specified number of objects with different names or other field values.

```
   newOpportunities.clear();
   for(Integer x=0; x<numberOfOpportunities; x++)
   {
      newOpportunities.add(
         new Opportunity(CloseDate = Date.Today().addDays(5),
                  Name = 'optest_' + String.valueOf(x),
                  StageName = 'Prospecting' ));
   }

   // Insert the test opportunities
   insert newOpportunities;

   List<Opportunity> otherOpportunities = new List<Opportunity>();
   for(Integer x=0; x<numberOfOtherOpportunities; x++)
   {
      otherOpportunities.add(
         new Opportunity(CloseDate = Date.Today().addDays(5),
            Name = 'optest_' +
```

```
                String.valueOf(x + NumberOfOpportunities),
                StageName = 'Prospecting' ));
    }

    insert otherOpportunities;
    // Combine the two for creating OpportunityContactRoles
    otherOpportunities.addall(newOpportunities);

    // Now insert contact roles
    List<OpportunityContactRole> ocrList =
        new List<OpportunityContactRole>();
    Integer contactNumber = 0;
    for(Opportunity op: otherOpportunities)
    {
        for(Integer ocrNumber = 0;
            ocrNumber < contactRolesPerOp; ocrNumber++)
        {
            ocrList.add(
                new OpportunityContactRole(OpportunityID = op.id,
                    ContactID = cts[contactNumber].id));
            contactNumber++;
            if(contactNumber >= numberOfContacts) contactNumber = 0;
        }

    }
    insert ocrList;
}
```

You can also initialize test data in a unit test by creating a method with the @test-Setup annotation as you saw earlier in the TestHeapAndSOQL class. While more efficient, the approach used here is more flexible, in that it allows each class using the initialization function to specify different numbers of objects. This approach also allows the initialization function to return references to the created objects to the test code without the need for a separate query. As is generally the case when there is more than one way to accomplish a task, you should choose the approach that is best for your particular scenario. Don't assume that the newer feature (in this case the @testSetup annotation) is always the best choice for every situation.

The next utility function takes a list of Opportunity objects, and makes sure that each one has one primary contact.

```
public static void validateOCRs(List<Opportunity> ops)
{
   // Get map for IDs
   Map<ID, Opportunity> opMap = new Map<ID, Opportunity>(ops);

   // Query for primary Contacts
   List<OpportunityContactRole> ocrs =
      [SELECT ID, OpportunityID from OpportunityContactRole
          where OpportunityID in :opMap.keyset()
          And IsPrimary= true];

   // Create set of opportunity IDs with primary contacts
   Set<ID> opportunitiesWithPrimaryContact = new Set<ID>();
   for(OpportunityContactRole ocr: ocrs)
      opportunitiesWithPrimaryContact.add(ocr.OpportunityID);

    // Now make sure every opportunity has a
   // primary contact role
    for(Opportunity op: ops)
      System.Assert(opportunitiesWithPrimaryContact.contains(op.id));
```

Unit tests are unique in that they have two sets of governor limits available: one set used for setting up data and verifying results, and one set for the test itself (the code between a call to the Test.StartTest and Test.StopTest methods). You'll typically call the ValidateOCRs function after calling Test.StopTest so it will be in the non-testing set of limits. Even so, it's best to write the setup and verification code to be as efficient as possible. Here's a demonstration of how use of an Apex subquery can eliminate a loop.

```
   List<Opportunity> opResults =
      [SELECT ID,
          (SELECT ID from OpportunityContactRoles
           where IsPrimary = true)
          from opportunity where ID in :opmap.keyset() ];
```

```
   for(Opportunity op: opResults)
      System.Assert(op.OpportunityContactRoles.size()==1);
}
```

With these utility functions in place, the tests themselves are easy to write. First, the bulkOpportunityTest test demonstrates how to tie the utility functions together into a functional test:

```
static testMethod void bulkOpportunityTest() {
   List<Opportunity> ops = new List<Opportunity>();
   // Note, you may need to adjust these numbers
   initTestObjects(ops, 100, 15, 15, 40);

   Test.StartTest();
   for(Opportunity op: ops) op.StageName ='Qualification';
   update ops;
   Test.StopTest();

   validateOCRs(ops);
}
```

You can get different test behaviors, and test different limits, by choosing different parameters to initTestObjects. You can also create several different tests that use different parameters, reducing the amount of code needed to implement your complete set of unit tests.

The bulkOpportunityTest test and utility functions validate the part of the requirements that ensures that a primary contact exists for opportunities that are already associated with contacts. But it doesn't test the condition where there are no contacts associated with an opportunity. The TestBulkPatterns.createTaskTest verifies that part of the functionality.

```
static testMethod void createTaskTest()
{
   Integer numberOfOpportunities = 100;
    List<Opportunity> ops = new List<Opportunity>();
   for(Integer x=0; x<numberOfOpportunities; x++)
   {
```

```
        ops.add(new Opportunity(CloseDate = Date.Today().addDays(5),
            Name = 'optest_' + String.valueOf(x),
            StageName = 'Prospecting' ));
    }

    insert ops;

    Test.StartTest();
    for(Opportunity op: ops) op.StageName='Qualification';
    update ops;
    Test.StopTest();

    List<Task> tasks =
        [SELECT ID, OwnerID, WhatID, Status, Subject, Type
            from Task
            where OwnerID = :UserInfo.getUserID()
            And Type='Other' And IsClosed = False
            And Subject = 'Assign Primary Contact' ];
    system.assertEquals(NumberOfOpportunities, tasks.size());
}
```

How do you ensure that the tasks being queried during the validation are those that were created during this execution context? It's a trick question – unit tests, by default, only see data that was created during the unit test. There are a few exceptions – for example, unit tests can see existing static resources and User objects (user data).

You can change this behavior and allow your unit tests to see existing organization data by using the SeeAllData=true attribute on the unit test. When you do so, you must be careful to differentiate in your tests between test data and existing data. A common way to do this is by maintaining a list of IDs for created test data and using it in queries to make sure you only validate records that you have created. Don't worry though, even when SeeAllData is true, any modifications you make to the database during a unit test are discarded when the test is complete.

Be careful if you are looking at older code – Test classes that are configured to run in API version 23 or earlier see all of the organization's data (the SeeAllData attribute did not exist at the time, and the option to hide an organization's data did not exist).

Evaluating Worst-Case Conditions

When designing code for bulk processing, it is important to evaluate the worst-case scenario for every part of the implementation. This starts with understanding the size of the data input. For triggers, this is generally 200 objects at a time.

Let's do a worst-case assessment of a very simple, non bulkified, translation of the requirements into pseudocode[1].

```
Look for a change in opportunity status
If the opportunity has no OpportunityContactRole objects, check if a
task to create a primary contact already exists.
    If it does, exit.
    If not, create the task and then exit.
Are any of the OpportunityContactRole objects primary?
    If so, exit.
    If not, get a list of the contacts associated
    with the opportunity.
    Query all of the OpportunityContactRole objects
    associated with those contacts.
    For each contact
        Count the number of primary
        OpportunityContactRole objects.
        Count the total number of
        OpportunityContactRole objects.
        Keep track of which contact best matches the
        criteria (most primary, then best total if
        primaries are equal).
    Find the the best qualifying contact, and set
    the original OpportunityContactRole for that
    contact to primary.
```

What happens if 200 opportunities are updated at once?

---

[1] Pseudocode, for those who are not familiar with the concept, is a way of describing software functionality without using the syntax of any particular language.

If this algorithm were implemented within a loop that enumerates those opportunities, everything in the algorithm could happen up to 200 times.

Let's look at this algorithm again:

```
Look for a change in opportunity status
If the opportunity has no OpportunityContactRole objects, check if a
task to create a primary contact already exists.
    If it does, exit
    If not, create the task and then exit.
```

That's a query for OpportunityContactRole objects.

In a worst-case scenario, this results in up to one query for existing Task objects and one DML operation to insert a new Task object.

```
Are any of the OpportunityContactRole objects primary?
```

How many OpportunityContactRole objects might be on an opportunity? It really depends on the type of organization and business. There's no theoretical upper limit, so you need to choose a realistic worst case – a worst case number that should work for any real organization. Let's assume that even the largest B2B organization won't exceed an average of 20 contacts per opportunity. So this test has a worst case of 20 loop iterations.

```
    If so, exit
    If not, get a list of the contacts associated
    with the opportunity.
```

Building the list of contact IDs is another 20 loop iterations.

```
    Query all of the OpportunityContactRole objects
    associated with those contacts.
```

How many opportunities might a given contact be involved in? Again, there's no theoretical maximum, so we need to come up with a realistic worst case. Let's say that as a worse case an average contact could be involved with 100 opportunities. So this would be a query that returns 100 results for each of 20 contacts.

```
For each contact
    Count the number of primary
    OpportunityContactRole objects
    Count the total number of
    OpportunityContactRole objects
    Keep track of which contact best matches the
    criteria (most primary, then best total if
    primaries are equal)
```

This becomes a 100-iteration loop.

```
Find the the best qualifying contact, and set
the original OpportunityContactRole for that
contact to primary.
```

This ends with a DML statement.

So to process a single opportunity, we have as worst cases:

- One Task Query + One DML operation

Or

- 2 x 20 iterations
- 1 Contact/OpportunityContactRole query @ 2000 records
- 20 x 100 iteration
- One DML operation

That seems easy enough, but what happens when you put it in a batch of 200 opportunities?

The task worst case becomes 200 queries or 200 DML operations – both exceed current limits.

The opportunity processing worst case becomes:

- 200 x 2 x 20 = 8,000 iterations
- 200 queries @ 400,000 records

- 200 x 20 x 100 = 400,000 iterations
- 200 DML operations

Obviously, we have a problem. The number of queries and DML statements is something you probably expected and know how to deal with. If your goal is to keep your CPU time below 1 second, that leaves you a bit under 3 microseconds per iteration. That's not a lot of time. It's not certain that this implementation would exceed limits even in a worst-case scenario, but the possibility exists, depending on how much functionality you need to place in each iteration loop.

Unlike the queries and DML statements, the number of records queried and CPU time is not easily reduced by just moving queries outside of a loop. These are issues that testing alone would not necessarily show, because the limits on unit tests prevent creation of very large numbers of records. Only incorporating a worst-case analysis as part of the design process allows you to anticipate these kinds of problems and be prepared to deal with them.

In the chapter on Limits, you learned that limit issues are generally addressed by trading off one limit against another. And indeed, the way you typically bulkify code with SOQL or DML operations inside of loops, is to use collections to prepare the necessary data and hold the results, moving the SOQL or DML out of the loop - trading additional code for a reduction in SOQL and DML operations.

But what do you do when you are already reaching limits on CPU time and number of records that can be retrieved by a query? How do you trade off one limit against another when your algorithm fails all limits in a worst-case scenario?

A Common Solution

Let's begin with a straightforward solution to the problem using common bulk design patterns. In the sample code, you'll see an implementation of the non-bulkified solution in method afterUpdateOpportunityAwful – a solution so hopeless that I won't even bother including the whole thing here. You'll need to reduce the number of test objects in the test class to even get it to run.

The code we will look at is implemented in method afterUpdateOpportunityCommon.

The method begins with a design pattern that is part of almost every bulk compatible trigger – a simple loop over the input data to identify which objects need to be processed.

```
public static void afterUpdateOpportunityCommon(
    List<Opportunity> newList, Map<ID, Opportunity> newMap,
    Map<ID, Opportunity> oldMap)
{
    // Pattern 2 - Straightforward common implementation

    Set<ID> opportunityIDsWithStagenameChanges = new Set<ID>();

    // Get OpportunityContactRoles
    for(Opportunity op: newList)
    {
        if(op.StageName != oldMap.get(op.id).StageName)
            opportunityIDsWithStagenameChanges.add(op.id);
    }

    // Quick exit if no processing required
    if(opportunityIDsWithStagenameChanges.size()==0) return;
```

In this case we build a set of IDs to the opportunities that have a stage change. We're not interested in any others. You'll see implementations of this pattern that use sets, lists and maps. It's really not critical which one you choose. The idea is to choose the one that captures the data that you actually need. In this case, the ID is sufficient because we already have a map (the newMap variable). There is some very small saving in heap space by using a Set instead of a map – but it's a minor issue.

If you detect that no records need to be processed, exit the code as quickly as possible. This improves efficiency and reduces the chance of errors later in the code. There are some developers who feel strongly that every function should have a single exit point. If you prefer that approach, consider using a try/catch/finally block instead of complex nesting of conditional statements, as shown in the following pseudocode.

```
function
   try
      Test condition
      If fail return

      continue operation
   catch
      rethrow error
   finally
      early return statement and any exceptions
      will all execute here
end function
```

The next step is to query all of the OpportunityContactRole objects related to these opportunities, so we can evaluate if any opportunities already have primary contacts, or if any of them have no primary contacts.

```
// Query for all related OpportunityContactRole
List<OpportunityContactRole> ocrs =
   [Select ID, ContactID, IsPrimary, OpportunityID
      from OpportunityContactRole
      where OpportunityID in :opportunityIDsWithStagenameChanges];

// Look for primary, or for no OCR on opportunities
Set<ID> primaryFound = new Set<ID>();
Set<ID> anyFound = new Set<ID>();

for(OpportunityContactRole ocr: ocrs)
{
   if(ocr.IsPrimary) primaryFound.add(ocr.OpportunityID);
   anyFound.add(ocr.OpportunityID);
}
```

As you recall, the worst-case assessment of 20 OpportunityContactRole objects for each opportunity could result in 4000 records being retrieved here – so while this query is safe, we know there are potential problems. For this implementation, we're going to remain aware of these issues, but not incorporate them into the solution.

One question that arises is whether it might make sense to split this into two queries – one that pulls primary contacts (IsPrimary = true), and the other that doesn't. Doing so adds one query and might save a line or two of code at best – so while it is potentially a legitimate trade-off, it has such minor effect that it's probably not worth worrying about.

Now you have two sets, one that contains the IDs of all opportunities with primary contacts, the other that contains the IDs of all opportunities with any contacts.

```
// Build list of opportunities with no contact role,
// and list with contact role but no primary contact role
// Use maps because it's an easy way to get the
// keyset for later queries
Map<ID, Opportunity> opsWithNoContactRoles = new Map<ID, Opportunity>();
Map<ID, Opportunity> opsWithNoPrimary = new Map<ID, Opportunity>();

for(ID opid: opportunityIDsWithStagenameChanges)
{
    if(!primaryFound.contains(opid))
    {
        if(anyFound.contains(opid))
            opsWithNoPrimary.put(opid, newMap.get(opid));
        else
            opsWithNoContactRoles.put(opid,newMap.get(opid));
    }
}
```

Here we load two new maps based on the primaryFound and anyFound sets. Astute programmers may recognize that there is another way we could do this. Instead of creating two new maps, we could remove entries from clones of the opportunityIDsWithStagenameChanges set, and from then on use the newMap variable to obtain records as needed thus eliminating this loop completely. You can see an implementation of that approach in the afterUpdateOpportunitySets method in the sample code. It's not at all clear which approach is more efficient in terms of CPU time – the results will vary based on the data being processed. While use of sets will tend to reduce the number of lines of code executed, removing items from a set is slower than adding items to a set.

Using sets is also less intuitive and harder to understand – especially for beginners. Which means the long-term costs to support and maintain the code might be slightly higher. It's important to not just trade-off limits against each other – you need to also trade them off against the overall lifecycle costs of the software.

Next comes the code to deal with opportunities without contact roles. We first query for any existing tasks on those opportunities, filtering as much as possible to ensure that we only receive the correct type of tasks.

```
// First deal with any opportunities without contact roles
if(opsWithNoContactRoles.size()>0)
{
    // Find out which ones have existing tasks
    List<Task> tasks =
        [SELECT ID, OwnerID, WhatID, Status, Subject, Type from Task
        where Type='Other'
        And WhatID in :OpsWithNoContactRoles.keyset()
        And IsClosed = False
        And Subject = 'Assign Primary Contact'    ];

    // Don't loop through opportunities - waste of time.
    // Loop through tasks to build set of IDs with tasks
    Set<ID> opsWithTasks = new Set<ID>();
    for(Task t: tasks)
    {
        // Get the opportunity
        Opportunity op =opsWithNoContactRoles.get(t.WhatID);
        // Make sure it's assigned to the right person
        if(t.OwnerID == op.OwnerID) opsWithTasks.add(op.ID);
    }
    // Now create new tasks
    List<Task> newTasks = new List<Task>();
    for(Opportunity op: opsWithNoContactRoles.values())
    {
        if(!opsWithTasks.contains(op.id))
        {
            newTasks.add(
                new Task(OwnerID = op.OwnerID, Type='Other',
```

```
                WhatID = op.ID,
                Subject = 'Assign Primary Contact',
                ActivityDate = Date.Today().AddDays(3) ));
            }
        }
    if(newTasks.size()>0) insert newTasks;
}
```

One question that you'll often face is choosing which object to loop through. In this case, we're checking each opportunity to see if it has a task. Logically, you might want to loop through each opportunity, and for each opportunity scan the task list to see if a task was found. This approach is fine in a single object scenario, but inefficient in a bulk pattern. In a worst case, where all of the opportunities have existing tasks, the inside of the loop could execute about 200x 100 = 20,000 times (if you have close to 200 tasks in the list, the average number of iterations to find one in a simple search will be about 100). Instead, loop through the tasks and add an entry to the opsWithTasks set to determine which opportunities already have a task. The inside of this loop executes a maximum of 200 times.

Only then do we scan through the opportunities and create the tasks for those opportunities that do not already have tasks.

The code includes a test to make sure that the task belongs to the owner of the opportunity. Why didn't we include an OwnerID filter in the query? Since we're querying on tasks for multiple opportunities, the filter would have little value. Sure, we could build a set of owners for all of the opportunities we are interested in and filter on that, but we'd still have to do this test in code for each specific opportunity – so there's little benefit.

Back to the implementation.

First, build a list of the contacts for the opportunities that have no primary contact.

```
if(opsWithNoPrimary.size()>0)
{
    // Get a list of the contacts
    List<ID> contactIdsForOps = new List<ID>();
    for(OpportunityContactRole ocr: ocrs)
```

```
    {
        if(opsWithNoPrimary.containskey(ocr.OpportunityID))
            contactIdsForOps.add(ocr.ContactID);
    }
```

Looping through all of the OpportunityContactRole objects and testing each one against the opsWithNoPrimary map is potentially inefficient. But to avoid this inefficiency we'd have to either create a map of lists (map of opportunity ID to list of OpportunityContactRole), or requery the Opportunities using a subquery to grab the contact roles. The former would cost more code than we would save. The latter would add a query and additional code to process each record. So though this code looks inefficient, it's actually a good solution.

In this case, we query on contacts, using a subquery to obtain all of the existing OpportunityContactRole objects for the contact. Note that this will requery OpportunityContactRole objects that we already have – an inefficiency to remember for the next attempt (trading off number of records queried against CPU time).

```
// Now query the contacts with their OpportunityContactRoles
Map<ID, Contact> contactsForOps =
    new Map<ID, Contact>(
        [Select ID, (Select ID, IsPrimary, OpportunityID
            from OpportunityContactRoles)
        from Contact where ID in :contactIdsForOps]);
```

Ultimately, we need to find the best OpportunityContactRole for each opportunity. As with the task example earlier, we need to choose the object for the loop. While you could test each opportunity for its OpportunityContactRoles, it's much more efficient to iterate over OpportunityContactRole and store the ranking of each one in maps that are indexed by Opportunity.

```
// Now figure out which of the OpportunityContactRoles
// should be set to primary
// Map of opportunity ID to the best OCR for that ID
Map<ID,OpportunityContactRole> bestOcrs =
    new Map<ID, OpportunityContactRole>();

// Map of opportunity to Total # OCRs on
```

```
// the current best opportunity contact
Map<ID,Integer> bestContactAllOcrCount = new Map<ID,Integer>();

// Map of opportunity to Total # primary OCRs
// on the current best opportunity contact
Map<ID,Integer> bestContactPrimaryOcrCount = new Map<ID, Integer>();

for(OpportunityContactRole ocr: ocrs)
{
    if(!opsWithNoPrimary.containskey(ocr.OpportunityID)) continue;
    Contact currentContact= contactsForOps.get(ocr.ContactID);
    Integer primaryCount = 0;
    for(OpportunityContactRole testOcr:
        currentContact.OpportunityContactRoles)
    {
        if(testocr.IsPrimary) primaryCount ++;
    }
    if(!bestOcrs.containskey(ocr.OpportunityID) ||
        primaryCount>bestContactPrimaryOcrCount.get(ocr.OpportunityID) ||
        (primaryCount ==
            bestContactAllOcrCount.get(ocr.OpportunityID) &&
            currentContact.OpportunityContactRoles.size()>
            bestContactAllOcrCount.get(ocr.OpportunityID)))
    {
        bestOcrs.put(ocr.OpportunityID, ocr);
        bestContactAllOcrCount.put(ocr.OpportunityID,
            currentContact.OpportunityContactRoles.size());
        bestContactPrimaryOcrCount.put(
            ocr.OpportunityID, primaryCount);
    }
}
```

There's a small inner loop where we count the primary OpportunityContactRoles for each contact. The total number of OpportunityContactRole objects can be determined by the size of the OpportunityContactRoles array (from the subquery).

Once we've completed the loop, the bestOcrs map contains the best OpportunityContactRole for each opportunity. Set it to primary and update them all in one DML operation.

```
    for(OpportunityContactRole best: bestOcrs.values())
        best.IsPrimary = true;
    update bestOcrs.values();
}
```

The techniques you've seen in this example (and the afterUpdateOpportunitySets method in the sample code), demonstrate the kinds of design patterns that you will typically see from an experienced Apex developer.

However, in this case, based on how we defined the problem and worst-case scenario, common bulk design patterns simply aren't good enough.

Experimenting with the test code demonstrates that this solution is fine in terms of number of SOQL calls. However, the CPU time use and the number of SOQL rows retrieved is a concern, though it's not clear yet how big a problem each one will be.

Query Optimization

Usually when you see issues with CPU time, the problem is usually either a nested loop, or a loop over a very large number of objects. In this case, we have a bit of both.

Ignore the first part of the code where the requirement for dealing with opportunities without contact roles is addressed – that code is not causing the problem.

In the second part that deals with opportunities without primary contacts, the outer loop iterates over OpportunityContactRole objects. In this scenario, with up to 200 opportunities with 20 contact roles each, that's a 4000-object loop. If you're targeting a maximum of 1 second of CPU time, that's 250 microseconds per object per iteration. That doesn't leave a lot of extra room.

Within this loop, there is another loop, that iterates over the OpportunityContactRole objects for a single contact to count the number of times it is the primary
contact. In our scenario that can be 100 objects. So, even though it is a very tight
loop, it alone is a major contributor to the CPU time used.

Can this be improved?

The AfterUpdateOpportunityBetterQueries demonstrates how to address both
SOQL rows and CPU time issues.

First, you can get rid of the inner loop by using SOQL aggregate functions. The
count function allows you to count the number of records that match the specified
filter, in this case: IsPrimary = true.

But SOQL aggregate functions can't be placed in a subquery. So to use this approach, the algorithm has to be redesigned. You still need to be able to obtain the
count based on the contact, so after doing the query, you'll need to copy the totals
into maps that are indexed by the contact ID.

```
// Get a list of the contacts
List<ID> contactIdsForOps = new List<ID>();
for(OpportunityContactRole ocr: ocrs)
{
    if(opsWithNoPrimaryWithContactRoles.contains(ocr.OpportunityID))
        contactIdsForOps.add(ocr.ContactID);
}


// Now get the totals count and primary count for each
// contact by using aggregate functions and grouping by contact
List<AggregateResult> ocrsByContact =
    [Select ContactID, Count(ID) total
    from OpportunityContactRole
    where ContactID in :contactIdsForOps
    Group By ContactID];
List<AggregateResult> primaryOcrsByContact =
    [Select ContactID, Count(ID) total
    from OpportunityContactRole where IsPrimary=true
    and ContactID in :contactIdsForOps Group By ContactID];
```

```
// Let's get the totals by contact for a faster loop
Map<ID, Integer> totalsByContact = new Map<ID, Integer>();
Map<ID, Integer> primaryByContact =new Map<ID, Integer>();
for(AggregateResult ar: ocrsByContact)
    totalsByContact.put((ID)ar.get('ContactID'),
    Integer.ValueOf(ar.get('total')));
for(AggregateResult ar: primaryOcrsByContact)
    primaryByContact.put((ID)ar.get('ContactID'),
    Integer.ValueOf(ar.get('total')));
```

What are the tradeoffs in this approach? There are two extra queries, but that only brings the total number of queries to four, so that's insignificant. There are two new loops that together iterate over twice the total number of contacts. In our worst-case scenario, that is 200 opportunities x 20 contact roles each. Even if each contact role is a distinct contact, that is 4000 rows. Both are not only very tight loops, they are performing map inserts, which are very efficient operations. This replaces a possible 4000 object x 100 iteration - An excellent trade.

What about the rest of the algorithm? Can we reduce the number of objects that are being iterated?

Yes and no.

You still need to check all 4000 possible OpportunityContactRole objects to see which is most efficient. But you can potentially reduce the amount of code within the loop further.

Previously, the sample looped over all OpportunityContactRoles, and did a test within the loop to determine whether to continue or not:

```
if(!opsWithNoPrimary.containskey(ocr.OpportunityID)) continue;
```

You can get rid of that line by using the Set approach and modifying the set to contain opportunities without primary contacts, but that do have some contacts.

```
// Look for primary, or for no OCR on opportunities
Set<ID> opsWithNoPrimaryWithContactRoles =
        opportunityIDsWithStagenameChanges.Clone();
Set<ID> opsWithNoContactRoles =
        opportunityIDsWithStagenameChanges.Clone();
for(OpportunityContactRole ocr: ocrs)
{
    if(ocr.IsPrimary)
        opsWithNoPrimaryWithContactRoles.remove(ocr.OpportunityID);
    opsWithNoContactRoles.remove(ocr.OpportunityID);
}
opsWithNoPrimaryWithContactRoles.RemoveAll(opsWithNoContactRoles);
```

Previously, the next step was to perform a query on Contacts, with a subquery on OpportunityContactRole objects. The subquery was used to count the number of OpportunityContactRole objects related to each contact.

Now that you have maps to look up the totals for contacts, you don't need a subquery on the OpportunityContactRole query. What you actually need is a way to obtain a list of OpportunityContactRole objects for each opportunity. You can change the query to opportunities with a subquery on OpportunityContactRole. You'll then be able choose which OpportunityContactRole to set as primary for each opportunity.

```
List<Opportunity> opportunitiesWithoutPrimary =
    [Select ID ,(Select ID, ContactID, IsPrimary
    from OpportunityContactRoles) from Opportunity
    where ID in :opsWithNoPrimaryWithContactRoles];
List<OpportunityContactRole> ocrsToUpdate =
    new List<OpportunityContactRole>();

for(Opportunity op: opportunitiesWithoutPrimary)
{
    OpportunityContactRole bestOcr = null;
    Integer primaryCount = 0;
    Integer totalCount = 0;
    for(OpportunityContactRole opOcrs: op.OpportunityContactRoles)
    {
```

```
    // Use intermediate variables to reduce
    // # of map accesses in loop
    Integer primaryCountForThisContact =
        primaryByContact.get(opocrs.Contactid);
    Integer totalCountForThisContact =
        totalsByContact.get(opocrs.contactId);

    if(bestOcr==null ||
        primaryCountForThisContact > primaryCount ||
         (primaryCountForThisContact == totalCount &&
        totalCountForThisContact > totalCount )) {
        primaryCount = primaryCountForThisContact;
        totalCount = totalCountForThisContact;
        bestOcr = opOcrs;
    }
  }
  bestOcr.IsPrimary = true;
  ocrsToUpdate.add(bestOcr);
}
update ocrsToUpdate;
```

In terms of the code itself, there will be little savings in the worst-case scenario where every opportunity needs to have a primary contact role assigned. However, in any case where only some of the opportunities need primary contact roles assigned, you'll definitely see a performance boost.

It may seem odd to do an Opportunity query just to essentially map from opportunities to OpportunityContactRole objects. After all, you already have the opportunities (it is an opportunity trigger), and you've already queried for the OpportunityContactRole objects. Why not create a map where the key is the opportunity ID and the values are lists of OpportunityContactRole objects?

```
Map<ID,List<OpportunityContactRole>>
```

This is another limits tradeoff. Building a map would save a SOQL query and reduce the number of query rows retrieved, but it seems likely that the extra loop would have an additional cost in CPU time. We'll take a closer look at this later. Right now, let's take a look at the results so far.

We've been discussing worst case scenarios. Our test class can't demonstrate the worst-case scenario because it isn't capable of creating enough test objects to reproduce that scenario – trying to do so would exceed the test setup limits. However, it does create enough objects to demonstrate the effectiveness of this approach.

Choosing the fastest of four runs using the afterUpdateOpportunityCommon method produced the following results:

- Number of queries: 2
- Number of query rows: 3265
- CPU Time: 3434 ms

With the same test conditions, averaging four runs using the afterUpdateOpportunityBetterQueries method produced the following results:

- Number of queries: 4
- Number of query rows: 3140
- CPU Time: 173 ms

That's a huge drop in CPU time! Not only will this dramatically reduce the risk of exceeding CPU limits, it will significantly improve the performance of the application.

Now let's take a closer look an approach discussed earlier that could serve to reduce the row count. Instead of requerying the Opportunities that don't have primary contacts with a subquery for the related OpportunityContactRole objects, let's try building a similar related list using data that has already been retrieved. You can see how this is done in the afterUpdateOpportunityBetterQueries2 example.

Instead of the query:

```
List<Opportunity> opportunitiesWithoutPrimary =
    [Select ID ,(Select ID, ContactID, IsPrimary
    from OpportunityContactRoles) from Opportunity
    where ID in :opsWithNoPrimaryWithContactRoles];
```

You can build a map from the opportunity ID to a list of related OpportunityContactRole objects as follows:

```
// Instead of requerying opps with a subquery of contact
// roles, build a map from opp ID to related contact
// roles for opportunties without primary contact roles
Map<ID, List<OpportunityContactRole>>
      opportunitiesWithoutPrimary =
      new Map<ID, List<OpportunityContactRole>>();
for(OpportunityContactRole ocr: ocrs)
{
   ID opid = ocr.OpportunityID;// Use temp var for speed
   if(opsWithNoPrimaryWithContactRoles.contains(opid))
   {
      if(!opportunitiesWithoutPrimary.containsKey(opid))
         opportunitiesWithoutPrimary.put(
            opid, new List<OpportunityContactRole>());
      opportunitiesWithoutPrimary.get(opid).add(ocr);
   }
}
```

This is a very common design pattern for building a map to a related list. Note how the code makes use of a temporary variable to hold the opportunity ID instead of accessing the object property multiple times.

Switching from an array of objects and related objects to a map of related lists does require some additional changes to the code. Instead of iterating over a list of objects, you enumerate over the opportunity IDs from the map's keys which are retrieved using the map keyset method.

```
for(ID opid: opportunitiesWithoutPrimary.keyset())
{
   OpportunityContactRole bestOcr = null;
   Integer primaryCount = 0;
   Integer totalCount = 0;
   for(OpportunityContactRole opOcrs:
      opportunitiesWithoutPrimary.get(opid))
   {
```

```
    // Use intermediate variables to reduce #
    // of map accesses in loop
    Integer primaryCountForThisContact =
        primaryByContact.get(opocrs.Contactid);
    Integer totalCountForThisContact =
        totalsByContact.get(opocrs.contactId);
    if(bestOcr==null ||
        primaryCountForThisContact > primaryCount ||
         (primaryCountForThisContact == totalCount &&
        totalCountForThisContact > totalCount )) {
        primaryCount = primaryCountForThisContact;
        totalCount = totalCountForThisContact;
        bestOcr = opOcrs;
        bestOcr.IsPrimary = true;
        ocrsToUpdate.add(bestOcr);
    }
  }
}
update ocrsToUpdate;
```

Logic would suggest that this approach will reduce the number of query rows but increase the CPU time, since there is a new loop over all of the OpportunityContactRole objects that includes creation of multiple list objects.

The minimum over four runs produces the following results:

- Number of queries: 3
- Number of query rows: 1540
- CPU Time: 378 ms

And indeed, the CPU time has increased. This increase will be unsurprising – unless you read previous editions of this book, where this example showed a decrease in CPU time! In the past, looping over a subquery collection was quite slow, so the cost of creating the opportunitiesWithoutPrimary map was offset by the speed advantage of map access over accessing a collection created via a subquery. Current benchmarks suggest that advantage has vanished. What has changed?

The most significant change in Apex from the time the previous edition was published is the transition to a new Apex compiler. That Salesforce was able to build and deploy a new Apex compiler without anyone noticing is certainly one of the greatest feats in software engineering I have ever heard of. It seems likely that the improvement in subquery performance relates to that, though it could well be related to other system optimizations.

In either case, it's a good reminder that the platform is constantly changing, and one must be very careful to verify and reevaluate best practices periodically.

Into the Future

The current implementation is already fairly solid. But you won't always be able to reduce CPU time through the use of SOQL aggregation. Here's another approach you can use.

One of the advantages of future (asynchronous) calls is that they have higher limits. But sometimes an even more important advantage is that they isolate your code from other operations taking place during the trigger. In this example, we are triggering on an opportunity update. There may be any number of other triggers, workflows and processes invoked by the same update, all of which will be consuming resources. Moving your code into an asynchronous operation isolates it from those demands. In this example, the only functionality competing for resources would be those triggered by task creation. Updating OpportunityContactRole objects will have no effect, as it's not currently possible to trigger on those objects. This isolation, along with the higher limits available during asynchronous operations, can dramatically reduce the chances of you hitting limits both now and in the future, as others add additional code and declarative functionality to the org.

 In this particular case, there is no reason why the operation has to take place immediately. So why not do it asynchronously?

Refactoring this code into a future call is remarkably easy.

The start of the function is changed as follows:

```
private static Boolean futureCalled = false;

public static void afterUpdateOpportunityFutureSupport(
    List<Opportunity> newList, Map<ID, Opportunity> newMap,
    Map<ID, Opportunity> oldMap)
{
    // Pattern 6 - with future support
    Set<ID> opportunityIDsWithStagenameChanges = new Set<ID>();

    // Get OpportunityContactRoles
    if(!System.isFuture())
    {
        for(Opportunity op: newList)
        {
          if(op.StageName != oldMap.get(op.id).StageName)
            opportunityIDsWithStagenameChanges.add(op.id);
        }
        if(newList.size()>50)
        {
            if(!futureCalled)
                futureUpdateOpportunities(
                opportunityIDsWithStagenameChanges);
            futureCalled = true;
            return;
        }
    }
    else
        opportunityIDsWithStagenameChanges.addall(newMap.keyset());
```

This implementation starts by detecting whether or not it is a future call. If not, it looks for the stage changes to obtain a list of effected opportunities (as before). In this example, there's a fixed threshold to determine whether to go with a future call or not – I'll come back to that shortly.

If a future call is needed, the set of opportunity IDs are passed as arguments to the future call, and the function exits. There's a static variable test to make sure the future call happens only once – just in case this trigger is reentered due to a DML update by another trigger, or a field update in a workflow.

If this is a future call, the opportunityIDsWithStagenameChanges variable is loaded with the IDs of the opportunities to process and the function continues as before.

The asynchronous function is quite simple:

```
@future
public static void futureUpdateOpportunities(Set<ID> opportunitiyIds)
{
    Map<ID, Opportunity> newMap = new Map<ID, Opportunity>(
            [SELECT ID, OwnerID from Opportunity
            where ID in :opportunitiyIds]);
    afterUpdateOpportunityFutureSupport(newMap.values(), newMap, null);
}
```

Remember to include any opportunity fields used within the afterUpdateOpportunityFutureSupport function in the Select query.

In this example, we used a fixed threshold to determine whether to perform a future call or not, but you have many other options. You can use custom metadata or a custom setting to make this number configurable. You can use a Limits function to determine dynamically whether you are approaching limits as the code runs. If you see that you are getting close, you can abort the operation and make the future call instead.

You don't have to make it an all or nothing decision. You could process the opportunities without contact roles (creating tasks as necessary) within the trigger, and only process those without primary contacts in the future call. This would be a great approach if, instead of creating tasks, you wanted to mark those records as errors (something that must be done immediately).

You could add some other optimizations at this point. For example, the futureUpdateOpportunities function could include a subquery on OpportunityContactRoles, thus allowing you to eliminate an extra query later.

This example used a future call, but we could have implemented this using queueable Apex as well. You'll learn more about the various asynchronous operations in chapter 7.

By the way, the ability to quickly refactor code as you saw here is yet another reason why all of your trigger functionality should be implemented in class methods.

Batch Apex

Future calls are a great way to handle CPU time limits, but in this example, we're also concerned about the limit to the number of records that can be retrieved in an execution context. Unfortunately, this limit is a tough one to test for – the number of records that you can insert using your test code is less than the limit on the number you can retrieve. So the only ways to detect potential record limit issues are by evaluating worst case scenarios (as we did earlier), or by running the tests on existing data in a large organization that happens to generate that worst-case scenario.

The way to handle processing of large numbers of records is to split them up into smaller batches using Batch Apex.

The trigger processing code uses almost exactly the same design pattern as the future call did, as shown in the afterUpdateOpportunityBatchSupport method:

```
private static Boolean batchCalled = false;

public static void afterUpdateOpportunityBatchSupport(
    List<Opportunity> newList, Map<ID, Opportunity> newMap,
    Map<ID, Opportunity> oldMap)
{
    // Pattern 7 - with batch support

    Set<ID> opportunityIDsWithStagenameChanges =new Set<ID>();

    // Get OpportunityContactRoles
    if(!System.isBatch())
    {
        for(Opportunity op: newList)
        {
            if(op.StageName != oldmap.get(op.id).StageName)
                opportunityIDsWithStagenameChanges.add(op.id);
```

```
    }
    if(newList.size()>100)
    {
        if(!batchCalled)
        {
            Database.executeBatch(new BulkPatternBatch(
                opportunityIDsWithStagenameChanges), 100);
        }
        batchCalled = true;
        return;
    }
}
else opportunityIDsWithStagenameChanges.addall(newMap.keyset());
```

The second parameter in the Database.executeBatch call specifies the size of the
batch to use. Choose a small enough size to ensure that you won't exceed the record
count limit.

The batch class itself is fairly simple. The query and set of opportunity IDs are initialized by the class constructor and are stored in the class. The execute method is
called with a subset of records based on the batch size. It then calls the AfterUpdateOpportunityBatchSupport method.

```
global class BulkPatternBatch implements Database.Batchable<sObject> {

    global final string query;
    global final Set<ID> opportunityIds;


    public bulkPatternBatch(Set<ID> opportunityIDsToUpdate)
    {
        opportunityids = opportunityIDsToUpdate;
        query = 'SELECT ID, OwnerID from Opportunity
                where ID in :opportunityids ';
    }

    global Database.QueryLocator start(Database.BatchableContext BC){
        return Database.getQueryLocator(query);
```

```
    }

    global void execute(
        Database.BatchableContext BC, List<sObject> scope){
        List<Opportunity> ops = (List<Opportunity>)scope;
        Map<ID, Opportunity> newmap = new Map<ID, Opportunity>(ops);
        BulkPatterns.afterUpdateOpportunityBatchSupport (
            ops, newMap, null);
        return;
    }

    global void finish(Database.BatchableContext BC){
    }
}
```

Keep in mind that test code can only execute a single batch iteration. So be sure that your test code batch size does not exceed the batch size specified in the Database.executeBatch method.

Other Approaches

What if you absolutely can't find a way to solve a limits issue? As you have seen, it is important to design your code based on worst-case bulk scenarios. But those worst-case scenarios have to be realistic. The very fact that there are limits means that you can rarely code against theoretical worst-case scenarios.

If you are a consultant developing code for a single organization, your job is relatively easy. You can run some reports against the actual organization. In this example, you would probably find that while one or two opportunities have twenty contacts, the average is actually two or three. And that the average number of opportunities for a given contact is also two or three. On finding that, you might generously allow for six of each and stop with the initial simple scenario (though not the awful one!)

But if you are writing software for a package to use on multiple organizations, your challenge is much greater – as you have to anticipate the realistic worst-case scenario for any organization.

What if even these approaches won't work? There are still other options to try.

- You can store intermediate information in custom objects. Then use scheduled Apex to query for those objects, executing the required operations in smaller batches than are even possible using Batch Apex. It might take a while though – as the number of scheduled operations is also limited.

- You can use an external service. An asynchronous call can make a callout into an external web-service. You can host external functionality there to perform complex tasks either immediately, or in the background. After completion of the background operations, your external service can use the API to update data within the Salesforce instance.

- If you are building a package, you can implement multiple solutions and choose the right one for a particular organization after deployment using your package configuration.

- You can build a standalone utility program that performs operations either using the API, or on data exported using the Apex dataloader.

Don't expect to come up with the perfect solution the first time around. It is very common for even the most advanced developers to assess multiple designs, and to even prototype and implement several different approaches in order to come up with the best solution for a particular problem. Adopting bulk patterns and considering limits from the start doesn't mean your first attempt will be your final implementation, only that your path to a good solution will be faster and your final implementation more likely to work well.

Bulk Patterns and Web Services

Apex allows you to expose methods as global web services using both SOAP and REST. Most of the examples illustrate how to do so using single object or single value parameters. Don't follow those examples.

In addition to the limits I have already discussed, inbound web service calls on most organizations are subject to 24-hour limits to the number of calls that can be processed. They are also subject to limits on the amount of data that can be transferred by a single call. These two limits help define the way you should design web service calls.

First, as with triggers, all web service calls should be designed for bulk processing. Both SOAP and REST web services support lists of primitive and SObject types as both parameters and return types. Your web service interface will be more efficient, easier to develop and support, and more scalable if you avoid single object patterns entirely and only build bulk web service calls.

At the same time, you should specify the maximum number of items in your parameter lists to ensure that you don't exceed other limits. In particular, be sure to keep an eye on CPU time limits – many of the functions used to support web services, such as serialization and encryption, are particularly CPU intensive. You should validate the length of input lists to make sure those limits aren't exceeded, and return or throw errors if necessary.

Part II – Application Architecture and Patterns

In Part I of this book, you learned to think in Apex. This means that when faced with a software challenge, you know that your solution must be built to fit within the constraints of one or more execution contexts, each of which has a set of limits. You know that, with rare exceptions, your design will have to handle large numbers of objects. You know that static variables in Apex work differently from other languages, and that difference is a critical and essential part of Apex programming.

These are the core, fundamental concepts that every Apex programmer has to not just know, but understand so deeply it becomes second nature.

Now that you can think in Apex, it's time to look at how one builds solutions in Apex. To do so, we will look at both architecture and common design patterns.

At first, I considered separating those into two parts of the book – chapters on architecture that focused on the higher-level structure of Apex applications, and chapters that discussed common software patterns. But after some thought, I decided to combine the two, mixing the discussion of high level design patterns with the code patterns used to implement them. I believe that viewing these together will help clarify the thought processes one can bring to Apex design.

This part of the book is also not a comprehensive treatment of every possible Apex design pattern. The number of subsystems left out, VisualForce, Lightning, Email, Chatter, and so on, probably exceed those that are included. However, as discussed in the introduction, the goal here is not to replace the Salesforce documentation, but rather to focus on, and elaborate on, the core language features. I think you'll find that your understanding of the design issues discussed in this part of the book will translate nicely to those other subsystems, and make them easier to learn and use effectively.

5 – Fun with Collections

You've already seen quite a few bulk patterns. The one thing they all have in common is extensive use of collections.

The Apex collection types: maps, sets and lists, all have their little quirks. Here are some of the issues that you may run into.

Using Maps to Obtain Sets

One of the most common operations in Apex involves retrieving a related list of objects. In this example, assume you have a list of contacts and wish to retrieve the related tasks. You certainly wouldn't use a loop to perform a query for each contact, as that would quickly fail in a bulk operation. Instead, you need a list or set of the contact IDs, so that you can retrieve all of the tasks for those contacts in one query. You could build the set and perform the query like this:

```
Set<ID> contactIds = new Set<ID>();
for(Contact ct: cts) contactIds.add(ct.id);

List<Task> tasks = [Select ID from Task where Whoid
                    in :contactIds Limit 500];
```

But in most cases, you'll prefer to do it like this:

```
Map<ID, Contact> contactMap = new Map<ID, Contact>(cts);

List<Task> tasks2 = [Select ID from Task
     where Whoid in :contactMap.keyset() Limit 500];
```

When you pass a list as a constructor parameter to a newly created map with an ID key, the map is created using the ID property of the object as the map key. Using a map in this manner is a slightly inefficient use of memory (assuming you don't actually need the map itself), but it is much more efficient than using a loop to populate a set (typically better than 5 times as fast).

Grouping Objects

You've already seen how you can use SOQL to group related objects. There are some cases, however, where you will find yourself needing to group objects using Apex code.

One example is where your algorithm requires you have all of the objects in a single array. In that case, you have a choice: use a Group By SOQL query and then loop through and build a single list of all the related objects, or do a SOQL query without the Group By term, and do your own grouping.

In some cases, you may need records with different groupings, and you may find it more efficient to do your own grouping than to perform multiple SOQL queries.

Finally, you may want to group on a term that isn't supported in SOQL at all. For example, let's say you want to look at all of the tasks for a group of contacts. These contacts may be specified in a trigger, a batch call, an external API call or even a VisualForce page. First, you want to perform a global operation on the tasks, where you don't care about the source. Next, you want to perform an operation on them grouped by the week in which they occur (displaying them in a VisualForce calendar, for example).

The solution is to create a map, where the key is the start date of the week and the value is a list of tasks.

```
// cts is the list of input contacts
Map<ID, Contact> contactMap = new Map<ID, Contact>(cts);

List<Task> tasks = [Select ID, ActivityDate, Description
    from Task where Whoid in :contactMap.keyset() Order
    By ActivityDate Desc Limit 500];

Map<Date, List<Task>> tasksByWeek = new Map<Date, List<Task>>();

for(Task t: tasks)
{
    // Perform global task operation here
```

```
    // Group by week
    Date weekStart = t.ActivityDate.toStartOfWeek();
    if(tasksByWeek.get(weekStart)==null)
        tasksByWeek.put(weekStart, new List<Task>());
    tasksByWeek.get(weekStart).add(t);

    // Perform week related operation here
}
```

Ordering the original list of tasks by ActivityDate results in each of the weekly task lists being in order as well.

This approach results in a sparse list of weeks. In other words – weeks for which there is no task do not have entries in the tasksbyweek map. In a calendar application, you could take a slightly different approach: initially creating entries for each week in the year, and filtering the task query to allow only tasks within that year. This would eliminate the need for testing the presence of a key/list while doing the grouping, which can lead to a slight efficiency improvement when processing large number of tasks.

Case Sensitivity

Keys on maps are case sensitive, except when they are not.

Generally speaking, the keys on a map are case sensitive. Thus the following test code succeeds:

```
static testMethod void caseSensitivity()
{
    Map<String,Integer> intMap =
        new Map<String,Integer>{'A'=>0, 'b'=>1,'C'=>2};
    system.assert(!intMap.containskey('a'));
    system.assert(!intMap.containskey('B'));
}
```

B is not b. A is not a.

However, there are some specific cases where a map is case insensitive. For example, when using dynamic Apex to obtain describe information.

```
static testMethod void caseOnDescribe() {
    // Get global describe
    Map<String, Schema.SObjectType> gd = Schema.getGlobalDescribe();
    System.Assert(gd.ContainsKey('CampaignMember'));
    System.Assert(gd.ContainsKey('campaignmember'));
    System.Assert(gd.ContainsKey('CAMPAIGNMEMBER'));
```

These asserts all pass, indicating that the lookup is case insensitive. This also applies when using the getMap method on SObject describe types.

Internally, the object names are stored in lower case, something you can easily verify by adding the statement system.debug(gd); and looking at the debug output for the map. This an interesting side effect if you use the following code:

```
    System.Assert(gd.keyset().Contains('campaignmember'));
    System.Assert(!gd.keyset().Contains('CampaignMember'));
    System.Assert(!gd.keyset().Contains('CAMPAIGNMEMBER'));
}
```

Though logically the statements gd.ContainsKey and gd.keyset().contains are equivalent, in this case the latter is case sensitive and the former is not.

These are issues to keep in mind when using dynamic SOQL – which is particularly common when creating packages.

As an aside, keep in mind that effective API 28 (Summer 13), the keys for the map returned by the getGlobalDescribe function always contain the namespace of the object if it is part of a managed package.

Avoid Using Objects as Keys

Apex allows you to use objects as map keys and to store objects in sets. But don't do it. Here's why.

Let's say you have a list of contacts, and you need to store an integer value for each object using a map. Your code might look something like this:

```
static testMethod void objectKeys()
{
    List<Contact>cts = new List<Contact>();
    for(Integer x=0;x<5;x++)
    {
        cts.add(new Contact(LastName = 'cttest_' + String.valueOf(x)));
    }
    insert cts;

    // Create a map keyed on contacts
    Map<Contact, Integer> contactMap = new Map<Contact, Integer>();

    for(Integer x = 0; x< 5; x++)
    {
        contactMap.put(cts[x], x);
    }

    system.assertEquals(contactMap.size(),5);
```

So far, so good. But let's say you modify the object, either directly or through a reference from a different variable. In this case, the sameContacts array contains references to the same objects. You then modify one of the fields on the object (either through the original reference or through the new one – it doesn't matter).

```
    // Create another list to reference these
    List<Contact> sameContacts = new List<Contact>(cts);

    for(Integer x = 0; x< 5; x++)
    {
        sameContacts[x].AssistantName = 'person' + string.ValueOf(x);
```

First, assert that the change applied to the object itself regardless of which array you use to reference it. Since we made a copy (not a clone), this works correctly.

```
system.assertEquals(cts[x].AssistantName,
    sameContacts[x].AssistantName);
```

Now use the object to look up its value in the contactmap. The value should be there and should retrieve the integer value, but it doesn't. In fact, the lookup returns null.

```
system.assertNotEquals(contactMap.get(cts[x]), x);
```

Go ahead and add the revised object into the map.

```
contactmap.put(sameContacts[x], x);
}
```

As this assert shows, entering the modified object caused a new entry to exist in the map. The contactmap size is now 10.

```
system.assertNotEquals(contactmap.size(),5);
}
```

You can see this same phenomenon with sets as well in the FunWithCollections.objectSets example in the sample code.

Apex uses a hash of the field values as the internal value to use when searching for the object in the map or set. Changing a field on an object changes this hash value, causing the same object to appear as two distinct objects when used as keys.

Given that one of the main purposes of maps and sets when used with objects is to hold them while they are being modified, using objects as keys or in sets is a sure way to create subtle and hard to find bugs.

The right design pattern is to use the object ID as the key or set value. A correct implementation of the objectKeys method is shown here:

```
static testMethod void objectKeysCorrect()
{
    List<Contact>cts = new List<Contact>();
    for(Integer x=0;x<5;x++)
```

```
{
    cts.add(new Contact(LastName = 'cttest_' + String.valueOf(x)));
}
insert cts;

// Create a map keyed on contacts
Map<ID, Integer> contactMap = new Map<ID, Integer>();

for(Integer x = 0; x< 5; x++)
{
    contactMap.put(cts[x].id, x);
}

system.assertEquals(contactMap.size(),5);

// Create another list to reference these
List<Contact> sameContacts = new List<Contact>(cts);

for(Integer x = 0; x< 5; x++)
{
    sameContacts[x].AssistantName = 'person' + string.ValueOf(x);
    system.assertEquals(cts[x].AssistantName,
        sameContacts[x].AssistantName);
    system.assertEquals(contactMap.get(cts[x].id), x);
    contactmap.put(sameContacts[x].id, x);
}
    system.assertEquals(contactMap.size(),5);
}
```

As you can see, the lookup within the final loop now works (assertEquals instead of assertNotEquals), and the final number of entries in the map is 5.

This presents an interesting dilemma when dealing with objects that you have not yet inserted (and thus have no ID). If the object has a unique field, such as account number, you may be able to use that field as a key. Otherwise, your best bet is to leave the objects in a list and reference them by location. In this example, where you want to associate an integer with each contact, use the position of the contact as the map key in a Map<Integer, Integer> map.

Keeping Track of Objects to Update

It's very common to update objects in triggers and other Apex code. It's always a good idea to only update those objects that are actually changed. That improves the efficiency and performance of your code, and reduces the number of DML records touched, helping you stay within limits.

Logically, the way to do this is simple: any time you update a field in an object, place that object in a collection of objects that need updating. Then, at the end of the Apex Code, update them all in a single DML operation.

For a simple trigger case, a list of objects to update might seem the best way to go.

```
List<Contact>contactsToUpdate = new List<Contact>();


for(Contact ct: cts)
{
   // Do various operations
   // If an update is needed:
   contactsToUpdate.add(ct);

}


if(contactsToUpdate.size()>0) update contactsToUpdate;
```

But as you'll see in the next chapter, there are good reasons to design your code so that you can add functionality to a trigger, or combine all of the updates required by several distinct triggers or classes into a single update operation. For this reason, you should always use a map that is keyed to the object ID (or other unique field).

```
Map<ID,Contact> contactsToUpdate = new Map<ID, Contact>();

// First set of operations
for(Contact ct: cts)
{
   // Do various operations
   // If an update is needed:
```

```
        contactsToUpdate.put(ct.id, ct);
}

// Second set of operations
for(Contact ct: cts)
{
    // Do various operations
    // If an update is needed:
    contactsToUpdate.put(ct.id, ct);
}

if(contactsToUpdate.size()>0)
    update contactsToUpdate.values();
```

You can't use a list, because you can't have the same object twice in a list during a DML operation. You can't use a set because, as you saw in the previous section, field modifications can cause two identical objects to be seen as unique, leading again to duplicate objects in the set.

The Contains Method

Both the List and Set collection have a "contains" method that allows you to determine if an element is in the collection.

Avoid using the List.contains method for very long lists. What is a very long list? That depends on many factors.

For example: it depends on what you are comparing – the harder it is to compare two elements, the greater the advantage of using a Set. That's because a Set uses a hashtable index to speed up searches. It's literally designed for that purpose. Whereas the List.contains method scans the list for the element you are looking for.

It also depends on how many contains operations you plan on doing. If you have a list, and only need to test a few elements, it's probably not worth converting it into a Set for this purpose. If your list is short, say, under 100 elements, staying with a list should be fine. However, if you have a list of more than 100 elements and expect to perform many contains method calls on the list, you may be better off converting the List into a Set, and performing the contains operation there.

The sample code includes two functions, FunWithCollections.ListOrSet and FunWithCollections.ListOrSetWithString that you can use as a template for your own benchmarking experiments.

Eliminating Duplicate Fields from Queries

Dynamic SOQL is used to query objects when you don't know ahead of time what fields will need to be in the query. You'll see a number of examples of dynamic SOQL later in the book. For now, just assume there is some logic that determines what fields to include. The catch is that you must be very careful not to include duplicate fields in the query. If your query is being generated dynamically, that's an easy bug to run into.

Imagine a case where the query logic has created a list with the following fields:

```
List<String> fieldList = new List<String>{'ID', 'Id',
                'lastmodifieddate', 'LastModifiedDate'};
```

The query might be assembled like this:

```
leads = Database.query('Select ' +
     string.join(fieldList, ',') + ' From Lead Limit 1');
```

If you ran this code, you'd get the exception "Query failure duplicate field selected: Id". You can see this in the sample code in the FunWithCollections.eliminateDuplicateFields function.

Clearly, unless your field list is hardcoded, it's a good idea to test for and remove any duplicates. By far the easiest way to do this is using a Set, as Sets ensure that every element is unique.

You might try to maximize efficiency by taking the following approach:

```
Set<String> fieldSet = new Set<String>();
String fields = string.join(fieldList,',');
```

```
fieldSet.addAll(fields.toLowerCase().split(','));
fieldList = new List<String>(fieldSet);
```

It starts by converting the list into a comma separated string. This is very safe with fields, as field API names can't include commas. Next, the entire string is converted into lower case. Remember, Sets are case sensitive, so this is a necessary step. The lower-case string is split back into a list and all its elements are added to the set. Finally, the Set, which now contains no duplicates, is converted back into a list, as the Set object does not have a join function.

It may seem like a lot of back and forth conversions, but each one is fairly efficient, so this solution is simpler and less likely to have errors than doing your own duplicate removal.

There is, however, one situation where this approach may fail – specifically, if you are in a namespaced org – that is, an org used for developing a package. Here's why:

Let's say you're developing in an org with a namespace of xyz and your custom object myobj has a custom field named project with API name project__c. In the namespaced org, that field can be referenced either as project__c or xyz__project__c. And it can be surprisingly easy for duplicates to appear, as developers will typically use the project__c form, but the describe information for the field (say, when you obtain a map of fields) will include the namespace.

Include both in the dynamic SOQL query, and you will see a duplicate field exception! And this duplicate will not be removed by the earlier code, as project__c and xyz__project__c are unique as far as a Set collection is concerned.

A better approach in this case would be as follows:

```
Set<String> fieldSet = new Set<String>();
String ourprefix = 'xyz' + '__';
for(String f: fieldList)
{
    f = f.toLowerCase();

    // Strip off your own namespace here if necessary
```

```
    if(!String.isEmpty(ourprefix) && f.startsWith(ourprefix))
    f = f.replace(ourprefix,'');

    // Optionally test for presense of the field using
    // describe info (not shown here)
    fieldSet.add(f);
}
fieldList = new List<String>(fieldSet);
```

Removing a namespace from a string is trivial – in this example you would just replace xyz__ at the start of the string with an empty string. In the sample code, the namespace is hard-coded. It is, however, preferable to write code that determines its namespace dynamically to allow for potential reuse. You'll learn how that's done in chapter 12.

6 – Triggers

It's a rare application that doesn't involve the creation of one or more triggers. There are other ways for Apex code to run in a system, but none of them are more important to do correctly. If you have an exception in a VisualForce controller, you may see an error message on a page. If you have an exception in a webservice class, calls to that class may fail. But if you have an exception in a trigger, your organization's users may no longer be able to perform even simple operations using the standard Salesforce user interface.

One Trigger to Rule Them All

The first and most important thing to know about triggers is that when you have more than one trigger of the same type, you cannot predict the order in which they will fire.

In a perfect world, this would not matter. Each trigger's code would be completely independent of the others and there would be no possibility that they could interfere with each other. In a perfect world, external factors, such as workflows or triggers written by other developers, couldn't interfere with the operation of your code.

But this is not a perfect world. You can't control the order in which triggers are fired. This can be a very serious problem. What if there is an order dependency with the triggers you've built? You may never know it, because you can't write test code that specifies the order in which your triggers are fired. If there is a problem, it might not appear until you've deployed the code into production. And even then, it may present itself as an intermittent error that is virtually impossible to catch in a debug log and is impossible to reproduce.

You also can't prevent other system administrators from creating triggers and workflows. If you are creating a package, you have no control over what exists on the target system. Learning to deal with these possibilities (as much as is possible) will be an ongoing theme throughout the rest of this book.

While you can't achieve perfect control over an organization, you can, at least, take control over your own code.

Figure 6-1 illustrates the non-deterministic nature of triggers, where the order in which they execute cannot be predicted.

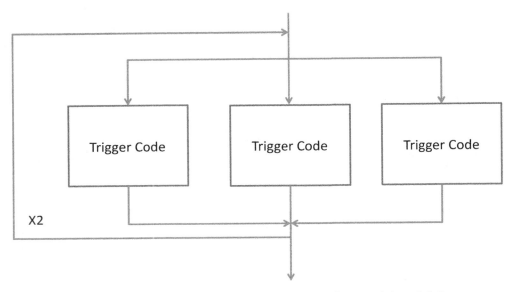

Figure 6-1 —The order in which triggers occur is non-deterministic

In Chapter 2, the discussion of static variables offered one reason to place trigger code into a class. Figure 6-2 illustrates how you can extend that approach to combining the functionality from several triggers into one.

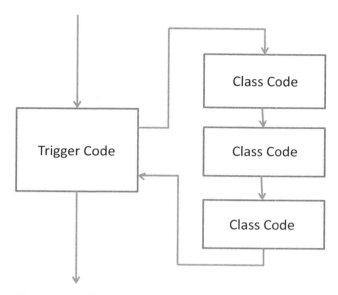

Figure 6-2 –The preferred design pattern for triggers

This approach guarantees you predictability within your application. But it has other benefits as well.

Let's say that this is an update trigger where each functional block may perform an update on a related object. If each functional block is in its own trigger, you can end up with three DML updates. Aside from drawing against your available limits, each of those updates will potentially spawn off additional workflows, processes and trigger executions. This is the true source of most CPU timeout errors in practice – each of the various triggers and declarative processes is efficient enough, but they are called and reentered so many times in an execution context that even the best code ultimately exceeds the limits.

Figure 6-3 illustrates a better approach. You can define a collection to hold all of the objects to be updated. The collection can be a static class variable, or you can pass it as a parameter to each of the class methods.

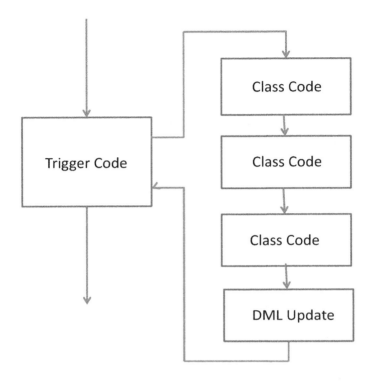

Figure 6-3 –One DML update can be shared among functional blocks

Once all the classes have completed their operations, a single DML update handles all of the updates at once.

Let's look at some approaches you can use to implement this design.

Managing the Data Updates

It is important for every Apex developer to review the Apex Developer Guide's section on triggers – there are quite a few special cases and subtle quirks listed. But for now, there are just two rules to always keep in mind for insert and update triggers (which are the most commonly used trigger types):

- Updating fields on an object in a before trigger is easy. All of the fields are present, and those that are updatable, can be updated.

- Updating fields on an object in an after trigger requires a DML operation and cannot be performed on the objects provided by the trigger. Those objects, found in the new, old, newMap and oldMap trigger context variables, have all their fields set to read-only.

To facilitate combining DML operations from multiple classes, you'll almost certainly want to create some form of centralized data handler. There are many design patterns for this, but we'll start with a very simple one shown in the example TriggerDMLSupport class.

The class has two static variables. The updatingPendingObjects variable is a Boolean that indicates to the system that an internal DML operation is currently in progress. This can be used by the various triggers to modify their behavior - for example, to skip trigger handling that is either unnecessary, or might spawn off additional DML operations. It is also used within the class to ensure that a DML operation does not invoke another one, even if the trigger framework tries to do so.

The opsToUpdate static variable is used by other classes to keep track of records that need to be updated. In this example, the class only handles opportunity objects. You'll learn how to extend this later in the chapter.

```
public static Boolean updatingPendingObjects = false;
public static Map<ID, Opportunity> opsToUpdate =
    new Map<ID, Opportunity>();

// Return a map of updatable opportunity records to use
// in after triggers
public static Map<ID, Opportunity>
    getUpdatableOpportunities(Set<ID> opIds)
{
    Map<ID, Opportunity> ops = new Map<ID, Opportunity>();
    for(ID opid: opIDs)
        ops.put(opid, new Opportunity(ID = opid));
    return ops;
}
```

The getUpdatableOpportunities method creates a map containing empty opportunity objects for each ID. The various trigger handler classes can then set field values for these objects for later update.

Finally, the updatePendingOpportunities function is called at the end of the trigger. It does not fire if called while currently updating objects – this helps reduce the chance of reentrancy. It continues to loop while there are any objects to update. This loop is not necessary in this particular example, but will come into play in later versions, as you will see.

```
public static void updatePendingOpportunties()
{
    if(!updatingPendingObjects)
    {
        while(opsToUpdate.size()>0)
        {
            List<Opportunity> updatingList = opsToUpdate.values();
            opsToUpdate = new Map<ID, Opportunity>();
            updatingPendingObjects = true;
            update updatingList;
            updatingPendingObjects = false;
        }
    }
}
```

Now that we have a basic data management class, it's time to develop the trigger architecture that will use it.

Architecture and Triggers

There are a number of viable architectures for implementing tightly controlled execution flow within a trigger.

Let's say you have two operations to perform during an after-update trigger on an opportunity. Either of these operations might need to perform an additional update on the opportunity or a related object (such as the account or primary contact). The code should be designed so that it is easy to add additional functionality to the trigger later - anywhere in the sequence of operations. In this example it will be an opportunity trigger where the first handler class updates the opportunity stage, and the second one updates the opportunity amount.

You could implement this functionality as follows:

In the trigger

```
trigger OnOpportunity on Opportunity (before insert,
    after insert, after update) {
    if(TriggerDMLSupport.updatingPendingObjects) return;
    Map<ID, Opportunity> updateableMap;
    if(trigger.isAfter) updateableMap =
        TriggerDMLSupport.getUpdatableOpportunities(
        trigger.newMap.keyset());
    TriggerArchitectureClass1.Entry1(trigger.operationType,
        trigger.new, trigger.newMap, trigger.old,
        trigger.oldMap, updateableMap);
    TriggerArchitectureClass2.Entry1(trigger.operationType,
        trigger.new, trigger.newMap, trigger.old,
        trigger.oldMap, updateableMap);
    TriggerDMLSupport.updatePendingOpportunties();
}
```

The first thing the trigger does is check to see if the trigger was caused by an internal DML operation – in other words, are we currently in the process of updating opportunities? Since it's our own operation, we certainly don't need to call those trigger classes again (at least not in this simple example).

The trigger uses the TriggerDMLSupport class to create a map of updatable objects for use by the after triggers, passing it as a parameter to each class. The two trigger handler classes are called, followed by the TriggerDMLSupport.updatePendingOpportunities method to perform the database operation on behalf of both classes.

The trigger handler class follows this pattern:

```
public static void entry1(TriggerOperation triggerType,
    List<Opportunity> newlist, Map<ID, Opportunity> newMap,
    List<Opportunity> oldList, Map<ID,Opportunity> oldMap,
    Map<ID, Opportunity> updateableMap)
{
    List<OpportunityStage> opStages = [Select ID,
        DefaultProbability, MasterLabel
        from OpportunityStage Order By SortOrder Asc];

    for(Opportunity op:newlist)
    {
        Opportunity updateableOp = (updateableMap== null)?
            null: updateableMap.get(op.id);
        switch on triggerType {
            when BEFORE_INSERT
            {
                op.stageName = opStages[1].MasterLabel;
            }
            when AFTER_INSERT
            {
                String targetStage = opStages[2].MasterLabel;
                if(op.stageName!= targetStage)
                {
                    updateableOp.stageName = targetStage;
                    // Mark for update if changed
                    TriggerDMLSupport.opsToUpdate.put(
                        updateableOp.id, updateableOp);
                }
            }
            when AFTER_UPDATE
            {
                String targetStage = opStages[3].MasterLabel;
                if(op.stageName != targetStage)
                {
                    updateableOp.stageName = targetStage;
                    // Mark for update if changed
                    TriggerDMLSupport.opsToUpdate.put(
                        updateableOp.id, updateableOp);
```

```
                }
            }
        }
    }
}
```

The TriggerArchitectureClass1 class, shown here, updates the opportunity stage based on whether it's a before insert, after insert or after update trigger. Yes, it's not a very realistic example – but the purpose for now is to confirm the update operation.

In this example the trigger operation type switch statement is inside of a single opportunity loop. You can certainly take the approach of having an outer switch statement with individual opportunity loops inside of each trigger operation condition, depending on the needs of your application and which approach makes more sense. We'll do that in the next example.

As you can see, the before trigger is easy – the stage is just updated on the trigger context objects directly. The after triggers examine the values on the opportunities provided by the trigger context, but update the objects contained in the updatableMap collection. Changed objects are added to the TriggerDML-Support.opsToUpdate map so that it knows which ones to update.

The TriggerArchitectureClass2 class is identical, except that it updates the amount values.

This approach isn't terrible. It does allow you to control the flow of execution and makes it easy to change the order of trigger handler classes or add or remove functionality. It does aggregate DML operations.

However, this approach does have some serious flaws. It is limited to aggregating updates to one type of object. What if one or more of the classes needs to update a related object such as the opportunity account? You would have to add another parameter to each of the class entry methods to keep track of the related objects that need to be updated. This approach also violates the principle of reducing the amount of code in triggers.

Let's try again.

Dispatchers and Data

The previous example was fine for updating records in after triggers as long as those records were included in one of the trigger collections. But in the real world, triggers may update other types of records, or records of the same type that were not included in the current trigger collection.

To handle these cases, we'll need a much more flexible data manager – one designed to handle any type of object, and that is able to support multiple types of objects at once.

The updated TriggerDMLSupport class now stores objectsToUpdate in a map of maps, where the key is the type of object.

```
public static Boolean updatingPendingObjects = false;
private static Map<Schema.SObjectType, Map<ID, SObject>>
    objectsToUpdate = new Map<Schema.SObjectType, Map<ID, SObject>>();
```

The getUpdateableObjects method has as its parameters the type of object to retrieve and the desired set of IDs. The function first makes sure there is a map for the requested object type in the objectsToUpdate map. If not, it creates one. Next it iterates through the provided Ids, returning any existing updatable objects, and creating new ones if a matching object does not yet exist. This is important, as it ensures that every class that calls this function with a particular ID will receive the same updatable object. Not only will this prevent duplicate record exceptions during the update, it also allows each class to see any previous updates made by other classes, which could be handy in some scenarios.

```
// Return a map of updatable SObject records
public static Map<ID, SObject> getUpdatableObjects(
    Schema.SObjectType objType, Set<ID> objIds)
{
    Map<ID, SObject> objMap = objectsToUpdate.get(objType);
    if(objMap==null)
    {
        objMap = new Map<ID, SObject>();
        objectsToUpdate.put(objType, objMap);
```

```
    }
    Map<ID, SObject> results = new Map<ID, SObject>();
    for(ID objId: objIds) results.put(objID,
        (objMap.containsKey(objId))? objMap.get(objId):
        objType.newSObject(objId));
        return results;
    }
```

The objectsToUpdate map is now private – we don't want classes touching it directly. Instead, they will call the new queueForUpdates method that puts the specified objects into the update map for their object type. This function figures out the object type from the first element in the list – we assume that all objects in the list are of the same type.

```
// We assume all objects are of the same type
// You can add some error checking here just in case
public static void queueForUpdates(List<SObject> toUpdate)
{
    if(toUpdate==null || toUpdate.size()==0) return;
    Schema.SObjectType objType = toUpdate[0].id.getSobjectType();
    Map<ID, SObject> mapForSObjectType = objectsToUpdate.get(objType);
    mapForSObjectType.putAll(toUpdate);
}
```

The updatePendingObjects function has been modified to update all of the pending object types. Otherwise, it's exactly the same logic as before. It still supports the possibility of the trigger framework adding objects to update during a DML operation, even though our example still does not do that.

```
private static Boolean updatesPending()
{
    for(Schema.SObjectType objType: objectsToUpdate.keyset())
    {
        if(objectsToUpdate.get(objType).size()>0) return true;
    }
    return false;
}
```

```
public static void updatePendingObjects()
{
   if(!updatingPendingObjects)
   {
      while(updatesPending())
      {
         for(Schema.SObjectType objType: objectsToUpdate.keyset())
         {
            Map<ID, SObject> objectToUpdateMap =
               objectsToUpdate.get(objType);
            if(objectToUpdateMap.size()==0) continue;
            List<SObject> updatingList = objectToUpdateMap.values();
            objectsToUpdate.put(objType, new Map<ID, SObject>());
            updatingPendingObjects = true;
            update updatingList;
            updatingPendingObjects = false;
         }
      }
   }
}
```

With the improved data manager in place, it's time to update the trigger framework. First, we'll move all of the code out of the trigger except for a call to the new TriggerDispatcher.handleTriggers method.

```
trigger OnOpportunity on Opportunity (
   before insert, after insert, after update) {
      TriggerDispatcher.handleTriggers(trigger.operationType,
      trigger.new, trigger.newMap, trigger.old, trigger.oldMap);
}
```

Now for the TriggerDispatcher class. First there's the handleTriggers function. There's a lot going on, so we'll look at it in sections.

The first thing you'll notice is that all of the parameters are SObject parameters instead of Opportunities. That's right – this one handleTriggers function can be called from any trigger. Which means the code in all of your triggers will be identical. How's that for simplification?

Next, as before, if we're currently performing a DML operation, the code exits immediately. This will change in later versions as we add more flexibility to the framework.

The method next figures out what object type it is processing by looking at the ID of the first object in either the oldList or newList collections. All objects in a trigger collection will always be the same type, so this is reliable.

```
public static void handleTriggers(
    TriggerOperation triggerType, List<SObject> newList,
    Map<ID, SObject> newMap, List<SObject> oldList,
    Map<ID,SObject> oldMap)
{
    if(TriggerDMLSupport.updatingPendingObjects) return;

    SObject firstObject =
        (triggerType == TriggerOperation.AFTER_DELETE ||
        triggerType== TriggerOperation.BEFORE_DELETE)?
        oldList[0]: newList[0];
```

Next, you'll see a switch statement on the first object in the collection. We won't actually use that object – we're just taking advantage of the switch statement's object type selection syntax here.

The dispatcher will have a separate section for each type of SObject supported, calling in sequence the various class handlers. If you want, you can also select handlers by trigger type. In this example, it is assumed that each individual class handler knows what types of triggers it can handle and will ignore the others.

There's one subtle Apex quirk that you see here. Apex can cast a List of SObjects to a list of a specific type using a standard casting operation. However, this won't work for maps, so the castMapToOpportunities helper function performs that task. You'll need a similar helper function for each object type supported by this framework.

```
    switch on firstObject
    {
        when Opportunity obj
```

```
        {
            // You can dispatch to different handlers by
            // trigger type as well
            TriggerArchitectureClass1.entry1(triggerType,
            (List<Opportunity>)newList,
            castMapToOpportunities(newMap),
            (List<Opportunity>)oldList,
            castMapToOpportunities(oldMap));
            TriggerArchitectureClass2.entry1(triggerType,
            (List<Opportunity>)newList,
            castMapToOpportunities(newMap),
            (List<Opportunity>)oldList,
            castMapToOpportunities(oldMap));
        }
    }
    TriggerDMLSupport.updatePendingObjects();
}

// Helper function, since we can't cast directly from a
// map of ID,SObject to a specific type
public static Map<ID, Opportunity> castMapToOpportunities(
    Map<ID, SObject> sourceMap)
{
    if(sourceMap==null) return null;
        return new Map<ID,Opportunity>(
            (List<Opportunity>)sourceMap.values());
}
```

Now let's look at the TriggerArchitectureClass2 entry handler. This handler sets the opportunity amount based on the type of the trigger.

The first thing you'll notice is that the individual class is now responsible for obtaining a map of updatable objects instead of the map being passed as a parameter. The function is not at all limited to using the current object type or the IDs of the opportunities in one of the trigger collections. It can and should use this approach for any objects that the class wishes to update.

```
public static void entry1(TriggerOperation triggerType,
    List<Opportunity> newlist, Map<ID, Opportunity> newMap,
    List<Opportunity> oldList, Map<ID,Opportunity> oldMap)
{
    Map<ID, Opportunity> updateableMap;
    List<Opportunity> opsToUpdate;
    if(triggertype == TriggerOperation.AFTER_INSERT ||
    triggertype == TriggerOperation.AFTER_UPDATE)
    {
        updateableMap =
            TriggerDispatcher.castMapToOpportunities(
            TriggerDMLSupport.getUpdatableObjects(
            Opportunity.SObjectType, newMap.keyset())));
        opsToUpdate = new List<Opportunity>();
    }
```

The previous example used the opportunity as the outer loop and the switch statement as the condition within that loop. In this example we'll flip that around, refactoring the code so that the trigger type is in an outer switch statement, where each when condition has its own opportunity loop. Again, both approaches are fine – choose the one that works best for your scenario.

The function builds a list of records to update, loading them into the opsToUpdate list. That makes it easy to queue them all for update with a single call to the TriggerDMLSupport.queueForUpdates function. You don't have to worry if an object is accidentally added more than once to the list – the duplicate entries will be removed when queueForUpdates adds them to the update map.

```
switch on triggerType {
    when BEFORE_INSERT
    {
        for(Opportunity op:newlist)
        {
            op.amount = 10;
        }
    }
    When AFTER_INSERT, AFTER_UPDATE
```

```
    {
        Decimal targetAmount = (triggerType==
            TriggerOperation.AFTER_INSERT)? 20 : 30;
        for(Opportunity op:newlist)
        {
            if(op.Amount!= targetAmount)
            {
                Opportunity updateableOp = updateableMap.get(op.id);
                updateableOp.Amount = targetAmount;
                // Mark for update if changed
                opsToUpdate.add(updateableOp);
            }
        }
    }
    TriggerDMLSupport.queueForUpdates(opsToUpdate);
}
```

This sample is much better than the previous one. We now have a very nice data manager that supports centralization of data updates. We have a trigger dispatcher function that can be called from every trigger.

But it's still not perfect. Right now, all of our triggers are shut down any time the application updates a record. That may not always be ideal. For example: what if there is a Lightning process or flow that modifies a different object? It's quite possible that we would want the application to process that trigger update. What if an external process fires a field update during your DML operation? Right now, the framework can't detect those, because the triggers are completely disabled.

What if you want to perform DML operations in a certain order? The whole point of controlling program flow is to do exactly that – control the order of operations. The current design doesn't allow that for DML updates.

Could one add additional features to the DML support class to handle these scenarios? Possibly, but by the time you've added handling of insertions, sequencing, keeping track of which class requested which update, and figuring out a way to decide which trigger handlers should be called during each update – well, you'll have built a rather complex piece of code that will likely be fragile, hard to learn, and frustrating for developers.

So let's go in a different direction.

Controlling Program Flow

Figure 6-3 and the previous examples illustrated the concept of caching DML updates across functional blocks. This is one good way to control your execution flow, as it eliminates additional trigger calls and workflows during your trigger processing.

However, there are cases where you will want to perform DML updates during trigger execution. One obvious example is where you want changes in the database from one block of code to be reflected in a query during a subsequent block. This scenario is illustrated in Figure 6-4.

The additional triggers and workflows fired by the DML updates will run additional Apex code. They might even reenter the current trigger (which would lead to an infinite loop on other platforms, but will be self-limiting on Force.com).

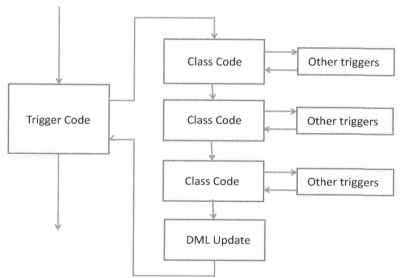

Figure 6-4 – DML operations have side effects

This raises the question: what do you actually want to have happen when your code performs a DML operation? Do you want to process those other triggers? Would you prefer to ignore them? One way or another, there's a good chance that you would want some special handling when they occur based on the knowledge that the trigger was raised due to your own DML call.

Our current example has two trigger handling classes that update two opportunity fields. Let's assume for a moment that there is a good reason for them to continue to work as they do. We'll just add one small change to the logic of the TriggerArchitectureClass1 file. Instead of always setting the opportunity stage to stage 3, it only does so if that would set a later stage. In other words, the code will never reset the stage to an earlier one. The condition for setting the stage is now:

```
if(op.stageName!= targetStage &&
    opLabelsToPosition.get(op.stageName) <
    opLabelsToPosition.get(targetStage) )
```

Next, we'll create a new class called WatchForStageUpdates. This class watches for opportunities whose probability is change from 20% or lower to 50% or higher. The probability field is driven by the opportunity's stage property. When the probability change is detected, the class creates a new task and updates the description of the opportunity.

```
switch on triggerType {
    When AFTER_INSERT, AFTER_UPDATE
    {
        List<Task> newTasks = new List<Task>();
        List<Opportunity> opsToUpdate = new List<Opportunity>();

        for(Opportunity op:newlist)
        {
            if((triggerType== TriggerOperation.AFTER_INSERT
                || oldMap.get(op.id).Probability <=20) &&
                op.Probability>50)
            {
                newTasks.add(new Task(ownerId = op.OwnerID,
                    WhatID = op.id,
                    ActivityDate = Date.Today().addDays(2),
```

```
                Subject='Opportunity stage update',
                Type='Other'));
            Opportunity updatingOp = new Opportunity(Id = op.id);
            updatingOp.Description = ((op.Description==null)? '':
                op.Description) + ' Stage update task on '
                + Date.Today().format();
            opsToUpdate.add(updatingOp);
        }
    }
    if(newTasks.size()>0) insert newtasks;
    if(opsToUpdate.size()>0) update opsToUpdate;
    }
}
```

Now we have a problem. Actually, multiple problems. The WatchForStageUpdates class has to see almost every trigger – including those that occur during a DML update of another class, or a workflow or process. So the current approach of blocking all triggers during a DML operation just won't work.

At the same time, we don't want the other two classes to fire during DML updates. Come to think of it, we may not want them firing during the WatchForStageUpdates DML operations either. So what kind of logic can we use to let these classes know what is happening in the framework so that they can decide whether or not to process the trigger?

An obvious solution is to use static variables to keep track of the state of the framework – we're already doing that with the TriggerDMLSupport.updatePendingObjects field. One could extend this pattern and use a separate static variable for each class. Add the following three static variables to the TriggerDispatcher class:

```
public static Boolean inTriggerArchitectureClass1 = false;
public static Boolean inTriggerArchitectureClass2 = false;
public static Boolean inWatchForStageUpdates = false;
```

Then set the corresponding variable each time a trigger handler function is called, and clear it after, like this:

```
inWatchForStageUpdates = true;
WatchForStageUpdates.processStageUpdate(triggerType,
    (List<Opportunity>)newList, castMapToOpportunities(newMap),
     (List<Opportunity>)oldList, castMapToOpportunities(oldMap));
inWatchForStageUpdates = false;
```

Now each class can determine for itself whether or not a DML operation is in progress either from the TriggerDMLSupport class or from the WatchForStageUpdates class. For example: The TriggerArchitectureClass1 entry1 method uses the following code to exit if a DML operation is in progress.

```
if(TriggerDMLSupport.updatingPendingObjects ||
    TriggerDispatcher.inWatchForStageUpdates) return;
```

You can look at the sample code for the "Controlling Program Flow" commit to see the complete solution, along with a unit test that validates the creation of a task for each opportunity when its probability goes over 50%.

As you see, it is possible to maintain a centralized trigger framework that tightly controls the order of execution, yet allows each class in the framework to choose exactly what trigger events it wants to detect.

That said, I expect many of you are horrified by this approach. Because while it does provide a great deal of flexibility, it is incredibly fragile. Any time you add a new trigger handler, you have to figure out whether or not to allow triggers during DML operations for every class that performs a DML operation. That's every class, not just those handling the same type of object, as you never know what other triggers or declarative constructs might do. If the new class performs a DML operation, you then have to examine every other class to potentially exclude that DML operation from trigger processing.

That means that each class might not only require code changes throughout the application, adding a class demands a deep understanding of the operation of every trigger handling class and the possible ways that they may interact. What a nightmare! What a rich source of potential bugs!

The only good thing you can say about it is that it's still better than having multiple triggers firing in random order.

Really Controlling Program Flow

It's not enough to control the order of execution within your application. It's not enough to be able to determine whether an internal or external DML operation is in progress and which trigger handler invoked it. The problem of application fragility is critically important. In the real world, if adding a new trigger handler requires careful thought and design to avoid unintended interactions and consequences, you're going to end up with a lot of unintended interactions and consequences. Because in the real world of Salesforce development, it is rare for developers to think beyond the specific functionality they are trying to implement. Those other triggers and processes are annoying distractions, and resolving any problems they cause is often seen as frustrating, inconvenient and a waste of time.

This is the normal situation in many Salesforce applications. We can do better. But to do so, we need to answer a fundamental philosophical question.

In traditional (simple) Force.com applications, you build a trigger by stating: "When the following database operations occurs, execute code that implements some desired functionality". This is illustrated in figure 6-5.

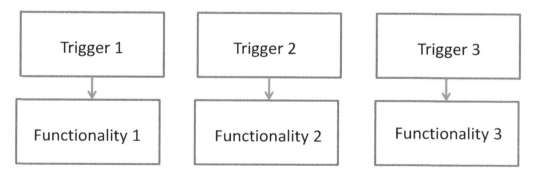

Figure 6-5 – Functionality is tied directly to a trigger

The functionality defined for each trigger is executed every time the trigger is invoked. However, that functionality might include other DML operations that in turn cause other triggers and workflows to execute – triggers and workflows that are completely out of your control. As a result, the real behavior of your application is not only unpredictable, it can vary as the system changes. The application is, as a result, extremely fragile over time.

The only way to address this is to change the original statement into a question: "I have some functionality that I wish to execute at certain times – when should I execute it?"

Your question as a developer is now: where do you answer that question?

In the current TriggerDispatcher implementation, the question is answered partly in the main dispatcher –when the trigger occurs, and partly in each class. This is illustrated in Figure 6-6. Each trigger is responsible for deciding what functionality needs to be called. As you add more and more complexity to the system, the conditions that have to be evaluated by the trigger handlers, or the main dispatcher for those handlers, become increasingly complex. Every time you add a DML statement anywhere in your code, you need to go back to the trigger handler code or dispatcher to decide what to do with any triggers that may result from that DML statement.

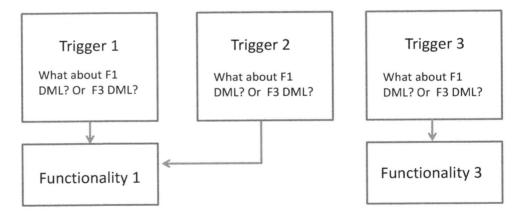

Figure 6-6 – A simple workflow can cause unintended consequences

For the next implementation, we're going to rearchitect the design to reflect a major philosophical choice. From now on, the rule will be that any piece of code that invokes a DML operation, has the right to determine how any of the triggers or workflows caused by that DML operation should be handled. The central dispatcher need only ask the question: "Was this DML operation caused by our application?" If so, dispatch the resulting triggers to the functional block that orig-inated the DML operation as shown in figure 6-7.

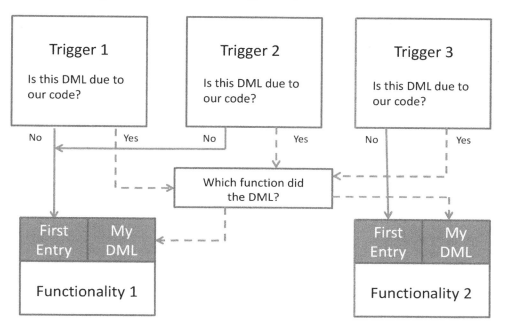

Figure 6-7– The execution decision lies with the originating functionality

Where this approach really shines over the previous one is the impact it has on the long-term stability and maintainability of the application. Where before, adding any new DML operation to the code requires that you review and potentially mod-ify the main decision code, now adding a new DML operation is perfectly safe – by default any resulting triggers or workflows will have no impact on the application because they will be quietly redirected to the originating code. On a project with multiple developers, or an application that evolves over time, this dramatically re-duces the chance of errors and unintended side effects, resulting in a much more stable application.

Think about this. When you add a new trigger handler that performs a DML oper-ation, by default no triggers in your application will be processed during that DML operation. If you do want specific triggers to be processed, that trigger handler can invoke them as needed, but the decision lies with each trigger handler as to how to process those triggers.

Yes, I'm repeating myself, but this may be the single most important concept in this chapter. A default behavior of bypassing trigger handling means that your other trigger handlers can't interact with the operation. They can't consume limits. They can't fire off other DML operations or updates. They can't produce unintended side effects.

Now, developers who are extending the application don't need to be aware of – don't need to even think of other trigger handlers or what else may be going on in the application. They can focus on their one piece of code. The result is a dramatic improvement in application stability, especially over time in projects that involve multiple developers.

Let's see how it's done.

To understand the following implementation, you'll need to be familiar with the concept of an interface. An interface is a set of property and function definitions. When a class implements an interface, it promises to implement each of those properties and functions. What makes interfaces particularly useful is that the interface also defines a type. A variable defined with that type can reference any class that implements the interface.

In this example we'll add the interface to the main TriggerDispatcher class.

```
public interface ITriggerEntry
{
    void mainEntry(TriggerOperation triggerType,
        Schema.SObjectType objectType,
        List<SObject> newList, Map<ID, SObject> newMap,
        List<SObject> oldList, Map<ID,SObject> oldMap);

    void inProgressEntry(TriggerOperation triggerType,
        Schema.SObjectType objectType,
        List<SObject> newList, Map<ID, SObject> newMap,
        List<SObject> oldList, Map<ID,SObject> oldMap);
```

```
    void inDmlEntry(TriggerOperation triggerType,
        Schema.SObjectType objectType,
        List<SObject> newList, Map<ID, SObject> newMap,
        List<SObject> oldList, Map<ID,SObject> oldMap);
}
```

The interface defines three entry points. The mainEntry function is the main entry point – called when an external trigger is processed. The inProgressEntry function is called when a trigger arrives caused by a DML operation invoked originally from within the trigger handler itself. The inDmlEntry function is called when a trigger arrives caused by a DML update from our TriggerDMLSupport class.

A public static variable, activeFunction, points to the instance of whatever trigger handler class is currently active.

```
    public static ITriggerEntry activeFunction = null;
```

Each of the trigger handling classes now needs some modification. First, it needs to implement the ITriggerEntry interface. All of the methods need to be changed from static to instance methods, as the dispatcher will be using instances of the trigger handler classes exclusively.

Because the ITriggerEntry interface methods all use SObjects, it's now up to the handler class to cast the collection parameters to the correct data type.

Here's what the start of the TriggerArchitectureClass1 class looks like after these changes:

```
public with sharing class TriggerArchitectureClass1
    implements TriggerDispatcher.ITriggerEntry {

    public void mainEntry(TriggerOperation triggerType,
        Schema.SObjectType objectType, List<SObject> newObjlist,
        Map<ID, SObject> newObjMap, List<SObject> oldObjList,
        Map<ID,SObject> oldObjMap)
    {
        if(objectType!= Opportunity.SObjectType) return;
        List<Opportunity> newList = (List<Opportunity>)newObjList;
```

```
    List<Opportunity> oldList = (List<Opportunity>)oldObjList;
    Map<ID, Opportunity> newMap =
    TriggerDispatcher.castMapToOpportunities(newObjMap);
    Map<ID, Opportunity> oldMap =
    TriggerDispatcher.castMapToOpportunities(oldObjMap);
```

The test to validate the object type is not really necessary here, as the mainEntry function will only be called by the dispatcher for specific object types. That said, it does make it clear that it's very possible for a trigger handler to support multiple object types – a nice improvement in flexibility over the previous approach.

The TriggerHandlerClass1 class is supposed to ignore any triggers that come in during DML updates by the TriggerDMLSupport class or any other trigger handlers. Where before we need code in the main entry class to exclude processing in those scenarios, this is no longer necessary. Triggers during DML updates are sent to the inDmlEntry function which simply returns – which is functionally equivalent to ignoring the trigger.

```
public void inDmlEntry(TriggerOperation triggerType,
    Schema.SObjectType objectType,
    List<SObject> newObjlist, Map<ID, SObject> newObjMap,
    List<SObject> oldObjList, Map<ID,SObject> oldObjMap)
{
}
```

Triggers during DML operations within other handlers will arrive at the mainEntry function only if the other handler explicitly requests it. And since this function does not itself perform a DML operation, the inProgressEntry function is never called. The function does have to be implemented however, as it is defined as part of the interface.

```
public void inProgressEntry(TriggerOperation triggerType,
    Schema.SObjectType objectType,
    List<SObject> newObjlist, Map<ID, SObject> newObjMap,
    List<SObject> oldObjList, Map<ID,SObject> oldObjMap)
{
}
```

Now let's look at the rest of the TriggerDispatcher function. The entry point, called from the various triggers, is unchanged, as it is retrieving one object to help determine the type of object being processed by the trigger.

```
public static void handleTriggers(TriggerOperation triggerType,
    List<SObject> newList, Map<ID, SObject> newMap,
    List<SObject> oldList, Map<ID,SObject> oldMap)
{

    SObject firstObject =
        (triggerType == TriggerOperation.AFTER_DELETE ||
        triggerType== TriggerOperation.BEFORE_DELETE)?
        oldList[0]: newList[0];
```

The activeFunction variable that you saw earlier keeps track of which handler class is active – processing trigger data. It is set each time the mainEntry function is called for a handler class. If it is not null at this point in the code, it means that this trigger is the result of a DML operation within that handler class. So instead of regular processing, we call the inProgressEntry function for the currently active handler.

```
    if(activeFunction!=null)
    {
        // Active function always gets all triggers
        activeFunction.inProgressEntry(triggerType,
        firstObject.getSObjectType(), newList, newMap, oldList, oldMap);
        return;
    }
```

The TriggerDMLSupport function still handles consolidation of object updates across handlers. Since it is updating objects, triggers are sure to follow, and because its operation takes place after the handlers have completed their work, the activeFunction variable will be null.

Which classes should see triggers that occur during these updates? That's entirely up to you. In this example application, the WatchForStageUpdates class needs to see these triggers, so it is the only class called in this example. The inDmlEntry point is used to allow the handler class to differentiate between regular trigger processing and processing during an internal DML operation. The activeFunctiton variable is set to the class instance to make sure that any subsequent triggers that occur during this processing are reflected back to the WatchForStageUpdates class.

```
if(TriggerDMLSupport.updatingPendingObjects)
{
    // During internal DML update, forward only to those
    // classes that need to see the trigger
    activeFunction = new WatchForStageUpdates();
    activeFunction.inDmlEntry(triggerType,
    firstObject.getSObjectType(), newList, newMap, oldList, oldMap);
    activeFunction = null;
    return;
}
```

The remaining trigger handling code is actually simpler than the previous solution. Instead of calling a series of static functions, one for each object being handled, we build a list of ITriggerEntry class instances to call. As with the activeFunction variable, the fact that all of these classes support the ITriggerEntry interfaces means that they can all be added to a list of ITriggerEntry objects.

Next, we iterate through the list, calling the invokeMainEntry function for each one.

```
switch on firstObject
{
    when Opportunity obj
    {
        List<ITriggerEntry> opportunityHandlers =
            new List<ITriggerEntry>{
                new TriggerArchitectureClass1(),
                new TriggerArchitectureClass2(),
                new WatchForStageUpdates()};

        for(ITriggerEntry handler: opportunityHandlers)
        {
```

```
            invokeMainEntry(handler, triggerType,
            firstObject.getSObjectType(), newList,
            newMap, oldList, oldMap);
        }
    }
}
TriggerDMLSupport.updatePendingObjects();
}
```

The invokeMainEntry function is very simple. It stores the current value of the activeFunction variable, sets activeFunction to the current handler instance, then on return restores the previous activeFunction value.

```
public static void invokeMainEntry(
    ITriggerEntry handler, TriggerOperation triggerType,
    Schema.SObjectType objectType,
    List<SObject> newList, Map<ID, SObject> newMap,
    List<SObject> oldList, Map<ID,SObject> oldMap)
{
    ITriggerEntry oldActiveFunction = activeFunction;
    handler.mainEntry(triggerType, objectType, newList,
                  newMap, oldList, oldMap);
    activeFunction = oldActiveFunction;
}
```

Why does the invokeMainEntry function store the previous value of activeFunction? Isn't it always null at this point? It is – if this function is called from within the TriggerDispatcher function. But this function is public. It can also be called from handler classes within their inProgressEntry or inDmlEntry functions to delegate trigger handling to a different handler. In that case, on return you would want to reset activeFunction to the calling class, not to null. To see this in action, let's take a look at the WatchForStageUpdates class.

Aside from the same changes required for the other handler classes, this class implements the three interface methods as shown here:

```
public void mainEntry(TriggerOperation triggerType,
    Schema.SObjectType objectType,
```

```
        List<SObject> newObjlist, Map<ID, SObject> newObjMap,
        List<SObject> oldObjList, Map<ID,SObject> oldObjMap)
{
    processStageUpdate(triggerType, objectType,
        newObjlist, newObjMap, oldObjList, oldObjMap);
}

public void inProgressEntry(TriggerOperation triggerType,
    Schema.SObjectType objectType,
    List<SObject> newObjlist, Map<ID, SObject> newObjMap,
    List<SObject> oldObjList, Map<ID,SObject> oldObjMap)
{
    TriggerDispatcher.invokeMainEntry(
        new TriggerArchitectureClass2(),
        triggerType, objectType, newObjList, newObjMap,
        oldObjList, oldObjMap);
}

public void inDmlEntry(TriggerOperation triggerType,
    Schema.SObjectType objectType,
    List<SObject> newObjlist, Map<ID, SObject> newObjMap,
    List<SObject> oldObjList, Map<ID,SObject> oldObjMap)
{
    processStageUpdate(triggerType, objectType,
        newObjlist, newObjMap, oldObjList, oldObjMap);
}
```

Both mainEntry and inDmlEntry call the main processStageUpdate handling function. Which is another way of saying that this handler processes normal triggers and those that occur during TriggerDMLSupport DML updates the same way.

The inProgressEntry function demonstrates how it is possible for one class to delegate trigger handling to another handler. This is where you see the real implementation of the answer to our question of who should decide which handlers are called during a DML operation within a handler. In this case, when a trigger occurs during the WatchForStageUpdates class DML operation, this class gets to decide which other handlers get to process that trigger. In this case, it's only the TriggerArchitecture2 class (though you could certainly forward the trigger to multiple classes).

You may thinking – what happens if an opportunity stage transition occurs during another class's DML operation? Does this mean it's necessary to add a similar invocation to TriggerDispatcher.invokeMainEntry for this class in every other handler's inProgressEntry class if I want to be sure this class always sees the trigger?

In the current design, yes. Again, it goes to that philosophical question. By default, only the handler that invokes a DML operation sees the triggers during that DML operation.

That said, it would be absolutely trivial to add some code to the TriggerDispatcher's handleTrigger function to always call selected trigger handlers no matter what. I'll leave the implementation of that approach to you. Just be careful to avoid calling them twice.

Now I'd like you to think for a moment about the ramifications of what is possible using this architecture.

- You now have absolute and total control over the sequence of operations within your application. You also know exactly when a trigger is caused by your application, or by some outside code, and where in your application it is occurring.

- You now have additional information in one central location as to what your code is doing. You'll see later how this can become very useful for diagnostics and for debugging.

- Code within triggers is normally difficult to refactor – the only way for a trigger to invoke code in another trigger is through a DML operation. With this architecture, refactoring trigger functionality is easy, and it's trivial for one "trigger function" to call another.

- Because you can create instances of "trigger" classes directly, you can simulate trigger functionality without actually performing a DML operation. That can offer additional flexibility when testing.

- Instead of using a single static variable to track the currently executing function, you can use a list to implement stack functionality. Later in this book you'll learn how to use a variation on this technique to implement a simple execution stack trace that can be invaluable for debugging – especially with managed packages.

- With all of your trigger functionality going through one central point, you can build a centralized exception handler. You'll learn later how this can dramatically improve your ability to monitor, diagnose and support your software, and improve your users' experience.

This example is a relatively simple implementation of a centralized architecture. There are numerous ways you can build on the concepts shown here. For example:

- Your classes have entry points for the initial trigger, for "in progress" triggers, and for triggers during DML updates. Why not an entry point for asynchronous and batch operations as well? This can dramatically simplify the effort required should you find later that you need to move some of your trigger functionality into a future call.

- Is there functionality that is common to many of your classes? Instead of an interface, consider using inheritance, where the base class implements the shared functionality and you use overrides for the mainEntry, inProgressEntry and inDmlEntry functions.

- Remember that you are now using class instances to implement functionality instead of static methods. That means you can use constructors and properties to pass additional information to the class instances before or during processing. You can use multiple constructors depending on whether the class is being created by the main dispatch function, a future function or a batch function.

- You can create hybrid approaches, where most of your trigger functionality is handled by dispatching execution to trigger classes, but selected triggers that you want to always handle a certain way are processed separately. Think of these as "always process" conditions. By incorporating that logic into the main dispatcher, you still have complete control over the order of execution.

- You can trivially add a global on/off switch to your entire application. This can be useful in many ways. For example: it can allow you to configure an application after installation but before turning it on. It's also handy for proving that your application is not at fault when certain problems occur – if you turn the application off and the problem still exists, it's not your problem.

- Interfaces can be defined as global. You can expose the ITriggerEntry entry interface as a global interface and define global methods that allow other applications to "inject" handlers into your trigger handling sequence. This makes it possible for cooperating applications to share the same program flow definition, eliminating once and for all the problem of indeterminate trigger ordering.

- Following up on the previous idea, you don't have to hard-code the sequence of trigger handler classes. You could define the classes that handle each trigger type in custom metadata or even a table. In fact, the Salesforce Nonprofit Starter Pack includes a feature they call "Table-Driven Trigger Management" (TDTM) that uses this type of architecture to allow the list and order of trigger handlers to be defined in the database.

As you continue reading, you'll find numerous examples of the benefits of choosing a software architecture that moves trigger code into classes and uses some form of centralized dispatching.

As you explore Apex programming in general, you will find other trigger frameworks that build and extend on these ideas, and that incorporate other ideas as well. What you see here is intended to be just a starting point, but hopefully one that is already useful in and of itself.

One question that sometimes arises is whether it makes sense to use a framework like this for quick and simple triggers? Let's face it, most Apex development is not part of an application, but rather a series of small triggers and classes that evolve over time. Can you justify the investment to build a centralized framework?

Yes – as long as you keep the framework simple. And if you really think about it, the framework shown here, for all of its power, is extremely simple – there's just not that much code. If you are a member of a team, you may be able to sell the rest of the team on using this approach once they see its value. If you are a lone consultant, who is called in periodically when work is needed, build a simple framework so you can at least manage your own code.

But if you are creating a large application or package, take the time upfront to design a solid architecture that is right for your application and build the corresponding framework. It will pay for itself many times over by simplifying your application and making it easier to understand, debug, maintain and support.

Triggers, Workflows and Processes - Oh My!

The framework we have now does an excellent job of controlling program flow within an application. But, Apex code does not exist in a vacuum. Declarative constructs such as workflows, processes, and lightning flows all share the same metadata.

That means they can impact each other.

While I haven't shown it in the book yet, those of you who have been looking through the sample code will have seen a unit test class for this code. In particular, the testStageUpdates class that creates five opportunities, inserts them, updates their stage to one with a probability higher than 50%, then counts the number of tasks to make sure that all five tasks were created. If you've been following along with the sample code, this would be a good time to run the test and verify that it passes.

Now create a new opportunity workflow rule called "Probability Over 50".

Set the evaluation criteria to:
```
Evaluate the rule when a record is created, and any time it's edited to
subsequently meet criteria
```

Set the rule criteria to:
```
Opportunity: Probability (%)greater than 50
```

Set the workflow action to a new field update called "Set Next Step". This field update set's the Opportunity NextStep field to a text string. In this example I used "Pay Attention!"

I know – updating a field when the stage changes is exactly what the WaitForStageUpdate trigger handler does. Logically you'd want to combine the two. But this is the world of Salesforce. When an admin wants to perform an operation like this that can be done in workflow they are not going to reach out to a developer. Nor are they always going to be even aware that a similar trigger handler exists. And that is as it should be – that's why workflows exist.

Except that when you enable this workflow, and try to run the testStageUpdates unit test, you'll get the following test failure:

```
System.AssertException: Assertion Failed: Expected: 5, Actual: 10
```

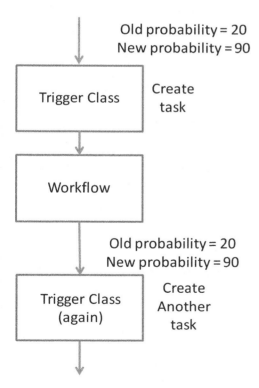

How is this possible?

The reason why this happens is subtle and is shown in Figure 6-8. The first time through the trigger, the old probability value is shown as 20 and the new value as 90 (the 20 comes from the stage setting in the TriggerArchitecture1 after-insert handler, the 90 is the new setting specified by the test class stage).

Logically, you might expect that the second time through the trigger the old value of the probability would be 90 - taking on the new value from the first time through. But in fact, the old trigger value remains the same – it reflects the field value at the start of the execution context.

Figure 6-8 – Trigger object fields are not updated between trigger invocations

When the workflow field update causes another trigger invocation, the code sees this as another field change, and creates another task.

A bit of defensive programming can avoid this problem. A simple solution might be to use a static variable to keep track of whether a task has already been created in this execution context, and simply exit if that static variable is set. However, that solution would not work in cases where it is the workflow itself that is doing a field update that you want to detect.

A more robust solution is to keep track of the correct "old" value – the value that was set during the previous trigger invocation.

Start by declaring a private static variable for the class.

```
private static Map<ID, Double> probabilityOverrides = null;
```

For each opportunity, calculate the true value of the old probability and use it in the condition that determines if a task needs to be inserted. If there is a value in the probabilityOverrides map, use it, otherwise, use zero (for inserts), or the true oldMap value provided by the oldMap trigger collection.

```
Double oldProbability = (probabilityOverrides.containskey(op.id))?
    probabilityOverrides.get(op.id) :
    ((oldMap==null)? 0: oldMap.get(op.id).Probability);
if((triggerType== TriggerOperation.AFTER_INSERT ||
    oldProbability <=20) && op.Probability>50)
```

Finally, as the last step inside the opportunity loop, add:

```
if(oldProbability != op.Probability)
    probabilityOverrides.put(op.id, op.Probability);
```

In this manner you can keep track of the "true" opportunity probability and use it in the comparison.

This is a good defensive solution for Apex code that needs to perform actions based on field changes.

It does, however, lead to two questions:

1. Is it really true that admins can use workflows and processes to break Apex code without realizing it?

2. Is there any alternative approach to applying paranoid defensive measures in Apex code?

As to the first question, yes, it is true. This is one of the defining characteristics of software development in Apex, and it has far reaching effects. You'll see more examples of this, and strategies for dealing with this issue later in the book, especially in chapter 13 that address the challenges of maintaining Apex.

As to the second question, I would argue there is no alternative to applying paranoid defensive measures to your Apex code, but there are things that you can do in Apex to help your admins to write better Apex code.

For this example, create two new opportunity fields.

- A DateTime field called "Description Updated" with API name Description_Updated__c.

- A Text field with length 40 called "Internal Update" with API name Internal_Update__c.

Now create a new opportunity workflow rule called "Opportunity Description Changed".

Set the evaluation criteria to:
```
Evaluate the rule when a record is created, and every time it's edited
```

Set the rule criteria to the formula:
```
Opportunity: ISCHANGED(Description)
```

Set the workflow action to a new field update called "Set Description Update Date". This field update sets the Opportunity Description_Update__c field to the formula Now().

When activated, you'll expect this workflow to fire, as the WatchForStageUpdates class updates the description. But what if the admin doesn't want the workflow to fire when we're doing the update? What if they really only want the Description_Update__c field to be set when a user changes the description? Right now it would be very hard to distinguish between the two updates.

You can make it easier.

Add the following line to the WatchForStageUpdates.processStageUpdate function right after the line that updates the description.

```
updatingOp.Internal_Update__c = 'WatchForStageUpdates - ' +
    String.ValueOf(DateTime.Now().getTime());
```

Now modify the rule for the "Opportunity Description Changed" workflow to be as follows:

```
ISCHANGED(Description) && NOT(ISCHANGED( Internal_Update__c ))
```

Each time the WatchForStagesUpdates class performs a DML operation, it will set the Internal_Update__c field to a different value, as the getTime() function increments once every millisecond. On a busy system you might want to add an additional random number just to be extra safe. The changed field will be detected by the ISCHANGED term in the workflow criteria formula and thus the workflow will know that this update is coming from the application and will not fire. You can verify this by running the testStageUpdates unit test in the developer console, and looking at the debug log, filtering on WF_FIELD_UPDATE to view the updating fields.

I think you'll agree that this is a rather useful capability to provide to admins and other declarative developers.

As it turns out, it can be far more than just useful. It can be a real lifesaver.

Remember, the whole purpose of controlling program flow in Apex is to minimize uncertainty and reduce unnecessary processing due to reentrancy –in terms of both executing code and DML updates.

Using this approach, it is possible for Apex to communicate to declarative code not just that a DML operation is coming from code, but exactly which code is performing the update. This allows declarative developers to avoid firing workflows and processes for updates that they know are irrelevant. Since most limit issues in well-designed code result from reentrancy caused by declarative constructs, this approach allows Apex developers and declarative developers to be partners in eliminating reentrancy problems and improving the efficiency of the org.

Additional Trigger Considerations

Here are a few additional issues and best practices related to triggers of which you should be aware.

Before vs. After Triggers

It is generally better to use before triggers where possible. The biggest advantage of before triggers is that any field changes you make to an object do not require a SOQL or DML operation – so they are easier on limits. In addition, during a before operation, you have access to all of the object's fields, so you don't have to keep track of the fields you are using and make sure they are included in the SOQL query. The biggest disadvantage of before triggers is that the object ID does not yet exist during a before-insert trigger. In addition, most formulas will not yet be updated based on the new field values during a before update trigger, or set at all during a before insert trigger.

Use after triggers when you need to reference formula fields or make sure that any related records (lookups, etc.) are set after an insert or update.

By the same token, use a before-delete trigger to be able to access existing related records (lookups, etc.) before they are deleted or reparented.

Always use after triggers to detect lead conversions. Depending on the lead settings, the before triggers may not even fire.

Missing Triggers

Before designing a solution based on triggers, make sure the triggers you want to use actually exist and fire. I already noted that before triggers may not fire on conversion depending on the lead settings. If you are a consultant, you can decide that the organization turn on those triggers and validation. However, if you are creating a package, you should not require this, and should be sure your application works with conversion before-triggers and validation turned off (though you should be sure to test your code both ways).

Some objects, such as the OpportunityContactRole object, have no triggers.

Delete triggers typically do not fire on cascade deletes. If you need to detect deletion of the child objects, you must create a before-delete trigger on the parent object and perform your desired operation on the child objects at that time (be sure to design this carefully – there may be a large number of child objects).

Reparenting of objects during a merge or conversion may not fire update or delete triggers. If you merge two contacts that each have a CampaignMember object to the same campaign, one of them will vanish without triggering a deletion.

Be sure to prototype and test your scenario sufficiently to make sure that the triggers work the way you expect before investing in a full implementation.

Beware of recursion – triggers or workflows that make changes that cause another trigger invocation. The Force.com platform will only let them go to a certain level, after which the triggers will simply not fire. This will rarely be a problem if you use a centralized trigger architecture such as that described in this chapter, as it lends itself to both minimizing the number of DML operations, and to ignoring subsequent trigger invocations. However, on a large system with multiple workflows and applications installed, you may find the organization is already experiencing recursion related issues before you write your first line of code.

7 – Going Asynchronous

In Chapter 4, you saw a very basic asynchronous (future) pattern, and how it could be used to defer the processing of an operation on a set of objects in order to overcome limits within an execution context. In this chapter, we'll take that basic concept, and see how far it can be extended.

Consider a scenario where you are managing work orders (using the WorkOrder object), and wish to add a field that contains the machine translation of the work order description, say, to Spanish. You want to build an application that will automatically populate a new custom field, DescriptionSpanish___c, on insertion or update of the WorkOrder object. To perform the translation, you'll use an external web service, such as Google Translate or Microsoft Translate.[2]

This scenario introduces a number of new limits. First, you can't actually make a callout to a web service during a trigger. You are also limited in the number of callouts that you can make during a single execution context, the amount of data you can pass to an external server in a callout, and the total amount of time for the external server to respond.

But don't let the fact that we are dealing with callout limits mislead you. The design patterns used to address these limits are exactly the same as those you would use to address other types of limits. The fact that they are more restrictive than most other limits only makes it easier to illustrate the approach.

Setting the Stage

Let's start by taking a look at the callout itself. Or rather, by the way that I'm going to cheat with regards to the callout.

---

[2] Readers of previous editions of the book may notice that this edition uses work orders instead of solutions for these examples. This is because Solution objects are not currently supported in Lightning, nor is that currently on the roadmap, and I wanted to ensure that this edition is fully Lightning compatible.

My first thought was to actually implement the translation. But Google Translate costs money, and Microsoft Translate requires a signup process – both of which are relatively easy and well documented, but would impose an annoying burden on readers. More important, the pages it would take to describe how to do this have nothing to do with the question at hand – that of asynchronous design patterns. So I decided to cheat and use the following simulation:

```
global class SimulatedTranslator {
    public static String translate(String sourcetext)
    {
        if(sourcetext==null) return null;
        HttpRequest req = new HttpRequest();
        req.setBody(sourcetext);
        req.setHeader('Content-Type','text');
        HttpResponse result = translate(req);
        return result.getBody();
    }
}
```

The translate override that has an HttpRequest object parameter takes advantage of the ability of the Salesforce platform to "mock" callouts when in test mode. This is implemented by the SimulatedTranslator.MockTranslator inner class shown here:

```
    global class MockTranslator implements HttpCalloutMock
    {
        global HTTPResponse respond(HTTPRequest req)
        {
            String requestBody = req.getBody();
            HttpResponse res = new HttpResponse();
            res.setHeader('Content-Type', 'text');
            res.setBody(requestBody + ' in Spanish');
            res.setStatusCode(200);
            return res;
        }
    }
```

The mock routine just returns the original text with the words " in Spanish' appended. Because we aren't actually implementing the callout, the translate method always calls the MockTranslator.respond method. If not in test mode, it calls the respond method explicitly. If in test mode, it attempts to send the request. However, as you will see, the test class uses the Test.setMock method to redirect callouts to the MockTranslator.respond method as well.

```
public static HTTPResponse translate(HTTPRequest req)
{
    // Just simulate the call for now -
    //remove this code if you've implemented real translation
    if(!Test.isRunningTest())
    {
        MockTranslator mock = new MockTranslator();
        return mock.respond(req);
    }
    // Replace following with call to translation service
    req.setEndpoint('http://api.salesforce.com/foo/bar');
    req.setMethod('GET');
    Http h = new Http();
    HttpResponse res = h.send(req);
    return res;
}
```

By using the ability of the platform to mock callouts in test mode, we can accurately see the behavior of the platform when making callouts in various scenarios without implementing a real callout, as it respects callout limits and restrictions.

A Simple (but Flawed) Implementation

The first step in the implementation should be familiar by now. We need a simple trigger that will call a class method. In this case we'll trigger both on insert and on update. Translation needs to occur on every insert, and on those updates where the Description field is changed.

```
trigger WorkOrderTrigger on WorkOrder (after insert, after update) {
    GoingAsync1.handleTrigger1(trigger.new, trigger.newMap,
```

```
        trigger.oldMap, trigger.operationType);
}
```

You may be wondering, why use an after trigger here instead of a before trigger? In this implementation, it's necessary to use an after-insert trigger because we need an ID as a parameter to the future call. It doesn't matter for the update trigger.

Here's the GoingAsync1 class (that handles the trigger processing for this first attempt).

```
// Simple protection from workflows and triggers
private static Boolean alreadyProcessed = false;

public static void handleTrigger1(List<WorkOrder> workOrderList,
    Map<ID, WorkOrder> newMap, Map<ID, WorkOrder> oldMap,
    TriggerOperation operation)
{
    if(alreadyProcessed) return;
    alreadyProcessed = true;
    if(operation == TriggerOperation.AFTER_INSERT)
        firstAttempt(newMap.keyset());
    else
    {
        Set<ID> textChangedIds = new Set<ID>();
        for(WorkOrder wo: workOrderList)
        {
            if(wo.Description!= oldMap.get(wo.id).Description)
                textChangedIds.add(wo.id);
        }
        if(textChangedIds.size()>0)
            firstAttempt(textChangedIds);
    }
}
```

This code is very straightforward. The alreadyProcessed static variable is a simple flag to prevent reentrance due to an external workflow or trigger. Since it's unlikely a workflow would be used to modify the work order description, it should be safe to use a single gating flag instead of a flag for each individual WorkOrder object in a batch.

For insert triggers, all of the records are processed. For update triggers, only those with changed Description fields are processed.

The firstAttempt future method is defined as follows:

```
@future(callout=true)
public static void firstAttempt(Set<ID> workOrderIds)
{
    List<WorkOrder> workOrdersToUpdate =
        [SELECT ID, Description, DescriptionSpanish__c
        from WorkOrder where ID in :workOrderIds];
    for(WorkOrder wo: workOrdersToUpdate)
        wo.DescriptionSpanish__c =
            SimulatedTranslator.translate(wo.Description);
    update workOrdersToUpdate;
}
```

As you can see, it queries the inserted or modified work orders, performs the simulated callout, and updates the work orders with the translated text. Note the use of the callout=true annotation that is required in order to allow future calls to make callouts.

The testWorkOrdersInsert test method validates the functionality:

```
private static Integer bulkTestSize = 10;

@isTest
private static void testWorkOrdersInsert() {

    List<WorkOrder> wos = new List<WorkOrder>();

    for(Integer x = 0; x<bulkTestSize; x++)
    {
        wos.add(new WorkOrder(
            Subject='work order ' + String.valueOf(x),
```

```
            Description = 'This is work order # ' + String.ValueOf(x) ));
    }
    Test.StartTest();

    Test.setMock(HttpCalloutMock.class,
        new SimulatedTranslator.MockTranslator());

    insert wos;
    Test.StopTest();

    Map<ID, WorkOrder> wosmap = new Map<ID, WorkOrder>(wos);

    List<WorkOrder> results =
        [Select ID, Description, DescriptionSpanish__c
        from WorkOrder where ID in :wosmap.keyset()];
    for(WorkOrder wo: results)
        System.AssertEquals(wo.Description + ' in Spanish',
            wo.DescriptionSpanish__c);
}
```

The test function inserts a specified number of work orders and then validates that the DescriptionSpanish__c has been set. The Test.setMock method redirects callouts to the SimulatedTranslator.MockTranslator class. You'll see that this code validates perfectly as is. But what happens if you increase the bulkTestSize variable to 200?

You'll see the error:

System.LimitException: Too many callouts: 101

At which point you hit a dead end.

You can't start another future call from within a future call. If you just stop processing at 100 callouts, you'll lose the list of work orders that still needs to be processed. And limiting the application to handling no more than 100 items in a batch is just not an option – the default batch size for triggers is 200.

This problem does not just apply to callouts. Future calls can fail for other reasons. What if an unexpected error occurs during the future call? What if a system error occurs? What if the external server is down, or the response time exceeds the maximum time that the system will wait for a response? And what about other code in the system - unless your code is part of an AppExchange managed package, you're sharing these limits with other application code – so your code may not have the full number of callouts or future calls available. In fact, it may not have any.

What if at some point in the future, somebody adds code to the system, or an application to the system, that tries to update a work order in a batch or future call? Now this code will fail because you can't call a future call from within a future call or most batch operations.

In all of these cases, you will lose the list of IDs of the work orders that need to be processed.

In short, this design pattern (passing a set of object IDs to process in a future call), though common, is fundamentally flawed.

Industrial Strength Future Calls

When looking for solutions to the previous approach, you might have thought about the possibility of storing a list of those work order objects that could not be processed somewhere for later use. If so, your instincts are good. But the answer isn't to just store a list of unprocessed objects when the limit is reached. Rather, it is to always store the complete list of objects that need to be translated. And while you could create a separate object just to keep track of pending translations, for now let's take an easier approach and do so with the help of a custom field on the WorkOrder object that we'll call TranslationPending___c.

On the trigger side, the code is going to be even simpler than before. The trigger itself is changed to use before triggers, because that will make it easy to set the TranslationPending___c flag. We also get rid of the newMap parameter as it is no longer needed.

```
trigger WorkOrderTrigger on WorkOrder (before insert, before update) {
    GoingAsync1.handleTrigger2(trigger.new, trigger.oldMap,
                              trigger.operationType);
}
```

The handleTrigger2 function is also simpler than its predecessor. It just sets the TranslationPending__c flag for each object that is inserted or has a change to the Description field, then requests an asynchronous operation.

```
public static void handleTrigger2(List<WorkOrder> workOrderList,
    Map<ID, WorkOrder> oldMap, TriggerOperation operation)
{
    if(alreadyProcessed) return;
    alreadyProcessed = true;
    for(WorkOrder wo:workOrderList)
    {
        if(operation == TriggerOperation.BEFORE_INSERT ||
            wo.Description!= oldMap.get(wo.id).Description)
            wo.TranslationPending__c = true;
    }
    secondAttemptRequestAsync();
}
```

The single future function has been replaced by no less than three new functions as follows:

```
public static void secondAttemptRequestAsync()
{
    if(system.isFuture() || system.isBatch() || system.isQueueable())
        secondAttemptSync();
    else
    {
        if(Limits.getFutureCalls()< Limits.getLimitFutureCalls()-3)
            secondAttemptAsync();
    }
}

@future(callout=true)
private static void secondAttemptAsync()
{
    secondAttemptSync();
}
```

```
public static void secondAttemptSync()
{
    Integer allowedCallouts =
        Limits.getLimitCallouts() - Limits.getCallouts();
    if(allowedCallouts<=0) return;
    List<WorkOrder> workOrdersToUpdate =
        [SELECT ID, Description, DescriptionSpanish__c from WorkOrder
        where LastModifiedDate > :DateTime.Now().addHours(-24)
        And TranslationPending__c = true LIMIT :allowedCallouts];
    if(workOrdersToUpdate.size()==0) return;
    for(WorkOrder wo: workOrdersToUpdate)
    {
        wo.DescriptionSpanish__c =
            SimulatedTranslator.translate(wo.Description);
        wo.TranslationPending__c = false;
    }
    update workOrdersToUpdate;
}
```

There's one function to request a future call, the actual future function, and then a synchronous implementation of the processing code that is called by the asynchronous function.

The secondAttemptRequestAsync method checks to make sure that you aren't already in an asynchronous context. If you are, it calls the synchronous version of the translation code. It can do this safely because if you're already in a future or batch context - callouts may be allowed, but another future call is not.

It also checks to make sure that you haven't already reached the maximum number of future calls. In fact, it always leaves a few extra to spare for other code. If it can't make a future call, it just exits, but that's ok. Remember, you've marked the work orders that need to be translated by setting the TranslationPending__c flag, and that won't be undone. If for some reason it's not possible to perform the translation right away, at least you haven't lost any information – the records will be translated next time.

When it comes time for the secondAttemptSync function to perform the translation, it first determines the number of callouts it is allowed to make (which may be zero, if the originating future call did not allow callouts), then uses a query to find WorkOrder records whose TranslationPending__c field is set. The query uses a limits statement to retrieve no more than the number of objects that can be processed. It also includes a conditional term based on the LastModifiedDate.

Limiting the queries to the last 24 hours has subtle consequences. Imagine that someone creates a validation rule that blocks work orders from being updated and nobody notices this for several days. Once the rule is fixed, records that were modified more than 24 hours ago won't be translated until someone modifies them again, even though their TranslationPending__c field is set.

This sounds like a bad thing, but imagine that there is some flaw that prevents a single record from being translated. Perhaps the translation would exceed the length of the DescriptionSpanish__c field (you may have noticed that this code does not include a test for this condition or an exception handler). Perhaps the callout raises an error for that particular data that you aren't handling – say, if it contains inappropriate language. Or maybe that particular WorkOrder record is corrupt and trying to update it causes an unexpected system error (yes, that kind of thing does happen). In any of these events, the error has the potential to freeze all translation, because the query will keep attempting to translate the failing record.

Except that with the 24-hour limit in place, the longest amount of time that translations can be frozen due to a failing record is 24 hours. After that, the query will exclude that record. So the date filter actually makes the code more robust, giving it the ability to recover from unexpected errors.

If you do run into a situation where you need to update older records, you have two options. You can use a tool to update records that have their TranslationPending__c field set, thus resetting the LastModifiedDate field. Or you can add some code to bypass that test based on the value of a custom setting.

This solution is not bad, but it still has one major flaw. The number of work orders that it can process is still smaller than the number of records that may have been updated, and there is still no mechanism for the future call to restart itself – to invoke another future call to continue processing.

Going Asynchronous with Batch Apex

Batch Apex provides a mechanism to process very large numbers of records. Given that our previous approaches both ran into trouble when the number of records that needed to be processed exceeded callout limits, it stands to reason that batch Apex can be a good alternative.

The batch class is defined in the GoingAsync2 class. It implements both the Database.Batchable interface and the Database.AllowsCallouts interface that is necessary if you wish to make callouts during the batch execute statement.

```
global without sharing class GoingAsync2 implements
   Database.Batchable<SObject>, Database.AllowsCallouts {

   global Database.Querylocator start(Database.BatchableContext bc)
   {
      return Database.getQueryLocator('SELECT ID,
         Description, DescriptionSpanish__c From WorkOrder
         Where TranslationPending__c = true');
   }
}
```

The class is declared without sharing, because you'll always want the translation to occur, regardless of the user context that the batch happens to be running in.

There is no filter based on the LastModifiedDate field. In batch Apex you don't have to worry as much about one bad record blocking processing of the rest of the records, though as you'll see shortly, additional steps have been taken to deal with this possibility.

More important, leaving the date filter out of the query enables new scenarios. For example: you could change the callout from one translation engine to another, use the data loader to set the TranslationPending__c flag on all of the records to true, then sit back as the batch process retranslates all of the work orders. In a more sophisticated solution you could use this approach to add translations to new languages – processing them all in one bulk operation.

The execute method is almost identical to what you've seen before:

```
global void execute(Database.BatchableContext BC, List<WorkOrder> scope)
{
    for(WorkOrder wo: scope)
    {
        wo.DescriptionSpanish__c =
            SimulatedTranslator.translate(wo.Description);
        wo.TranslationPending__c = false;
    }
    Database.update(scope, false);
}
```

One change is the use of Database.update instead of the simple update call. This ensures that validation or other exceptions that might cause one record update to fail won't impact the others in the batch.

Another problem with the previous approaches was their inability to chain – to continue processing any remaining callouts after exceeding current limits. This is less of a problem with batch Apex, as it is able to process all of the records that need translation, but what about records that are not picked up by the original query? Records that are added or modified while the batch is running?

This scenario can be handled easily in the batch Finish method. It first performs a query to find the start time of the current batch, then a query to find out if there are any records that still have their TranslationPending__c flag set. If so, it calls the startBatch method that you'll see shortly. Unlike future calls, batch Apex can chain to and execute another batch when called from the finish method.

```
global void finish(Database.BatchableContext BC)
{
    AsyncApexJob thisJob = [Select Id, CreatedDate
        from AsyncApexJob where id = :BC.getJobId()];
    List<WorkOrder> stillPending =
        [SELECT ID From WorkOrder Where TranslationPending__c = true And
        LastModifiedDate> :thisJob.CreatedDate Limit 1];
    if(stillPending.size()>0) StartBatch(true);
}
```

Starting a Batch Process

In our example, the batch is started by the GoingAsync1.handleTrigger3 method that, after setting the TranslatePending__c field (as you've seen before), also makes a call to the GoingAsync2.startBatch method that actually starts the batch process. It only starts the batch if it finds at least one record that needs to be translated.

```
public static void handleTrigger3(List<WorkOrder> workOrderList,
    Map<ID, WorkOrder> oldmap, TriggerOperation operation)
{
    if(alreadyProcessed) return;
    alreadyProcessed = true;
    Boolean foundOne = false;
    for(WorkOrder wo:workOrderList)
    {
        if(operation == TriggerOperation.BEFORE_INSERT ||
            wo.Description!= oldMap.get(wo.id).Description)
        {
            wo.TranslationPending__c = true;
            foundOne = true;
        }
    }
    if(foundOne) GoingAsync2.StartBatch(false);
}
```

If you look in the Salesforce documentation for information on launching a batch process, the example code looks something like this:

```
GoingAsync2 ga = new GoingAsync2();
Database.executeBatch(ga, 200);
```

As it turns out, this is a good way to get into trouble. A better way can be seen in the static GoingAsync2.startBatch method. The method uses a common design pattern where a static variable flag identifies whether the batch has already been started in this execution context and exits if it has. It also uses the isBatchActive method to determine if the batch is currently running. The forceStart flag bypasses this test so that the function can be used to restart the batch when called from the batch finish method (as the current batch is still technically running during the finish method).

The scope of the batch, which defines the number of records that will be sent to each batch execute statement, is set to the callout limit. This ensures that each batch execute statement does not have to worry about this limit. Because each batch execute statement exists in its own execution context, you shouldn't have to worry about other application code making callouts.

```apex
private static Boolean batchRequested = false;

public static void startBatch(Boolean forceStart)
{
   if(!forceStart && (batchRequested || isBatchActive('GoingAsync2')))
      return;

   GoingAsync2 ga = new GoingAsync2();
   Integer batchSize = Limits.getLimitCallouts();
   if(batchSize>200) batchSize = 200;
   try
   {
      Database.executeBatch(ga, batchSize);
   } catch(Exception ex)
   {
      return;
   }
   batchRequested = true;
}

public static Boolean isBatchActive(String classname)
{
   List<String> inactiveStatuses =
      new List<String>{'Completed','Aborted','Failed'};
   AsyncApexJob[] activeJobs =
      [select id, CompletedDate, Status, ExtendedStatus,
         ApexClassID from AsyncApexJob where
         ApexClass.Name = :classname
         and JobType='BatchApex'
```

```
      And Status Not in :inactiveStatuses
      Order By CreatedDate Desc Limit 1];
   return activeJobs.size() >0;
}
```

The Database.executeBatch statement is in an exception handler and simply exits if it is not able to start the batch. The most common reason for a failure here would be if there are already five batches currently executing on a system and the Apex flex queue is full – a highly unlikely scenario.

As before, if the batch does fail to execute, nothing is lost – as the WorkOrder records still have the TranslatePending__c field set. Barring a serious problem, the translation will be picked up next time the batch is run.

At first glance, batch Apex seems to address all of the issues of the previous solutions. It is robust and able to handle large numbers of records. It supports chaining, so is able to handle records added while others are being processed.

There are, however, several problems with this approach. While it may be great for processing large numbers of records, it is inefficient for updating single records. It also takes a lot of code, and given that you may have many operations that need to be done asynchronously, you could end up with dozens of batch classes. Finally, batch Apex is relatively slow. It can be minutes between the time you start a batch and the time it starts processing records. And while it's true that Salesforce provides no performance guarantees on any asynchronous operation – they all run as system resources become available – future calls do tend to run very quickly whereas batch Apex is known to run at a much lower priority.

Going Asynchronous with Queueable Apex

CAUTION!

The following section includes design patterns for asynchronous operations with queueable Apex and chaining.

Used incorrectly, it is possible to create code that will spawn large numbers of execution threads very rapidly.

Because it is impossible to update a class that has a queueable Apex job queued or executing, and it is possible to queue jobs faster than they can be aborted (even using anonymous Apex), you can place an org in a state where you cannot abort your code execution. Your code can run forever (or until aborted due to the 24-hour limit on asynchronous calls).

Queueable Apex code should always be gated by an on/off switch settable via a custom setting or other means that does not require a metadata change (i.e. do not use custom metadata for this purpose).

Trust me on this – you really don't want to find yourself in this situation.

Wouldn't it be great if there was an asynchronous operation that combined the best features of future calls with the best features of batch Apex? Salesforce heard the request and delivered queueable Apex. Queueable Apex is as fast, or faster than regular future calls. And it's chainable, with certain restrictions. And it's much easier to use than batch Apex.

You define a queueable class by implementing the queueable interface as shown in the GoingAsync3 example. If you wish to make callouts, you must also implement the Database.AllowsCallouts interface.

You add an instance of the class to the batch execution queue using the system.enqueueJob method as shown in the GoingAsync1.HandleTrigger4 example that replaces the batch call from the HandleTrigger3 example with:

```
if(foundOne && (Limits.GetLimitQueueableJobs() -
          Limits.GetQueueableJobs() > 0))
   system.EnqueueJob(new GoingAsync3());
```

The GoingAsync3 class does the translation. It uses an application on/off switch implemented as a custom setting. I won't go into detail on how it is implemented here – that will be covered in chapter 9. Otherwise the function is similar to what you've seen before.

```
public without sharing class GoingAsync3
    implements queueable, Database.AllowsCallouts {

    public void execute(QueueableContext context)
    {
        // On/off switch
        if(!AppCustomSetting.appEnabled) return;

        Integer allowedCallouts =
            Limits.getLimitCallouts() - Limits.getCallouts();

        if(allowedCallouts<=0) return;
        List<WorkOrder> workOrdersToUpdate =
            [SELECT ID, Description, DescriptionSpanish__c from WorkOrder
            where LastModifiedDate >:DateTime.Now().addHours(-24)
            And TranslationPending__c = true LIMIT :allowedCallouts];
        for(WorkOrder wo: workOrdersToUpdate)
        {
            wo.DescriptionSpanish__c =
                SimulatedTranslator.translate(wo.Description);
            wo.TranslationPending__c = false;
        }
        Database.Update(workOrdersToUpdate, false);

        if(workOrdersToUpdate.size()== allowedCallouts &&
```

```
Limits.getLimitQueueableJobs() -Limits.getQueueableJobs() > 0)
try
{
    system.enqueueJob(new GoingAsync3());
} catch(Exception ex)
{
    // Alternate chaining mechanism
}

    }
}
```

Due to the limits on the number of classes you can chain (which varies by type of org), and the possibility that other classes in the execution context may have queued a job, we not only check the limits to see if chaining is possible, but enclose the System.enqueueJob method inside of an exception handler.

What do you do if chaining is not allowed? How can you ensure that your work will complete? I'll address that later in this chapter as we take an even deeper look at queueable Apex.

Queueable Apex jobs have other advantages. They have job Ids, so you can keep track of them, check result status and abort jobs if necessary. You can even prioritize them using the Salesforce UI, though frankly I'd be skeptical of any application that creates so many queueable jobs that you would need to do so. The more asynchronous jobs you have running, the more opportunities for concurrency errors to occur – you'll read about those in the next chapter.

Right now, let's take a step back. You've seen several different approaches for implementing asynchronous operations. Future calls seem easy, but are not robust. They can fail in many ways, and if they do, it's easy to lose data associated with the call.

Batch Apex is powerful, and can handle large numbers of records, but is overkill for smaller jobs and can be very slow.

Scheduled Apex is another mechanism for performing asynchronous operations that was very important in the past, but plays a much more limited role today. I'll come back to that topic later in this chapter.

Queueable Apex combines the best features of future calls and batch Apex. It is easy to implement. You could implement separate queueable classes for each type of asynchronous operation in your application. However, just as you learned in chapter 6 that there are advantages to centralized trigger handling, it turns out that there are some very real benefits to centralized asynchronous processing as well, and queueable Apex forms the foundation of some fascinating design patterns that make it possible.

Centralized Asynchronous Processing

Earlier in this chapter, you learned that the only way to be absolutely certain that data is not lost when an asynchronous operation fails, is to store the information about the request somewhere. In our example, the request was stored in the TranslationPending__c field on the WorkOrder object. Creating a separate object just to keep track of translation tasks would surely be wasteful.

But let's do it anyway.

Create a new object called AsyncRequest.

- Label: AsyncRequest, Plural: AsyncRequests
- Object Name: AsyncRequest__c
- Description: Stores asynchronous requests
- Record Name: Async Request Name
    - Data Type: Auto Number
    - Display Format: ar-{0000}
    - Starting number: 0
- Allow Reports
- Uncheck: Allow activities, Track field history, Chatter
- Uncheck: Allow Sharing, Bulk and streaming API Access (optional)

Add the following custom fields:

- Picklist named 'AsyncType', with a single value 'Translate Work Order'
- Long text area named 'Params', length 131072
- Checkbox field named 'Error', unchecked by default
- Long text area named 'Error Message', length 32768

Change the WorkOrderTrigger back to an after-insert, after-update trigger as follows:

```
trigger WorkOrderTrigger on WorkOrder (after insert, after update) {
    GoingAsync1.handleTrigger5(trigger.new, trigger.newMap,
        trigger.oldMap, trigger.operationType);
}
```

In the GoingAsync1 class, create the HandleTrigger5 function, which is very similar to the original HandleTrigger1 function.

```
public static void handleTrigger5(List<WorkOrder> workOrderList,
    Map<ID, WorkOrder> newMap, Map<ID, WorkOrder> oldMap,
    TriggerOperation operation)
{
    if(alreadyProcessed) return;
    alreadyProcessed = true;
    List<AsyncRequest__c> newAsyncRequests =
        new List<AsyncRequest__c>();

    List<String> textChangedIds = new List<ID>();
    for(WorkOrder wo: workOrderList)
    {
        if(operation == TriggerOperation.AFTER_INSERT ||
            wo.Description!= oldMap.get(wo.id).Description)
            textChangedIds.add(wo.id);
        if(textChangedIds.size()>100)
        {
            newAsyncRequests.add(new AsyncRequest__c(
                AsyncType__c = 'Translate Work Order',
                Params__c = string.Join(textChangedIds,',')));
```

```
            textChangedIds.clear();
        }
    }

    if(textChangedIds.size()>0)
        newAsyncRequests.add(new AsyncRequest__c(
            AsyncType__c = 'Translate Work Order',
            Params__c = string.Join(textChangedIds,',')));

    insert newAsyncRequests;
}
```

The handleTrigger5 function iterates over the work orders, looking at all work orders on insert, and those where the Description has changed on update. It builds a list of the IDs of the work orders that need to be translated, and then joins them into a comma separated string. It breaks up the request into groups of 100, which is the current callout limit. You can't use the Limits.getLimitCallouts method here because it would return zero (it being a trigger context). Finally, the function creates the necessary AsyncRequest__c objects with an AsyncType__c value of "Translate Work Order", and inserts them.

The insertion of the AsyncRequest__c objects is detected by a new trigger called OnAsyncRequestInsert, that is defined as follows:

```
trigger OnAsyncRequestInsert on AsyncRequest__c (after insert)
{
    if(Limits.getLimitQueueableJobs() -
    Limits.getQueueableJobs() > 0)
    try
    {
        GoingAsync4.enqueueGoingAsync4(null);
    } catch(Exception ex)
    {
        // Ignore for now
    }
}
```

The enqueueGoingAsync4 method is a utility function that actually enqueues the job – you'll see why we do it that way shortly. This may seem like a lot of effort to queue up a request to process a set of WorkOrder objects to translate. The GoingAsync4 class, that implements the queueable interface, doesn't get any easier.

The execute method begins with a query for a single AsyncRequest__c object.

```
public void execute(QueueableContext context)
{
    // On/off switch
    if(!AppCustomSetting.appEnabled) return;
    List<AsyncRequest__c> requests;
    try
    {
        requests = [Select ID, AsyncType__c, Params__c
            from AsyncRequest__c
            where Error__c = false And
            CreatedById = :UserInfo.getUserId()
            Limit 1 for update];
    }
    catch(Exception ex) { return; }
    if(requests.size()==0 ) return;

    AsyncRequest__c currentRequest = requests[0];
```

There are a few interesting things about this query. First, it filters for the Error__c field being false. This small change carries huge consequences. It means that our AsyncRequest__c object actually has two distinct purposes: it holds the requests for pending asynchronous operations, and it holds error information for those that failed with exceptions! Think about it – instead of asynchronous errors causing lost data, or obscure error messages in system logs that are discarded over time (usually right before you need them), all of the information from the original request is stored along with the exception information in as much detail as you wish to keep. And the data is reportable using standard Salesforce reporting! You can even build workflows on it that detect errors and send out notifications!

Next, there is a filter so that the job only processes the AsyncRequest__c objects that were created in the current user context. This is another small difference with potentially huge consequences. It means that you can implement a class to process individual requests and declare that class "with sharing" and thus respect the sharing rules of whoever requested the original async operation. Any tests for field and record level security that you make will reflect the user that originated the request. This allows you to easily implement a wide variety of security architectures - something that is difficult to do when using batch Apex or scheduled Apex to process requests that may have been placed by many different users (as was the case in our previous solutions that used the TranslationPending__c flag).

Finally, this query has the "For Update" qualifier, which means that no other instance of the GoingAsync4 class can access the record while you are processing it. As you'll learn in the next chapter, this can dramatically reduce the chances of concurrency errors. If this instance, or another instance of the class times out with a concurrency error, who cares? The current execute method will chain to requeue the class if necessary.

I hope you're beginning to see that all of this extra work might actually be worthwhile. Hang on – it only gets better from here.

Once the request is made, the function examines the AsyncType__c field and passes the AsyncRequest__c object to the appropriate function to process the request. In this case, it's a new GoingAsync4.translate function that you'll see shortly. The really important part of this function is that there is no limit to the number of AsyncType__c values you can specify (well, Salesforce does actually limit picklists currently to 1000 entries, but you can always use a text field instead in the unlikely event you have more than 1000 types of asynchronous operations).

So yes, you've invested some extra work to build a more sophisticated queueable Apex class, but that one class now forms the infrastructure for handling most of your asynchronous functionality! Talk about efficiency.

The error handling system is also quite elegant. If the routine that handles a request succeeds, the framework deletes the AsyncRequest__c object, emptying it from the recycle bin so that the large number of objects being processed doesn't interfere with normal recycle bin processing of objects people might need – like leads and contacts.

If, however, the method handling a request throws an exception, the routine traps the exception and marks the AsyncRequest__c object as an error, setting its Error__c field and storing the exception message in the ErrorMessage__c field. The record is then updated and available for later examination.

```
try
{
    if(currentRequest.AsyncType__c=='Translate Work Order')
        translate(currentRequest);

    // Add more here

    delete currentRequest;
    // Optional
    database.emptyRecycleBin(
        new List<ID>{currentRequest.id});

}
catch(Exception ex)
{
    currentRequest.Error__c = true;
    currentRequest.Error_Message__c = ex.getMessage();
    update currentRequest;
}
```

All that's left is making sure that the GoingAsync4 class is queued up again if necessary. First, the function performs a query similar to the first one, except that it excludes the current request and does not use the For Update option to lock the record, since the only concern here is to detect if there is another record pending.

If a request is found, the function attempts to enqueue the class again. If that fails, typically because of a chaining limit exception, it calls the tryToQueue function as a backup – a function that performs an unexpected trick as you will soon see.

```
List<AsyncRequest__c> moreRequests = [Select ID, AsyncType__c, Params__c
    from AsyncRequest__c where Error__c = false
    and ID <> :currentRequest.id
    and CreatedById = :UserInfo.getUserId() Limit 1 ];
```

```
if(moreRequests.size()==0) return;

try
{
    enqueueGoingAsync4(context.getJobId());
}
catch(Exception ex)
{
    tryToQueue();
}
```

The tryToQueue method provides a backup mechanism for enqueueing the GoingAsync4 class. The odd thing is, that it is a future call. Everyone knows that you can't make a future call from a batch call and you can't create a batch from a future call. Except, it turns out that when it comes to queueable Apex, you can do both.

```
@future
private static void tryToQueue()
{
    // On/off switch
    if(!AppCustomSetting.appEnabled) return;
    try
    {
        if(Limits.getLimitQueueableJobs() -Limits.getQueueableJobs() > 0)
            enqueueGoingAsync4(null);
    }
    catch(Exception ex)
    {
        // Wait for someone else to make a request...
        // Or maybe use scheduled Apex?
    }
}
```

Was this by design? Was it an oversight on the part of the designers that will go away someday? Who knows? At the time this book was published, this works.

But what if that changes? Well, here too you can catch the exception and try yet another backup mechanism for requeuing the class. You can, for example, start a Scheduled Apex class whose sole purpose is to start queueable Apex jobs.

And if even that approach fails? Remember, no data has been lost. The asynchronous request remains on the system, and eventually a new asynchronous request will come in and process the existing request.

The enqueueGoingAsync4 method calls system.enqueueJob to create the queueable Apex job, but first it checks to make sure a job isn't already queued.

```
public static void enqueueGoingAsync4(ID currentJobId)
{
    List<AsyncApexJob> jobs = [
        Select ID, Status, ExtendedStatus from AsyncApexJob
        where JobType = 'Queueable' And
        (status='Queued'  Or Status='Holding')
        and CreatedById = :userinfo.getUserID() and
        ApexClass.Name='GoingAsync4' and
        ID!= :currentJobId Limit 1 ];
    // Exit if already have one queued that isn't this one.
    if(jobs.size()==1) return;

    system.enqueueJob(new GoingAsync4());
}
```

The reason for this approach is subtle. What if you have a batch operation that is processing hundreds of records, and during that record processing you want to start an asynchronous operation? This is admittedly an unlikely scenario, but it can happen in ways you don't anticipate if another application or process that uses batch Apex interacts with yours.

Entering large numbers of AsyncRequest__c objects isn't a problem. And creating a large number of queueable Apex jobs isn't a problem either except for the fact that we're using a For Update query to prevent concurrency errors (such as trying to process the same asynchronous request twice). In theory, creating large numbers of queueable Apex jobs that block each other shouldn't be a problem – in that each one should wait in turn until it either obtains an AsyncRequest__c record or times out. However, as it turns out, all of those queries blocking each other impose quite a load on the system, and Salesforce operations really frowns upon that. So this scenario will likely prompt a nasty Email from them complaining that you are using too many system resources and cause them to place a delay on queueable apex in that org.

The approach shown here avoids that problem by making sure that you don't add a new queueable job if one already exists for that class and user, which is fine, because you can rely on the chaining mechanism to ensure that the AsyncRequest__c objects are ultimately processed.

As you've seen, centralizing asynchronous operations using a framework such as this one has numerous benefits. It is very robust, though not quite indestructible, with great ability to recover from most exceptions. What's more, it naturally implements an asynchronous diagnostic system – an area that is usually exceedingly painful. By filtering on the requesting user, it enables sophisticated security scenarios. It reduces the chances of DML lock errors by locking access to individual requests and, in most cases, to the records referenced by those requests.

And above all, thanks to queueable Apex, it is fast and efficient.

Variations

What you've read so far represents the foundation for a centralized asynchronous processing framework. Here are a few things to consider as you look at building your own.

What would it take to retry an asynchronous operation after it has failed and its Error__c field has been set? All you need to do is clear the Error__c field! The record will be picked up next time the execute method runs for the originating user. You can, if you wish, use an update trigger on the AsyncRequest__c object to watch for resetting the Error__c field and queue up the Apex class at that time. You could even modify the query to accept both the user who created the AsyncRequest__c object and the person who last modified it (using the LastModifiedById field) to make sure it runs promptly.

The one type of exception that is not trappable using exception handlers are limit exceptions. If an asynchronous request for a particular AsyncRequest__c object causes a limit exception, the entire framework can get stuck as it tries over and over to process that request.

One approach to dealing with this problem is to be careful to use limit functions to check usage during each supporting function then processes the requests. If you see yourself approaching a limit, throw an exception to abort the operation and let the framework flag the AsyncRequest__c object as an error.

Here's another trick that works as a backup. While it is true that you can't trap limit exceptions, in the case of queueable Apex, you can detect them after the fact. You can query the AsyncApexJob object for classes that have a JobType of Queueable and that failed for the current user. If the most recent job was a failure, especially if you see more than one failed job of this type, it's a pretty safe bet that the current record is the one that is consistently failing. You can then mark it as an error and go on to the next one.

What would it take to add a StartTime field to the AsyncRequest__c object and modify the filter so that it pulled only AsyncRequest__c objects whose start time has been met? Doing so would let you effectively schedule asynchronous requests just by setting that StartTime field. The only trick would be to make sure someone or something enqueued the Apex job for the next pending request. That remains the legitimate task of scheduled Apex.

Going Asynchronous with Scheduled Apex

Scheduled Apex provides a mechanism to schedule an Apex class to run at a set time. It has a rather interesting history.

Originally, it was advisable to avoid using scheduled Apex. This is because when you had a class scheduled using scheduled Apex, it was impossible to update that class. The class was locked because the platform internally stores a serialized instance of that class. Worse, the platform also prevented updates to any classes that were referenced by the scheduled class. This meant that many of your code updates required the additional step of deleting any scheduled jobs and then restarting them after the update.

The problem was even worse if you were building an AppExchange package. It made it virtually impossible to push patches and updates to your users.

Then Salesforce added a new option called "Deployment Settings" which offers the option shown in figure 7-1

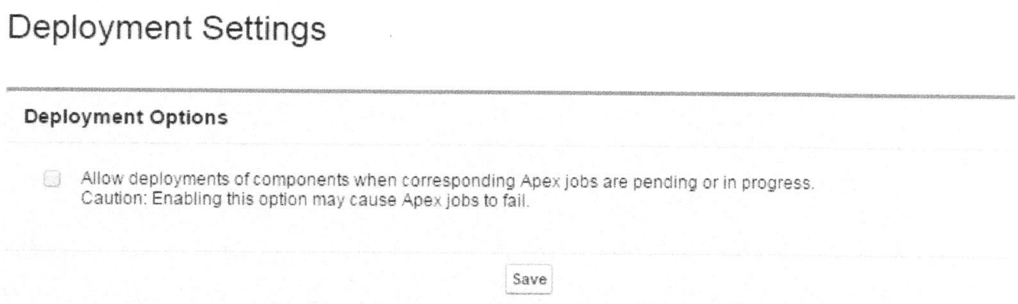

Deployment Settings

Deployment Options

☐ Allow deployments of components when corresponding Apex jobs are pending or in progress.
Caution: Enabling this option may cause Apex jobs to fail.

Save

Figure 7-1 – Deployment Settings

Checking this option allows you to deploy updates even if Apex jobs are pending, at the risk of them failing. This option is off by default.

You can eliminate the need to select this option by adopting the following design pattern for all scheduled Apex classes. The idea is to create a simple Apex class that is schedulable, that will call into other code, but not reference that code. This schedulable class will be locked when scheduled, but it won't lock any other code in your application. With luck, it will never need to be updated. What's more, package installations and upgrades are intelligent enough to recognize that a class has not changed, and will not attempt to update it – thus the fact that the class is locked will not interfere with package deployments and push updates.

The ScheduledDispatcher class demonstrates this principle.

```
global class ScheduledDispatcher Implements Schedulable {

    public Interface IScheduleDispatched
    {
        void execute(SchedulableContext sc);
```

```
    }

    global void execute(SchedulableContext sc)
    {
        Type targetType = Type.forName('GoingAsync5');
        if(targetType!=null) {
          IScheduleDispatched obj =
            (IScheduleDispatched)targettype.newInstance();
            obj.execute(sc);
        }
    }
}
```

The class defines an interface that can be referenced by another class. When the system scheduler calls the execute method, the code uses the Type.forName method to first obtain the type object for the class that will implement the desired functionality, then uses the newInstance method to create an instance of that class. As long as the class implements the IScheduleDispatched interface, you will be able to call its execute method.

In this example, the delegated class is the GoingAsync5 class. The scheduled operation starts the GoingAsync4 batch and aborts the scheduled job. You can use this approach to implement some of the design ideas suggested earlier. You could use it as a backup to queue the GoingAsync4 class if chaining completely fails. You could use it as part of a mechanism for scheduling AsyncRequest__c objects, setting the target scheduled time based on the earliest non-immediate request.

```
public without sharing class GoingAsync5
    implements ScheduledDispatcher.IScheduleDispatched {

    public void execute(SchedulableContext sc)
    {
      // When used as a backup to start the async framework
      system.enqueueJob(new GoingAsync4());
      // Always abort the job on completion
        system.abortJob(sc.getTriggerID());
    }
```

```
public static String getSchedulerExpression(Datetime dt) {
  // Don't try to schedule Apex before current time + buffer
  if(dt < DateTime.Now().AddMinutes(1))
    dt = DateTime.Now().AddMinutes(1);
    return ('' + dt.second() + ' ' + dt.minute() + ' ' +
    dt.hour() + ' ' + dt.day() + ' ' +
    dt.month() + ' ? ' + dt.year());
}

public static void startScheduler(
  DateTime scheduledTime, String jobName)
{

  // Is the job already running?
  List<CronTrigger> jobs =
    [SELECT Id, CronJobDetail.Name, State, NextFireTime
       FROM CronTrigger
       WHERE CronJobDetail.Name= :jobName];
  if(jobs.size()>0 && jobs[0].state!='COMPLETED' &&
   jobs[0].state!='ERROR' && jobs[0].state!='DELETED')
  {
    // It's already running/scheduled
    // Depending on your design you might want to
    // exitor abort and reschedule if the requested
    // start time is earlier
    return;
  }

  // If the job exists, it needs to be deleted
  if(jobs.size()>0) system.abortJob(jobs[0].id);

  try
  {
    System.schedule(jobName,
    getSchedulerExpression(scheduledTime),
                    new ScheduledDispatcher());
  } catch(Exception ex)
  {
```

```
            system.Debug(ex.getMessage());
            // Log the error?
            // Or throw the error to the caller?
        }
    }
}
```

The only tricky part of this code is the startScheduler function – a utility function intended to be called externally. It begins by checking if the scheduled job already exists – you can't create a new scheduled job with the same name as one that is running. If a job with this name is already running, you have a number of choices. You can just exit, assuming the existing job will serve the same purpose as the current request. You can throw an error. Or you can check the current scheduled time against the requested time, and abort the current job if the requested time is earlier than the scheduled time of the existing job.

Even if the existing job has been completed, you need to delete it if you wish to create a new job with the same name – that's the job of the system.abortJob call.

Finally, the System.schedule method creates the scheduled Apex job. The getSchedulerExpression function returns a properly formatted expression for the System.schedule method. It also ensures that the scheduled time is after the current time, adding a buffer of one minute. It is essential that you never schedule an Apex job before the current time – doing so will not only fail with an exception, it has been known to create asynchronous job entries that are stuck forever in the queued state, making it impossible to update or delete the scheduled Apex entry point (in this case the ScheduledDispatcher class) even if you've configured the system to allow updating of classes with jobs in progress.

At this point it is unlikely that the call will fail, as the code has already tested for the most common error conditions. However, there is a limit to the number of jobs that can be scheduled at once, and exceeding that limit will cause an exception. You should consider how you want to handle that situation.

Going Asynchronous with Platform Events

Platform events represent the newest form of asynchronous processing on the Salesforce platform. Platform events implement a message queue.

A message is defined by creating a platform event object. These event objects can have fields that define the event information. Only certain primitive field types are currently supported: text, checkbox, date, datetime and numbers.

When you insert an event into the system, it can be read asynchronously by one or more listeners – functional elements that subscribe to platform events and process them when they arrive. Each event can have multiple listeners.

Message queues are most often thought of as a means of integration with external systems. Indeed, platform events can be created and subscribed to by external systems. External system integration is really beyond the scope of this book, so I won't be going into those types of applications for platform events.

Normally, Apex developers won't use platform events for general purpose asynchronous programming. The mechanisms you've read about so far in this chapter are far superior. There are, however, two aspects of platform events that are unique and make it possible to perform tasks that can't be accomplished using the other asynchronous systems.

First, unlike regular asynchronous operations, platform events are not part of an execution context's transaction.

You already know that when an execution context fails due to an unhandled exception, any changes that were made during that execution context are reverted[3]. This includes the creation of asynchronous operations – any asynchronous requests made in a failed execution context will not be executed. This can make diagnostics a challenge, in that any diagnostic information you record in the database during execution of a failed context will be reverted as well. This is a particularly difficult

---

[3] This is almost always true. At this time there are some edge conditions with Lightning processes and CPU timeouts where this can fail.

challenge when it comes to dealing with untrappable limit exceptions such as CPU timeout errors, where the maximum debug log size is exceeded as well.

Because platform events are not part of the execution context's transaction, they are not reverted if the execution context fails due to an unhandled exception. This makes them uniquely useful for event logging, especially when it comes to diagnosing limit exceptions.

The second place where platform events are exceedingly useful is when it comes to building Lightning components and applications. Pages built on the Lightning framework are implemented as a single page application running on a browser. Lightning components can easily call Apex and wait for asynchronous responses to specific requests, but there is no built-in mechanism to watch for system changes that are not reflected by events built-in to the lightning framework.

However, Lightning components and applications can subscribe to platform events, offering a mechanism for Apex code to communicate asynchronously with running Lightning applications and components.

You'll find an example of using platform events in chapter 10 in the discussion of debugging and diagnostics, and an example of using platform events to communicate with a Lightning component in chapter 9.

8 – Concurrency

> Regarding the sample code for this chapter:
>
> Unlike other chapters that are branched from master in the git repository, the sample code for this chapter branches off the chapter 7 branch, as parts of it build on those samples

There are two errors possible in Apex that many developers will never see. The first is:

```
EXCEPTION_THROWN [32]|System.QueryException: Record Currently
Unavailable: The record you are attempting to edit, or one of its
related records, is currently being modified by another user. Please try
again.
```

The second is:

```
FATAL_ERROR System.DmlException: Update failed. First exception on row 0
with id .............; first error: UNABLE_TO_LOCK_ROW, unable to obtain
exclusive access to this record: []
```

If you have never seen either of these errors, count yourself lucky. I encourage you to read this chapter regardless. It will help you to design more robust code should you ever find yourself having to implement an application that demands a high degree of reliability and fault tolerance. And it will help you to avoid panic should you run into either of these errors in the future.

If you have run into either of these errors, I think you will find this chapter helpful.

Introduction to Concurrency

If you come to Apex from another language, you are likely already familiar with the concept of concurrency from your experience with multithreading. Then again, I have met a fair number of developers who use languages that support multithreading, who don't really understand the nature of what they are dealing with. So, for the benefit of those who don't have extensive experience with the topic, I'm going to take a somewhat more introductory approach here than I have in other chapters.

The problem of concurrency in real life may be quite familiar to you. Let's say that you and your spouse have a joint checking account with a balance of $100. You're both shopping for gifts for the holidays. You find the perfect gift, and just to be safe, check your account balance and confirm that it is indeed $100. Knowing this, you confidently write a check for $75 for your gift. At exactly the same moment, your spouse does exactly the same thing.

Both of you "know" that you have a balance of $100. So each of you spends $75, confident that the checks are good. But together you've spent $150 and one of those checks is going to bounce.

This is a classic concurrency problem. It can happen any time that two separate operations are able to access a shared resource.

Of all the software bugs that are possible, none are harder to solve than concurrency problems.

Here's why.

What are the chances that two sales reps will happen to be modifying the exact same field on the same object at the same time? What are the chances that two asynchronous processes or incoming service calls will do the same? On a smaller or lower traffic system, the odds might be a million to one against. So a concurrency related bug might only happen once every few years.

How do you detect, reproduce and debug a problem that occurs so infrequently? It's virtually impossible.

In many applications, when these problems do occur, they aren't even recognized. Someone notices some data that is incorrect and assumes it was edited in error. In many cases it's not a big deal. But if you're building a financial application, these errors can be serious – money can literally appear or disappear, seemingly at random.

The cost to identify concurrency bugs, reproduce them, and fix them, can be virtually unlimited. The only real way to address concurrency issues is at design time.

From a language perspective, Apex is not a multithreaded language. There is no shared data. There is no ability to create traditional threads. All static variables are the equivalent of what in the multithreading world is called "thread local storage" – they are specific to one thread and one execution context.

However, Force.com asynchronous processes do run in separate threads and can be concurrent. And those processes can access the database. So concurrency issues can occur – especially on high traffic systems, or systems that support many asynchronous processes or incoming service calls.

For this reason, it is essential that you understand concurrency and how to deal with it in your code.

Optimistic Concurrency

Let's examine a concurrency scenario from the Salesforce world.

Imagine a $20,000 opportunity that has two related contacts. Each contact is working with a separate sales person. At exactly the same time each contact calls their sales rep and gives them the good news – they're going to spend an extra $10,000 as shown in figure 8-1.

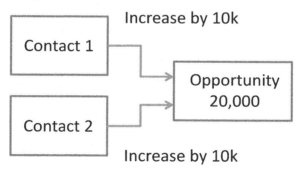

Figure 8-1 – Two contacts each increase an opportunity by 10K

The sales reps, thrilled, immediately go to their computers. On seeing that the current value of the opportunity is 20K, they edit the opportunity and set it to 30K as shown in figure 8-2.

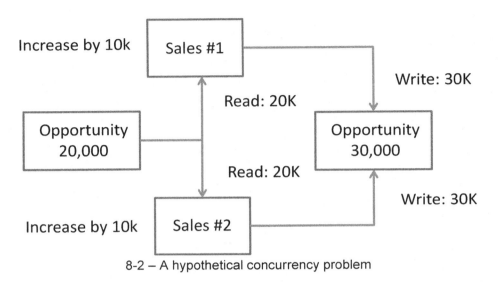

8-2 – A hypothetical concurrency problem

Because each sales person sees the current value as 20K, and updates the opportunity to 30K, nobody will realize that the opportunity should have been 40K unless the sales reps happen to compare notes.

Those of you with experience with this kind of scenario might see a problem with this example. In practice, if two sales reps try to update an opportunity at once, when the second sales rep tries to save the data, an error message will be displayed in the Salesforce user interface. The error will be the first one I listed: "The record you are attempting to edit, or one of its related records, is currently being modified by another user. Please try again."

That's because the Salesforce user interface is clever and implements the scenario as shown in figure 8-3:

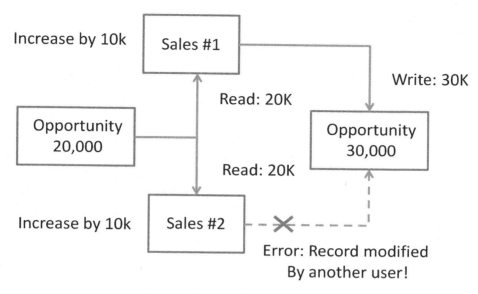

8-3 – Optimistic Record Locking

When the second user tries to update the opportunity, the system detects that the opportunity has been updated by another user since the edit session began and blocks the update. Salesforce is using a type of record locking approach called optimistic record locking (though purists will note that this is not true optimistic locking at the database level). This approach assumes that there won't be any concurrency issues, trusting on the ability of the system to detect them and report an error when they occur.

The ability of Salesforce to detect concurrency issues is limited. For one thing, it only applies to different users. If you have two asynchronous or external service calls running in the same user context, and a concurrency issue comes up, it will typically not be detected. If Apex code modifies a record that is being edited in the user interface by a different user, Salesforce will detect that another user modified the record and report an error. However, in the unlikely event that another user modifies a record between the time your Apex code queries a record and updates it, the concurrency error will not be detected.

This means that if you are building a very high reliability application that supports asynchronous operations, you must either implement your own concurrency error detection, or use pessimistic record locking.

Pessimistic Record Locking (For Update)

For cases where you want to be certain that your execution context has sole access to a record, you can use a technique called pessimistic record locking. This is implemented by adding the "For Update" term to your SOQL query.

When you lock a record with a "for update" query, any other thread that attempts to read that record will block – it will wait until the execution context that locked the record completes. Once the first execution context is finished, the blocked thread will be allowed to continue as shown in figure 8-4. In this example, Sales rep #2 will not be able to query the opportunity until Sales rep #1 has completed editing the record.

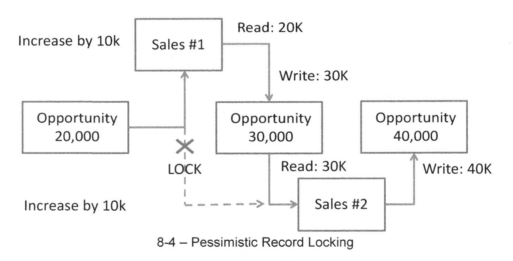

8-4 – Pessimistic Record Locking

What happens if the code processing Sales Rep #1 takes a very long time, say more than 10 seconds? At that point the block on Sales Rep #2 times out and you get the notorious UNABLE_TO_LOCK_ROW error.

In reality, it's not necessary for one process to hold a lock on a record to cause this error. If you have many processes attempting to access the same record, each one will be unblocked in turn as the previous one completes. But if any process is blocked for too long, it will time out with the UNABLE_TO_LOCK_ROW error.

One of the most common ways this can happen is if you have data skew in your organization.

For example: normally each account might have a relatively small number of contacts. But let's say that you have a "catch-all" account to hold contacts that don't have a specific account. In this case you can end up with one account with a very large number of contacts.

Any time you insert a contact or change the owner on a contact, Salesforce locks the parent account to maintain data integrity. So that catch-all account might spend quite a bit of time being locked. Worse, those operations may involve recalculating sharing rules, which is potentially very time consuming when you have a large number of contacts. If another thread tries to update the parent account or any of its related contacts, you may see an UNABLE_TO_LOCK_ROW error.

Your Apex code also locks records in two ways. First, it locks a record when you use "For Update" in a query. Second, it locks a record when you update it. Why is this? Because if Apex code terminates with an exception, the system reverts the entire transaction. If the platform did not lock the records, other processes could modify those records and the revert operation would cause those changes to be lost without notice or warning. This lock is held until the execution context ends.

On low traffic systems, and systems with small applications, chances are good you will never see a locking error. That's because the ten second lock timeout is really a very long time. However, on high traffic systems, or systems with large applications, UNABLE_TO_LOCK_ROW errors can appear, and they can become painfully common.

There are two key design principles that you can use to minimize the chances of this error occurring even on high traffic systems:

- Avoid data skew
- Defer DML updates until near the end of the execution context

Handling DML lock errors

It is impossible to guarantee 100% that DML lock errors will not occur on a system. The question is, how should you handle them?

For synchronous operations, say triggers or UI operations, the answer is usually simple – don't handle them at all. Lock errors will be raised and the DML operations will return an error result. If it's a user operation, the user will see an error message inviting them to try again later. Any other changes made during the operation will revert and no harm will be done.

But what if the lock errors occur during an asynchronous operation? By default, the best you can hope for is a system Apex error message that provides minimal insight as to where the errors occurred, and no information regarding the data being processed. In other words, you will see data loss – not what you want to have happen in a high reliability system.

For a high reliability system it is not enough to minimize the chances of DML lock errors – you need a detection, reporting and recovery mechanism as well. That's what we'll look at next.

Reproducing DML Lock errors

It's hard to write code for an error condition that rarely occurs. It's even harder to test it. So the first order of business in learning how to deal with these errors is to find a way to reproduce them.

Because concurrency errors involve timeouts, the first step is to find a way to create a nice long delay in Apex. Fortunately, this is not difficult. The stage was already set in chapter 3 where we discussed CPU time limits and the fact that some built-in operations can take a significant amount of time to run.

The Concurrency1.delay method uses JSON serialization of a long array to generate a delay. The actual length of the delay will vary. Though the delay parameter is called "seconds", it's a very rough approximation. In our tests we'll use trial and error to pick numbers that are long enough to generate timeouts without exceeding CPU time limits.

```
public static void delay(Integer seconds)
{
    List<Integer> largeArray = new List<Integer>();
    for(Integer x =0; x<10000; x++) largeArray.add(x);
    for(Integer counter = 0; counter<seconds * 4; counter++)
    {
        String s = json.serialize(largeArray);
    }
}
```

Unlike much of the code in this book, you can't do concurrency testing in a unit test. Unit tests serialize asynchronous requests, running them all synchronously after the Test.stopTest function is called.

To use the tests that follow, you must create an opportunity named "Concurrency1"

The two main methods in the Concurrency1 class are the incrementOptimistic and incrementPessimistic methods.

```
@future
public static void incrementOptimistic(double amount,
    Integer delayBefore, Integer delayFromQuery, Integer delayAfter)
{
    if(delayBefore>0) delay(delayBefore);
    List<Opportunity> ops = [Select ID, Amount From Opportunity
            where Name = :opportunityName];
    for(Opportunity op: ops)
            op.Amount = (op.Amount==null)? amount: op.Amount + Amount;
    if(delayFromQuery>0) delay(delayFromQuery);
    update ops;
    if(delayAfter>0) delay(delayAfter);
}

@future
public static void incrementPessimistic(double amount,
    Integer delayBefore, Integer delayFromQuery, Integer delayAfter)
```

```
{
    if(DelayBefore>0) delay(delayBefore);
    List<Opportunity> ops = [Select ID, Amount From Opportunity
            where Name = :opportunityName For Update];
    for(Opportunity op: ops)
        op.Amount = (op.Amount==null)? amount: op.Amount + Amount;
    if(delayFromQuery>0) delay(delayFromQuery);
    update ops;
    if(delayAfter>0) delay(delayAfter);
}
```

Both of these methods implement the following algorithm:

- Delay *delayBefore* seconds
- Query the opportunity record
- Delay *delayFromQuery* seconds
- Increment a field and update the opportunity record
- Delay *delayAfter* seconds

The incrementPessimistic method uses the "For Update" term in the query to support pessimistic record locking.

These two functions allow you to experiment and reproduce all kinds of locking scenarios. All you need to do is open an anonymous Apex window in the developer console, and execute two or more (up to ten) of these functions at once.

Let's start with some of the optimistic locking scenarios.

Open the Concurrency1 opportunity that you created and set the value in the Amount field to zero.

In your anonymous Apex window, enter:

```
Concurrency1.incrementOptimistic(10,0,2,0);
Concurrency1.incrementOptimistic(10,1,0,0);
```

When you execute these commands, the two future calls will start running concurrently. The first one will query the value of the amount, wait two seconds, and update the record, adding 10 to the original amount. The second method will wait one second, query the record and update it immediately, adding 10 to the original amount. You may need to repeat this test to see the results, as there is no guarantee that both future operations will start at the same time.

Both of these methods increment the Amount by ten, so one would expect the end value to be 20. But the resulting value will be only ten. You've effectively reproduced a concurrency error by stretching out the time of the operations.

Now let's reproduce a lock error.

Try executing the following in your anonymous Apex window:

```
Concurrency1.incrementOptimistic(10,0,0,25);
Concurrency1.incrementOptimistic(10,1,0,0);
```

The first method immediately adds 10 to the amount and updates the opportunity record. It then waits over 10 seconds before exiting (you may need to tinker with the value of the DelayAfter parameter – too short and it may not timeout, too long and you may see CPU timeout limits instead of DML lock errors).

The second method waits one second, then attempts to update the record. However, it is blocked by the first method. After about 10 seconds, the second method aborts with a DML lock (UNABLE_TO_LOCK_ROW) error.

Now let's look at a pessimistic locking example.

Reset the opportunity amount field to zero, then execute the following anonymous Apex:

```
Concurrency1.incrementPessimistic(10,0,2,0);
Concurrency1.incrementPessimistic(10,1,0,0);
```

This is the same scenario you saw earlier with the first optimistic locking example. But this time the amount field does increment to 20. That's because the second method call is blocked and waits until the first one completes before it reads the record. The record thus contains the value as updated by the first method call.

But what if the first method takes too long to finish and the second method is blocked for too long? You can illustrate that scenario with the following code (again, you may need to tinker with the actual timeout value).

```
Concurrency1.IncrementPessimistic(10,0,20,0);
Concurrency1.IncrementPessimistic(10,0,20,0);
```

One of the methods should fail with the following exception:

```
System.QueryException: Record Currently Unavailable: The record you are
attempting to edit, or one of its related records, is currently being
modified by another user. Please try again.
```

You can experiment with these functions to reproduce a variety of locking scenarios. You also now have a tool that can allow you to create lock errors and thus create, test and debug code designed to handle them, instead of just having to simulate those errors in unit tests.

Reprocessing DML lock errors

When you run into a DML lock error in a synchronous operation, you may prefer to just let the error occur and allow the user or caller to handle the error. But if you want to handle these errors in an asynchronous operation, you have only two options – log the error, or try to recover from the error.

In either case, the first thing you have to do is capture the error. This is done by replacing the Update statement with the following code as illustrated in the incrementOptimisticWithCapture method:

```
List<Database.SaveResult> dmlResults = Database.Update(ops, false);
List<Opportunity> failedUpdates = new List<Opportunity>();
for(Integer x = 0; x< ops.size(); x++)
{
```

```
Database.SaveResult sr = dmlResults[x];
if(!sr.isSuccess())
{
    for(Database.Error err: sr.getErrors())
    {
        if(err.getStatusCode() == StatusCode.UNABLE_TO_LOCK_ROW)
        {
            failedUpdates.add(ops[x]);
            break;
        }
    }
}
}

if(failedUpdates.size()>0)
{
    // Do a logging or recovery operation here
}
```

The Database.Update statement has a parameter *opt_allOrNone* which can be set to false to indicate that the code should return an error result rather than throwing an exception. On return, the software tests each result to see if any failed. If the failure was due to a DML lock, the opportunity is stored in an array. We set the *opt_allOrNone* false because in a bulk update it's very likely that the concurrency error would only apply to one or two records in the batch.

There are other types of DML errors that can occur here, so in a real application you might want to extend this code to detect and handle different errors. For example: while it might make sense to retry a DML failure due to a DML lock, you would likely want to log an error caused by a validation rule, as retrying it later is unlikely to work.

Things get more complex if you are updating related objects at the same time. In that case you may prefer to keep the *opt_allOrNone* field true and use the DML savepoint capability to wrap your DML operation inside of a transaction. But that's an entirely different topic, and beyond the scope of this chapter.

Logging DML lock errors in this scenario is straightforward – just use a custom object to store any failure information that you wish to track. While the opportunity record may be locked, that won't prevent you from inserting a new custom object. You'll read more about diagnostic logging in chapter 10.

The interesting thing about a DML lock error is that it is recoverable. Even though this update timed out, one would expect that at some time in the future the update will succeed. So it's quite reasonable to try again sometime in the future. Because you're in a future or batch context already, you can't just perform a future call. However, by remarkable coincidence, you already have a very nice asynchronous processing system that was implemented in chapter 7.

All it takes are a few simple changes to the AsyncRequest__c object:

- Add a currency field NewAmount__c with 2 digits to the right of the decimal
- Add a currency field OriginalAmount__c with two digits to the right of the decimal
- Add a lookup to an opportunity field TargetOpportunity__c
- Add picklist value "Amount Update" to the AsyncType__c field.

The recordRecoveryInformation method creates a new AsyncRequest__c object for each failed opportunity:

```
@testvisible
private static void recordRecoveryInformation(
      List<Opportunity> failedOps, double amount)
{
   List<AsyncRequest__c> requests = new List<AsyncRequest__c>();
   for(Opportunity op: failedOps)
   {
      requests.add(new AsyncRequest__c(
         AsyncType__c = 'Amount Update',
         NewAmount__c = op.Amount,
         OriginalAmount__c = op.Amount - amount,
         TargetOpportunity__c = op.id ));
   }
```

```
    insert requests;
}
```

This method is called from the IncrementOptimisticWithCapture method as follows:

```
if(failedUpdates.size()>0)
{
    // Do a logging or recovery operation here
    recordRecoveryInformation(failedUpdates, amount);
}
```

There's a bit of a "cheat" here, where I determine the original value of the opportunity by subtracting the amount that was previously added. In a real application, you would likely keep an array of original values around in case you wanted to save them when failures occur. Why save the original value? You'll see that shortly.

The GoingAsync4.execute method needs to be modified to query the new AsyncRequest__c object fields:

```
requests = [Select ID, AsyncType__c, Params__c, NewAmount__c,
    OriginalAmount__c, TargetOpportunity__c
    from AsyncRequest__c
    where Error__c = false And CreatedById = :UserInfo.getUserId()
    Limit 1 for update];
```

Now all that remains is to modify the execute statement to process the new type. First, add a branch call to a new updateAmounts function:

```
try
{
  if(currentRequest.AsyncType__c=='Translate Solution')
      translate(currentRequest);

  if(currentRequest.AsyncType__c=='Amount Update')
      updateAmounts(currentRequest);
```

Next, define the updateAmounts function as follows:

```
public void updateAmounts(AsyncRequest__c request)
{
    List<Opportunity> ops =
        [Select ID, Amount from Opportunity
         where ID = :request.TargetOpportunity__c for update];
    // The op may have been deleted
    if(ops.size()==0) return;
    Opportunity op = ops[0];

    // Implement update scenario here
}
```

As you can see, adding processing for a new type of asynchronous operation is very simple. You can also see that I'm breaking the cardinal rule here – using a single object pattern instead of a bulk pattern.

Even though this subsystem is designed to only execute one object at a time, I was sorely tempted to build this using a bulk pattern - creating a separate list of opportunity IDs to query, then doing the query, then processing them one at a time and doing a final update. But the truth is that doing so would make this particular example considerably harder to read and understand.

Now comes the big question. What fits into that block titled "**Implement update scenario here**"

Well, it depends.

You could do a simple amount update like this:

```
op.Amount = request.NewAmount__c;
```

But there's a problem with this approach. What if somebody else has updated the opportunity amount in the meantime? In that case, you're just trading a DML lock error for a concurrency error.

You could say that what you really want to do is increment the amount field regardless of the current value. In that case you can do the following:

```
op.Amount += (request.NewAmount__c - request.OriginalAmount__c);
```

This avoids the concurrency error by redefining the nature of the asynchronous operation from saving a value to incrementing a value.

Another approach is to validate the current value of the opportunity against the original opportunity value – checking if some other process may have updated the amount.

```
if(op.Amount!= request.OriginalAmount__c)
{
    // Concurrency error - throw an exception here
    throw new AsyncUpdateException(
        'Amount on opportunity update has changed');
}
```

The exception is a simple exception class that extends the standard exception class as follows:

```
public class AsyncUpdateException extends Exception {}
```

What you are doing here is a very traditional form of optimistic locking – where you test to see if there is a concurrency issue before performing an update. In this case, if you see the value of the amount has changed, you can assume that there is a concurrency issue. You can then raise an exception, that tells the asynchronous framework to mark the AsyncRequest__c object as an error which can be analyzed later.

When it comes to updating the opportunity, as hard as it is to imagine, it's still possible to run into yet another DML lock error. However, in this case it's easy enough to handle – if you see a DML lock error, you can just clone the AsyncRequest__c object and insert the clone to request another try. That way, next time the async routine runs, your code will try the update again. Here's one way you can implement this:

```
try
{
    update op;
}
catch(DmlException dex)
```

```
{
    if(dex.getDmlType(0) == StatusCode.UNABLE_TO_LOCK_ROW)
    {
        insert request.clone();
        return;
    }
    throw dex;
}
// Any other exception will not be caught
```

Try experimenting with the incrementOptimisticWithCapture function using anonymous Apex in the developer console. For example, try:

```
Concurrency1.incrementOptimisticWithCapture(10,0,0,25);
Concurrency1.incrementOptimisticWithCapture(10,1,0,0);
```

Depending on the timing, and your current implementation of the recordRecoveryInformation method, you'll either see that the Opportunity value has been incremented to 20, or an AsyncRequest__c object has been created with an error status indicating that it was not able to update the opportunity.

Dealing with concurrency can be a huge headache. The only thing worse is not dealing with it in organizations and applications where it is really needed.

Many Apex developers can get away with ignoring this issue. It is rare on many systems. And to be perfectly honest, in many organizations the data in the org is so inaccurate anyway that an occasional undetected concurrency error will never be noticed and never matter.

But if you are building an application that demands a high level of reliability and accuracy – say, a financial application, you should at the very least be aware of potential concurrency issues, and design your application with them in mind.

9 – Application Configuration

Most non-trivial applications make use of some form of configuration. Packaged applications and other code that is intended to be used in multiple organizations make heavy use of configuration to allow software to adapt to different orgs and meet the needs of different customers, each of which may have unique requirements.

Even software intended for use in a single org may implement configurability to anticipate changes in business needs or to customize information for production, sandbox, scratch and developer orgs.

Configuration is also used to allow users to adjust individual preferences, and to provide non-administrators with the ability to customize an application's behavior.

Storing Configuration Data

There are three common ways to store configuration data: database objects, custom settings and custom metadata. There are a number of factors that you should consider when choosing which one is right for your application.

Cost and efficiency of reading data

Both custom settings and custom metadata can be read efficiently without it counting against query limits. Standard objects are subject to query limits.

The ability to protect settings

Managed package vendors are able to protect settings from being viewed or modified on systems on which they are installed. This can be an essential part of maintaining reliable and secure operation in an application. At the very least it reduces or eliminates the need to write defensive code to handle the possibility that someone might tamper with the configuration data. Custom settings can be protected at the object level, and custom metadata at the object and individual field level.

Data types and validation

Standard objects support the most data types, though custom metadata has the unique ability to reference other custom metadata objects, entities and fields. Custom settings are the most limited in this regard. Custom settings do not support validation rules.

The ability to programmatically write configuration data

Simple applications often rely on the setup user interface for setting configuration data. There are, however, advantages to building configuration pages that write configuration data programmatically. In addition to offering a richer user interface, you can perform complex validations beyond what is supported by validation rules. Custom user interfaces are often required for protected configuration data in packages, as those aren't visible in the setup menu.

Database objects and custom settings can be modified using standard DML operations. Custom metadata is harder to update and currently can only be modified by privileged users such as system administrators.

Deployment and transferring configuration data between orgs

Standard data can be deployed using data import and export tools such as the Data Loader. Custom metadata can be deployed using change sets or other metadata deployment tools. Custom settings have no built-in deployment or transfer mechanism beyond being copied during most sandbox refreshes.

So which should you choose?

Both custom settings and custom metadata can be read without consuming limits, which, along with their support for data protection in packages, makes them the first choice for most applications. Custom metadata is particularly useful for in-house development due to its ability to be easily deployed from development orgs and sandboxes to production.

Hierarchical custom settings remain the first choice for settings that vary based on user and profile.

Salesforce has been strongly pushing custom metadata over list custom settings, to the point where on new orgs you can't even create list custom settings without explicitly enabling the feature in the schema settings for the org. And indeed, they are superior in almost every way. They are efficient, and they can be deployed using change sets and other metadata tools. As metadata, they can be included in source control in Salesforce DX. But they aren't quite perfect yet.

There are three scenarios where list custom settings remain the preferred approach:

- It is not yet possible to programmatically delete custom metadata using Apex. If your configuration data involves maintenance of lists of data and you are building custom configuration pages instead of using the setup user interface, it will be easier to implement using list custom settings than custom metadata – which would require more complex object management due to the inability to delete records.

- If you intend to build custom configuration pages to allow non-administrators to customize configuration, custom settings currently remain the preferred choice. Salesforce is working on fine-turning permissions to make it possible for non-administrators to modify custom metadata, but this is not yet available. Be sure to check for updates on AdvancedApex.com for possible changes in this area.

- Use a custom setting for your application's on/off switch. This allows you to shut off your application even if you are unable to deploy metadata – which can occur if your application makes heavy use of asynchronous operations.

Accessing Custom Settings and Custom Metadata

Accessing custom settings and custom metadata is easy and efficient – so easy and efficient that developers are sometimes tempted to access them directly in their code as needed. This is a terrible idea.

In this section you'll learn a correct way to work with both custom settings and custom metadata – the design patterns for both are almost identical. I won't go so far as to say that this is the only correct way to access configuration data, but be sure the approach you choose addresses the challenges that are discussed here.

One of the major driving factors behind configuration data design patterns is support for unit tests. Unit tests should not be dependent on the values of configuration data – if they are, even simple configuration changes might cause tests to fail. This is of particular concern with custom metadata, which, unlike custom settings and most database objects, is visible to unit tests.

Unit tests can also run with the SeeAllData attribute set to true, an option that makes database objects and custom settings visible to the unit test. Use of this option is strongly discouraged and will be discussed further in chapter 11. For now, the possibility that this attribute is set means that unit tests must have the ability to ignore existing configuration data and to work with either default configuration data, or configuration data set by the test itself.

Indeed, unit tests must have the ability to set configuration data, and both custom settings and custom metadata pose unique challenges in this regard.

There is a subtle problem that can occur if your test code inserts, updates or deletes custom setting objects. By default, unit tests can run asynchronously. When more than one test tries to insert or update a custom setting object, you can see intermittent record locking errors. This can express itself as Apex test failures or extremely long test times. If this occurs, you can configure an organization to disable parallel testing – but it is far better to avoid modifying custom settings in unit tests.

As for custom metadata, the problem is less subtle – you simply can't create or modify custom metadata in a unit test.

These issues are best addressed by centralizing all access to custom settings and custom metadata. It's best to make sure that custom setting and custom metadata configuration data is always wrapped in a class, with individual field settings exposed as properties of the class.

In chapter 7, we made use of this approach in the AppCustomSetting class that serves as a wrapper for the AppConfig__c object. This object has two Boolean fields: AppEnabled__c, which you've already seen, and EnableDiagnostics__c, which will be used later in the book. Let's take a closer look.

The class holds a copy of the AppConfig__c object that will be loaded as needed. The field is marked with the @testvisible attribute. This allows unit tests to override the default configuration data as needed.

```
public without sharing class AppCustomSetting {

    @testvisible
    private static AppConfig__c testConfig = null;
```

The getAppConfig function returns the custom setting object. It is also marked as testvisible to make it easy for unit tests to retrieve and possibly modify the default configuration data.

Unit tests always see either an existing test object, or a newly created default object. Outside of unit tests, code will always see a valid configuration object – either one that exists, or a newly created default object.

```
    @testvisible
    private static AppConfig__c getAppConfig()
    {
        if(Test.isRunningTest() && testConfig!=null) return testConfig;

        AppConfig__c theobject = AppConfig__c.getInstance('default');
        if(theObject==null || Test.isRunningTest())
        {
            theObject = new AppConfig__c();
            theObject.name = 'default';
            theObject.EnableDiagnostics__c =
                (Test.isRunningTest())? true: false;
            theObject.AppEnabled__c = true;
            if(!Test.isRunningTest()) Database.Insert(theobject);
            else testconfig = theObject;
        }
        return theObject;
    }
```

Each custom setting field has its own property

```
public static Boolean diagnosticsEnabled
{
    get
    {
        return GetAppConfig().EnableDiagnostics__c;
    }
}

public static Boolean appEnabled
{
    get
    {
        return GetAppConfig().AppEnabled__c;
    }
}
}
```

There is some argument in favor of refactoring the code for a clearer separation of the code that runs in a test context versus a regular context, instead of using multiple Test.isRunningTest() conditions as shown here. Though more cluttered and less efficient, the code shown here does centralize the object initialization, which can be an advantage on custom settings with many fields. But it's more of a stylistic choice than a question of best practices.

Now let's look at the corresponding design pattern for custom metadata.

Custom metadata object fields are read-only. You'll see later in this chapter how custom metadata can be written from Apex. This means that unlike custom settings, we can't cache a custom metadata object – as we can't set its fields. Instead, we create an inner class whose fields correspond to those of the custom metadata type. The object has two constructors, one takes a custom metadata object and uses it to set the object fields, the other just takes the desired name of the object and sets fields to their default values.

```
public class MDSettingClass
{
    public Boolean BooleanSetting;
    public String TextSetting;
```

```
   public String Name;

   public MDSettingClass(MDSetting__mdt source)
   {
       BooleanSetting = source.BooleanSetting__c == true;
       TextSetting = source.TextSetting__c;
       Name = source.DeveloperName;
   }

   // Constructor that sets default values
   public MDSettingClass(String MDName) {
       Name = MDName;
       BooleanSetting = false;
   }
}
```

The ConfigCustomMetadata class then follows a pattern similar to that of the custom setting, except that it always caches a copy of the configuration data. What you're seeing here is a traditional limit tradeoff – while there is no limit cost to querying the custom metadata object, the fact that our code copies its data into a writable object means there is a certain amount of computation required. Holding a cached copy here will improve performance at the cost of some heap space. If you have many custom settings or they hold larger amounts of data, you will probably take the alternate approach of querying the data each time it is needed.

As you can see, reading a custom metadata object is done using a query. Even though it uses the standard query syntax, it does not count as a query for calculating limits.

```
@testvisible
private static MDSettingClass cachedConfig = null;

public static MDSettingClass getConfig()
{
    if(cachedConfig!=null) return cachedConfig;

    List<MDSetting__mdt> settings = [Select DeveloperName, MasterLabel,
        BooleanSetting__c, TextSetting__c from MDSetting__mdt
```

```
        where DeveloperName = 'Default'];

    if(settings.size()==0 || Test.isRunningTest())
    {
        cachedConfig = new MDSettingClass('Default');
        return cachedConfig;
    }
    cachedConfig = new MDSettingClass(settings[0]);
    // If configuration data is large, don't cache it
    // outside of test mode

    return cachedConfig;
}
```

Unlike the custom setting example, the custom metadata code does not attempt to write a default custom metadata object if one does not yet exist. We could do so, but as you'll see, the process of writing custom metadata is more complex than it is for custom settings.

The rest of the class is identical to what you saw earlier – properties that reflect the fields on the custom metadata object.

```
public static Boolean BooleanSetting
{
    get
    {
        return getConfig().BooleanSetting;
    }
}

public static String TextSetting
{
    get
    {
        return getConfig().TextSetting;
    }
}
```

These examples work with single custom setting and custom metadata objects – a very common scenario. There's little difference when it comes to handling lists of objects – an exercise I leave for you.

Writing Custom Settings

Custom settings are written using a standard DML statement. If you wish to modify an existing custom setting, you must first query it using the getInstance method or a SOQL statement such as this one:

```
List<AppConfig__c> settings =
[Select ID, Name, BooleanSetting__c, TextSetting__c from AppConfig__c
where Name = :settingName];
```

The only reason I'm showing the SOQL approach here is that it's the one you'll use when adapting this technique to write multiple custom setting objects. This SOQL query does count against your limits.

While it is possible to protect (and hide) custom settings in managed packages, custom settings do not otherwise support sharing, CRUD or FLS security. Editing custom settings in the setup UI does require setup privileges.

You can build a custom configuration page in VisualForce or Lightning to support validation and editing of custom settings by less privileged users (in which case you would configure the security of the configuration page). Custom configuration pages are essential if you wish to allow users to edit protected custom settings – as those are not visible in the setup UI.

When using VisualForce, you should wrap the custom setting in a class and use form fields such as <apex:inputText> to edit the class properties. Do not edit the custom setting fields directly using the <apex:inputField> tag. This tag enforces the same security requirements as the setup UI when it comes to editing custom settings, so you won't be able to allow access to less privileged users.

The sample code includes a Lightning application that demonstrates a simple custom setting configuration page. Lightning component development is beyond the scope of this book, so I won't go into details about the markup and controllers.

The sample includes a container application ConfigurationApp, a status component called StatusComponent that displays the success or failure of a save operation, and the ListSettingConfiguration component that is the actual configuration form. While I won't show you all of these components here, I will go into the Apex controller and the helper class that calls it. Brace yourself – I will have to show you some JavaScript.

You may wonder, if reading and writing custom settings is so simple, why do I even bother explaining it? The reason follows from what you learned in the previous chapter about concurrency. While concurrency errors can be annoying, they are far better than allowing multiple users to overwrite each other's data. As you saw, optimistic concurrency detection in Salesforce is supported at the UI level. If we're going to build a configuration page to edit custom settings, it really should have a similar form of concurrency protection.

For this reason, the ConfigController class that is used by our Lightning helper to retrieve the current settings returns two copies of the configuration object. In this case it's just easier to clone an object in Apex than it is in JavaScript. It also creates a new default object if one does not currently exist.

```
// Return 2 copies of the same object –
//one to track as the original value
@auraEnabled
public static List<AppConfig__c> getCSListObject(String settingName)
{
    List<AppConfig__c> settings = [Select ID, Name,
        BooleanSetting__c, TextSetting__c
        from AppConfig__c where Name = :settingName];
    List<AppConfig__c> results = new List<AppConfig__c>();
    results.add((settings.size()==0)?
        new AppConfig__c(Name = settingName, BooleanSetting__c = false,
                TextSetting__c = null): settings[0]);
    results.add(results[0].clone(true, false, false, false));
    return results;
}
```

The helper class, ListSettingConfigurationHelper.js, implements the getCurrentRecord method that retrieves the current custom setting records. It stores two copies in the component. One will be edited directly by the component fields. The other will hold the original value at the time this function was called.

```
getCurrentRecord : function(component, event, configObjectName) {
    var action = component.get("c.getCSListObject");
    action.setParams({ "settingName" : configObjectName });
    action.setCallback(this, function(response) {
        var state = response.getState();
        if (state === "SUCCESS") {
            var setting = response.getReturnValue();
            component.set("v.configObject", setting[0]);
            component.set("v.originalObject", setting[1]);
        }
        else if (state === "ERROR") {
            var errors = response.getError();
            if (errors) {
                if (errors[0] && errors[0].message) {
                    console.log("Error message: " +
                    errors[0].message);
                }
            }
        } else {
            console.log("Unknown error");
        }
    });
    $A.enqueueAction(action);
},
```

When saving the configuration data, the helper's saveRecord method passes both the current and original values of the custom setting to the Apex controller.

```
saveRecord : function(component, event, configObjectName) {
    var action = component.get("c.saveCSListObject");
    var configObject = component.get("v.configObject");
    var originalObject = component.get("v.originalObject");
    action.setParams({ "configObject" : configObject,
```

```
            "originalObject" : originalObject,
            "settingName" : configObjectName });
    component.find('status').set("v.message", null);
    action.setCallback(this, function(response) {
        var statusComp = component.find('status');
        var state = response.getState();
        if (state === "SUCCESS") {
            statusComp.set("v.message","Config saved");
            statusComp.set("v.success", true);
        }
        else if (state === "ERROR") {
            var errors = response.getError();
            if (errors) {
                if (errors[0] && errors[0].message) {
                    statusComp.set("v.message",errors[0].message);
                }
            }
        } else {
            statusComp.set("v.message","Unknown error");
        }
    });
    $A.enqueueAction(action);
}
```

The Apex controller performs a number of concurrency tests before attempting to upsert the new custom setting. First it makes sure that some data was actually provided. If an ID exists on the custom setting, it must be present on the original object and unchanged. Finally, the field values of the original object must match the current custom setting value – a difference here indicates that the custom setting on the system has been changed.

```
@auraEnabled
public static void saveCSListObject(AppConfig__c configObject,
    AppConfig__c originalObject, String settingName)
{
    if(configObject == null || originalObject == null)
        throw new AuraHandledException('No data provided');
    AppConfig__c currentValue = getCSListObject(settingName)[0];
```

```
Boolean concurrencyError = false;
// If it's a new object,
// the existing value must also be null
if(configObject.id != currentValue.id) concurrencyError = true;
if(!concurrencyError && configObject.id!=null )
{
    if(originalObject.AppEnabled__c != currentValue.AppEnabled__c ||
        originalObject.EnableDiagnostics__c !=
        currentValue.EnableDiagnostics__c)
        concurrencyError = true;
}
if(concurrencyError) throw new
    AuraHandledException('The setting you are trying to
    save has been modified - restoring original values');

    upsert configObject;
}
```

It may seem overkill to implement concurrency detection for a configuration page, and in some cases it probably is. However, it is important for you know how to do this if one day you find the need. And as someone who has built many configuration pages, I can assure you that the need does arise.

Custom Setting Quirks

I haven't said much about hierarchical custom settings. They are very similar to list custom settings except for the presence of the setupOwnerId field. This field corresponds to the scope for the custom setting – user, profile or organization wide. For retrieving or setting the default (organization) custom setting value, use the org ID as the value of the setupOwnerId field.

For list custom settings, the name field must be unique for each object. This is enforced by the system – any attempt to create two list custom setting records with the same name will fail.

If you do get two list custom setting records with the same name in an org, the getInstance method will fail with an error. I'm sure you're wondering how that is possible, given that the system enforces unique names. I wish I could answer that question. That particular error should never occur. Yet it does.

When it does, you can resolve the issue by querying all of the records for a custom setting and iterating through them. Create a set and add each name into the set after checking if it is already present. If already present, mark the record for deletion. The code will look something like this:

```
for(SObject s: customsettingrows)
{
    String thisname = String.ValueOf(s.Get('Name')).ToLowerCase();
    if(thenames.contains(thisname)) {
        objstodelete.add(s);
    } else {
        thenames.add(thisname);
    }
}
if(objstodelete.size()>0) Database.Delete(objstodelete);
```

Writing Custom Metadata

As before, the focus here will be on the helper class and Apex controller. We will, however, have to go a bit deeper into the world of Lightning to deal with the added complexity that is involved when writing custom metadata. As with the previous example, we'll handle concurrency as well.

Let's begin as before with reading the existing custom metadata. As you may recall from earlier in this chapter, we can't use the actual MDSetting__mdt object as a parameter or return type with the controller methods – there's little use in passing an object whose fields are read-only. So instead we'll use the ConfigCustom-Metadata.MDSettingClass wrapper that we created earlier.

The Lightning platform does a great job of serializing and deserializing SObject records, but classes are trickier. So we avoid the issue by passing serialized strings back and forth and doing our own JSON serialization.

Retrieving the record is easy. On the Apex controller side, we query for the record, then return either the serialized record, or a serialized default record.

```
@auraEnabled
public static String getCustomMetadataObject(
    String MDName)
{
    List<MDSetting__mdt> settings = [Select DeveloperName,
    MasterLabel, BooleanSetting__c, TextSetting__c
    from MDSetting__mdt where DeveloperName = :MDName];
    return(JSON.serialize((settings.size()==0)?
        new ConfigCustomMetadata.MDSettingClass(MDName):
        new ConfigCustomMetadata.MDSettingClass(settings[0]))
    );
}
```

Unlike the custom setting example, where the Apex controller returned two copies of the record, in this example we leave it for the helper function to deserialize the data twice, thus creating two distinct copies.

```
getCurrentRecord : function(component, event, configObjectName) {
    var action = component.get("c.getCustomMetadataObject");
    action.setParams({ "MDName" : configObjectName });
    action.setCallback(this, function(response) {
    var state = response.getState();
    if (state === "SUCCESS") {
        var setting = response.getReturnValue();
        component.set("v.configObject", JSON.parse(setting));
        component.set("v.originalObject", JSON.parse(setting));
    }
    else if (state === "ERROR") {
        var errors = response.getError();
        if (errors) {
            if (errors[0] && errors[0].message) {
                console.log("Error message: " + errors[0].message);
            }
        }
    } else {
```

```
    console.log("Unknown error");
  }
});
  $A.enqueueAction(action);
  },
```

Writing custom metadata is considerably more complex than updating a custom setting. Doing so requires use of classes defined in the Metadata namespace. But it's not just that writing metadata is more complex than updating a custom setting record – the real challenge is that updating metadata records in Apex is asynchronous.

Lightning components have no problem calling Apex controller methods that are synchronous. The controller method completes, and a callback function is invoked in the Lightning component. But that call back occurs as soon as the Apex controller method returns. There is currently no provision for asynchronous Apex operations.

There are a number of approaches that can be used to handle asynchronous Apex callouts and batch or queueable operations. Apex callouts can be handled by invoking them by way of a VisualForce remote action and a bit of messaging between Lightning and VisualForce. Queueable and Batch apex operations can be monitored using a JavaScript timer and some polling. Neither approach works for custom metadata at this time.

This is an area where things are likely to change soon, so be sure to monitor AdvancedApex.com for updates. For now, the best way for a Lightning component to detect completion of a metadata update is through the use of platform events.

The MetadataDeployComplete__e platform event has four fields:

- ErrorMessage is a text field containing an error message if an error occurs.
- JobID is a text field that contains the metadata job ID.
- Status is a text field containing the value of the DeployStatusEnumeration that reflects the status of the metadata operation.
- Success is a Boolean field indicating whether the metadata operation was successful.

The Apex controller will post this platform event when the metadata operation completes, which in turn will invoke a callback on the Lightning component that is listening for the event.

That's the concept. Now let's see how it's done.

The CustomMetadataConfigurationHelper.saveRecord function is straightforward. The action parameters are reserialized into JSON strings using the JavaScript JSON.stringify method.

If the asynchronous custom metadata operation succeeds, the job ID is stored in the metadataJobId attribute. It will be used later to match the platform event to the component that is waiting for it.

If a concurrency error occurs, the spinner, which is set by the controller, is hidden. We use a spinner here because metadata update operations can take a while, so it's important to provide feedback that the operation is in progress.

```
saveRecord : function(component, event, configObjectName) {
   var action = component.get("c.saveCustomMetadataObject");
   var configObject = component.get("v.configObject");
   var originalObject = component.get("v.originalObject");
   action.setParams({
      "configObjectJSON" : JSON.stringify(configObject),
      "originalObjectJSON":JSON.stringify(originalObject),
      "MDName" : configObjectName });
   component.find('status').set("v.message", null);
   action.setCallback(this, function(response) {
      var state = response.getState();
      var statusComp = component.find('status');
      if (state === "SUCCESS") {
         var jobID = response.getReturnValue();
         component.set("v.metadataJobId", jobID);
      }
      else if (state === "ERROR") {
         var errors = response.getError();
         if (errors) {
            if (errors[0] && errors[0].message) {
```

```
                  console.log("Error message: " + errors[0].message);
                  statusComp.set("v.message",errors[0].message);
                  this.getCurrentRecord(component, event,
                          configObjectName);   // Reload
                  this.showSpinner(component, false, null);
              }
          }
      } else {
          console.log("Unknown error");
      }
   });
   $A.enqueueAction(action);
},
```

Now let's look at the Apex controller. The first part of the function works very much like the custom setting code. The MDSettingClass object is deserialized from the JSON string. Its values are then tested against an existing setting if one exists.

```
@auraEnabled
public static String saveCustomMetadataObject(
    String configObjectJSON, String originalObjectJSON, String MDName)
{
    if(configObjectJSON == null || originalObjectJSON == null)
        throw new AuraHandledException('No data provided');

    ConfigCustomMetadata.MDSettingClass configObject =
    (ConfigCustomMetadata.MDSettingClass)JSON.deserialize(
    configObjectJSON,
    ConfigCustomMetadata.MDSettingClass.class);
    ConfigCustomMetadata.MDSettingClass originalObject =
    (ConfigCustomMetadata.MDSettingClass)JSON.deserialize(
    originalObjectJSON,
    ConfigCustomMetadata.MDSettingClass.class);

    // See if it exists?
    List<MDSetting__mdt> currentObject = [
        Select DeveloperName, MasterLabel,
        BooleanSetting__c, TextSetting__c
```

```
    from MDSetting__mdt where DeveloperName = :MDName];
Metadata.CustomMetadata customMetadataRecord;

if(currentObject.size()>0)
{
    // If one already exists,
    // see if any of the values have changed
    if(originalObject.BooleanSetting !=
        currentObject[0].BooleanSetting__c ||
        originalObject.TextSetting !=
        currentObject[0].TextSetting__c)
    {
        throw new AuraHandledException('The setting you
            are trying to save has been modified -
            restoring original values');
    }
```

We can't update the record that was queried. Instead, we have to retrieve it in metadata form, or create a new object in metadata form if one does not already exist.

```
    // Get the existing object as metadata
    List<String> componentNameList =
        new List<String>{'MDSetting__mdt.' + MDName};
    List<Metadata.Metadata> components =
        Metadata.Operations.retrieve(
        Metadata.MetadataType.CustomMetadata, componentNameList);
    customMetadataRecord =
        (Metadata.CustomMetadata)components.get(0);
    }
else {
    // It's a new object
    customMetadataRecord = new Metadata.CustomMetadata();
    customMetadataRecord.fullName = 'MDSetting__mdt.' + MDName;
    customMetadataRecord.label = MDName;
}
```

Next, we have to set the individual fields in the metadata record. This is done using a new setMetadataField method that was added to the MDSettings object. You'll see it shortly. Then the deployment is set up and enqueued, and an Apex callback method is specified that will be called when the metadata update is complete.

```
configObject.setMetadataFields(customMetadataRecord.values);
Metadata.DeployContainer mdContainer =
    new Metadata.DeployContainer();
mdContainer.addMetadata(customMetadataRecord);
ID jobID = Metadata.Operations.enqueueDeployment(
    mdContainer, new MDCallback());
return String.valueOf(jobID);
}
```

The setMetadataFields method on the MDSettings object copies the field values from the object into the list of CustomMetadataValue records that hold field values in the correct metadata format. The setFieldValue method either updates an existing value or inserts a new one.

```
public void setMetadataFields(List<Metadata.CustomMetadataValue> values)
{
    setFieldValue(values, 'BooleanSetting__c', BooleanSetting);
    setFieldValue(values, 'TextSetting__c', TextSetting);
}

private void setFieldValue(List<Metadata.CustomMetadataValue> values,
    String fieldName, Object fieldValue)
{
    // Check for existing field
    for(Metadata.CustomMetadataValue cmvalue: values)
    {
        if(cmvalue.field == fieldName)
        {
            cmvalue.value = fieldValue;
            return;
        }
    }
```

```
Metadata.CustomMetadataValue customField =
    new Metadata.CustomMetadataValue();
    customField.field = fieldName;
    customField.value = fieldValue;
    values.add(customField);
}
```

When the metadata update operation is complete, the MDCallback.handleResult function is called. This class creates a new platform event object, copies the results of the metadata operation into its fields and publishes it using the Eventbus.publish method.

```
public void handleResult(Metadata.DeployResult result,
    Metadata.DeployCallbackContext context)
{
    MetadataDeployComplete__e mdevent = new MetadataDeployComplete__e();
    mdevent.Success__c = result.success;
    mdevent.JobID__c = result.id;
    mdevent.Status__c = string.valueOf(result.status);
    if(!result.success)
    {
        if(result.errorMessage!=null)
        {
            mdevent.ErrorMessage__c = result.errorMessage;
        }
        else {
            List<Metadata.DeployMessage> errors =
                result.details.componentFailures;
            mdevent.ErrorMessage__c = errors[0].problem;
        }
    }

    Database.SaveResult eventResult = EventBus.publish(mdevent);
    if(!eventResult.success)
    {
        system.debug('Failed to publish event');
    }
}
```

I'm not going to go into detail as to how a lightning component can listen for a platform event. You'll find the sample code in the MetadataDeployEventListener component. This component is almost identical to the example in the "Build an Instant Notification App" Trailhead module. I strongly recommend it as a great way to learn more about platform events. When our version of the component receives the event, it fires the MetadataDeployEvent Lightning application event that is registered to be handled by the CustomMetadataConfiguration component.

When the event fires, it is ultimately handled by the controller and the helper's metadataComplete function. The controller checks to see if the event's jobId matches the one stored in the metadataJobId attribute. That ensures that each component receives the metadata completion event for the metadata update it invoked. It then calls the helper.metadataComplete method and stops further propagation of the event, as each event corresponds to a single component. Finally, we reload the data to ensure that the original object is updated so that we don't get false concurrency errors, and hide the spinner.

```
metadataCompleteEvent: function(component, event, helper) {
    if(component.get("v.metadataJobId") == event.getParam("jobId"))
    {
        helper.metadataComplete(component, event);
        event.stopPropagation();
        var configObjectName = component.get("v.configObjectName");
        // Reinitialize
        helper.getCurrentRecord(component, event, configObjectName);
        helper.showSpinner(component, false, null);
    }
}
```

The helper's metadataComplete function retrieves the event parameters and displays a success or failure message.

```
metadataComplete: function(component, event) {
    var success = event.getParam("success");
    var status = event.getParam("status");
    var statusComp = component.find('status');
    if(success)
    {
```

```
        statusComp.set("v.message", "Metadata saved succesfully");
        statusComp.set("v.success", true);
    } else
    {
        statusComp.set("v.message",
        event.getParam("errorMessage"));
    }
},
```

Thinking About Application Configuration

In this chapter you learned how to create custom configuration pages that work with custom settings and custom metadata. But in a sense, this chapter isn't about configuration pages at all – it's really about understanding how to think broadly about design issues and combine different platform technologies to come up with solutions.

Think what we covered in this chapter:

- How to design with unit tests in mind
- How to wrap an object inside of a class
- How to build an Apex controller for Lightning
- How to build concurrency handling into a Lightning UI component
- How to handle asynchronous Apex operations
- How to use platform events
- How to serialize and deserialize data
- How to work with custom settings
- How to read, retrieve and deploy custom metadata

It is a fitting conclusion for part II of this book, as it truly reflects what it means to think about application architecture and patterns.

Part III – Testing, Debugging and Deployment

The best design patterns, architectures, and coding practices aren't worth anything if you can't successfully deploy your application. When it comes to testing, debugging and deploying applications, these are exciting times for Salesforce developers.

With the appearance of Salesforce DX – the new Salesforce developer experience, along with packaging 2.0, a new and more modern approach for developing and distributing software is available – one that overcomes many of the limitations of previous methodologies.

Because Salesforce DX supports modern software development methodologies such as source control, automated test and build systems and continuous integration, there is a tendency among some to just want to blindly adopt those methodologies with Salesforce. This can be a mistake.

Salesforce is a cloud platform. But it is not an Infrastructure as a service (IaaS) or even Platform as a Service (PaaS) offering such as those provided by Amazon Web Services, Azure and the Google Cloud Platform. And while Salesforce is a Software as a Service (SaaS) vendor, the development platform isn't quite SaaS either, as it is a true development platform that allows creation of software that is independent from Salesforce's own applications.

I've taken to calling it Software Platform as a Service (SPaaS) – something that falls between SaaS and PaaS. It is different from other platforms, and as such the best practices for developing software, even with Salesforce DX, are different in some ways from the best practices on other platforms. In the chapter that follows, you'll become familiar with those differences and how they can and should impact your development process.

In the introduction to this book I emphasized that it is not a rehash of the documentation and that I expect it to be used as a supplement, not a replacement, for the platform documentation. Keep this in mind as you read the next few chapters, as I will not elaborate (beyond a brief mention) on unit test strategies that are recommended in the documentation (but not always followed). I won't describe the

Developer Console (which has improved considerably over time), and I won't walk you step by step through Salesforce DX, packaging or deployment.

Instead, you'll learn that there are actually many types of unit tests, and the design patterns you should use will depend both on the type of unit test, and on the way you plan to deploy the application.

You'll learn how you can build debugging features into your application to supplement the capabilities built into the platform and get around some of its limitations.

And you'll learn design patterns and best practices for deployment that vary by deployment type. In particular, you'll learn design patterns that are critical for deploying reliable and maintainable packages.

One more thing before we proceed.

You may have already noticed a common theme in the past few paragraphs, one that represents another way in which the Salesforce platform is unique. There is a tendency for most developers to write code first and then worry about deployment. Even where deployment is considered early in the design, it is rarely a major factor in the design and architecture of an application. But on the Force.com platform, the type of deployment you intend to do has a huge impact on design. Design patterns that represent best practices for a consultant building a custom solution for a specific organization, are in some cases radically different from the design patterns that are best practices for a developer creating a managed package for the AppExchange. The chapters that follow will address both types of deployment, and how that choice will impact your design efforts.

10 – Debugging and Diagnostics

When it comes to testing, debugging and diagnostics, it's very tempting to start the conversation with unit tests. The fact that you have to develop unit tests to deploy Force.com applications almost demands that every Apex developer engages in test-driven development to some degree.

However, I'm going to hold off the in-depth discussion of unit test design patterns until the next chapter, even though you will inevitably use unit tests as part of your debugging efforts. It's important not to confuse goals with the means used to attain them, and unit tests are just one tool – a means to an end.

What really are your goals when dealing with debugging and diagnostics? And what is the difference between them?

Debugging is the process of figuring out why software is working incorrectly and fixing the problem. To debug software, you really want to have the following:

- A way to reproduce the problem
- A way to capture data about the problem
- A way to modify the code to try different ways of solving the problem

Diagnostics generally refers to the second bullet - capturing data about the operation of the software. Let's look at the first two of these issues in the context of an Apex application.

Reproducing Problems

Your first step in debugging any problem is to find a way to reproduce it. Since debugging is an iterative process, you'll want to be able to reproduce it easily and quickly – you may need to reproduce it many times before you can fully resolve the issue.

During development, the easiest way to reproduce an error is using test classes. Remember that you can use the SeeAllData attribute on a test class to view or hide existing data in an organization. You can (and should) create "throwaway" test classes as needed to debug specific problems.

You can run anonymous Apex in the Developer Console and Salesforce DX. It is often faster to run an anonymous Apex script than it is to edit and run a test class. This, along with its additional capabilities, makes it particularly useful for iterative debugging. Unlike test classes, anonymous Apex works on actual data – so you will probably want to delete any objects that you create during the test.

When it comes to debugging bulk code, don't forget to look beyond just unit tests. The various data import and bulk operations available using the Salesforce user interface can be useful, as can the Apex Dataloader. Salesforce DX has a rich set of data commands, all of which can be included in your command line scripts. You can also use the API to set up or clear data, or even perform tests using languages such as Python, Java, C# or VB .NET.

Sometimes, of course, you'll just have to do things by hand with the Salesforce user interface.

What if you can't reliably reproduce a problem? This can happen for a number of reasons:

- The issue is load dependent – you may be hitting timeouts that only occur when the Salesforce instance you are using is heavily loaded.
- The issue is sequence dependent – there are many situations on the Salesforce platform where the order of results or operations is indeterminate. Examples include queries without an Order By clause, the order of objects within a bulk operation, and the order of triggers.
- Synchronization issues when multiple threads (multiple users or asynchronous operations) are taking place.

In these cases, you may have to rely on diagnostics - capturing information about problems when they occur.

Diagnostic Data

If you are coming to Apex from another language, in particular a desktop environment such as Visual Studio or Eclipse, you may feel that when it comes to obtaining information about a running application you are taking a step back into the dark ages – or at least back a decade or two.

For one thing, the ability to do real-time debugging is very limited, though much better than it was just a few years back. An Apex debugger does exist and does support basic debugging operations such as breakpoints and viewing data. It does support debugging of managed packages on customer sandboxes. But it does have a number of significant limitations when compared to what you would expect to see on other platforms:

- It can only debug synchronous code. You're out of luck when it comes to debugging batch, future, scheduled and queueable asynchronous operations.
- It does not support watchpoints or conditional breakpoints.
- It is a paid feature – only the higher-end paid orgs have licenses to the Apex debugger. That means developers who only have access to developer orgs are out of luck. A debugger license is good for a single debugging session at any one time. If you want to run two sessions simultaneously, you'll need two licenses.

The reasons for these limitations are easy to understand. Apex code runs in a shared environment. Allowing code to freeze a thread or lock the database is very hard to do. Perhaps someday Salesforce will provide developers with organization instances inside of virtual machines where this might be possible, but in the meantime, it's rather amazing that they've been able to provide the level of Apex debugging that they have.

If a debugger is your first and primary tool for diagnosing problems, you're sure to find debugging Apex extremely frustrating. Experienced Apex developers tend to rely instead on the debug logs. They are the primary source for capturing runtime data from Apex. The debug logs have the following characteristics:

- They are limited in size.
- You can control the level of detail of the data you are capturing at the class level. Capture enough detail and you can view the values of variables – but you are more likely to exceed the maximum log size.
- You can use the System.Debug statement to add debug data to the log.
- The Developer Console has the ability to extract and organize data from the debug logs, but only if the debug logs don't exceed a certain size (that is typically smaller than the maximum debug log size).
- The Apex Replay Debugger is a rather elegant Visual Studio Code plugin that simulates a debugging session using data from a log file.
- The platform stores only a limited amount of debug log data. If you exceed that amount you must delete older debug logs to free up space.
- When instructed to capture debug logs, the monitoring continues for a limited time or number of logs. Continuous logging is possible for the current user using the Developer Console, though the amount of log data stored is limited.
- Debug logs are generated for a particular running user.
- Debug logs do not capture detailed data from managed packages unless you are the package owner and log in via the Subscriber portal.

As a result of these characteristics, it's not unusual to find yourself in the following debug cycle:

- Reproduce the error to obtain a log file and find a problem.
- If the execution context fits into a log file captured with a high degree of detail, examine the log file using your preferred tools to figure out the problem.
- Otherwise, add some debugging code.
- Override the detail level of one or more classes so as not to exceed the maximum debug log size.
- Repeat

Another common variation of this technique takes advantage of the fact that the system.debug statement allows you to specify a logging level. For example:

system.debug(logginglevel.info,...) will output the debug message even if the logging level is set to info. This is particularly useful when benchmarking, or when you find yourself unable to capture the information you need because of debug log size limits.

Though sometimes frustratingly slow, this approach does work for debugging during development. But it borders on useless in other scenarios:

- Because debug log monitoring is time limited, they are not effective for monitoring the ongoing operation of an application. In other words, if you are trying to track down an intermittent exception, you cannot count on debug monitoring to capture the data you need.

- Debug logs are of limited use for debugging managed packages. In particular, when developing a managed package, the debug log excludes most debug information when running the managed package after deployment to a test system. And you must do this kind of testing because there are occasionally bugs that can appear in a managed package only after it is deployed.

- Debug logs are useless for tracking down package installation errors – they simply aren't available at that time.

Instrumenting Apex - I

How important is the ability to monitor and capture diagnostic data on a deployed application?

That depends.

If you are a consultant building an organization specific solution, it can be hard to justify the added investment in diagnostic code, even though (as you will see), the investment can result in faster debugging.

If you are building a managed package for distribution, instrumentation is critical. Any investment in diagnostic code will pay for itself many times over in reduced support costs.

Our example will build on much of the code you've seen up until now. A single trigger, OnOpportunity, will dispatch triggers to class DiagnosticsMain. This class is based on the concepts for central dispatching covered in Chapter 6. Two sets of functionalities are implemented for this trigger: the functionality from Chapter 4 in which contact roles are processed during an opportunity stage change, and the functionality from Chapter 6 in which tasks are created during an opportunity probability change. I won't include all of the listings here because you have already seen them (the previous code is largely copied verbatim into the new sample classes). The example architecture is shown in Figure 10-1.

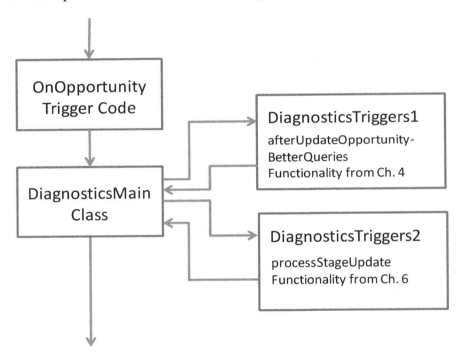

Figure 10-1 – Base example for instrumentation

The instrumentation is designed to capture information during an execution context. In addition to simple text debug information, it incorporates the ideas of levels – where each time you enter a function the level number increments, and each time you exit a function the level number decreases. This acts as a simple call stack.

The DiagnosticsInstrumentation class starts by defining some static variables along with the DiagnosticEntry class that contains the current level and description of a diagnostic entry. The stackTrace list is similar, but instead of capturing diagnostic messages, it just keeps track of the function for the current level.

```
public without sharing class DiagnosticsInstrumentation {

    public static Boolean diagnosticsEnabled =
        AppCustomSetting.diagnosticsEnabled;

    private static List<DiagnosticEntry> diagnosticLog;
    private static Integer currentLevel = 0;

    private static List<String> stackTrace = new List<String>();
    public static string exceptionTrace = '';

    private class DiagnosticEntry
    {
        Integer level;
        String description;

        public diagnosticEntry(string entryDescription)
        {
            level = currentLevel;
            description = entryDescription;
        }
    }
}
```

The diagnosticEnabled flag makes it possible to enable or disable the diagnostic system – you may remember it was the second field in the AppConfig__c custom setting that we used in earlier chapters. This is important because the diagnostics code does consume CPU time, and in later implementations, performs SOQL and DML calls as well. So you'll want to be able to disable the diagnostics in cases where limits are an issue.

Four main diagnostic functions are defined as follows:

```
public static void push(String functionName)
{
    debug('Entering: ' + functionName);
    currentLevel+=1;
    stacktrace.add(functionName);
}

public static void debug(String debugString)
{
    if(!diagnosticsEnabled) return;
    if(diagnosticLog==null) diagnosticLog =
        new List<DiagnosticEntry>();
    diagnosticLog.add(new DiagnosticEntry(debugString));
}

public static void pop()
{
    if(currentLevel>0) currentLevel-=1;
    if(currentLevel==0) System.Debug(LoggingLevel.Info,
        'Diagnostic Log\n' + currentLog());
    if(stackTrace.size()>0) stackTrace.remove(stackTrace.size()-1);
}

public static void popAll()
{
    while(currentLevel>0) pop();
}
```

The push function should be called at the start of every function, and the pop function on exit (though you may want to avoid putting them in small functions that are called frequently to avoid capturing too much data). The pop function includes a test to make sure the level can't be decremented below zero – that prevents errors in cases where you forget to include a push statement for a function or one of its entry points, or accidentally call pop twice. The push function adds the current function to the stackTrace stack, the pop function removes the top function from the stack. Thus, the last entry in the stackTrace list always shows the current function.

popAll is used for exception handling – you'll see why later.

Finally, there's a function to display the current diagnostics log:

```
public static String currentLog()
{
    if(diagnosticLog == null) return null;
    String spaces = '                              ';
    String result = '';
    for(DiagnosticEntry de: diagnosticLog)
    {
        Integer endIndex = 3 * de.level;
        if(endIndex >= spaces.length())
            endIndex = spaces.length()-1;
        result += spaces.substring(0,endIndex) +
                  de.description + '\n';
    }
    return result;
}
```

In addition to adding the push and pop statements, in this example add a debug call right before the main trigger processing in the DiagnosticsMain.handleTriggers function (that is called by the triggers):

```
DiagnosticsInstrumentation.push(
    'handleTriggers TriggerObject: ' + firstObject.getSObjectType() +
    ' Operation ' + triggerType);
```

In the TestDiagnostics1 unit tests, it's not necessary to enable the diagnostics as they are enabled by default in test mode. It is a good idea to add a debug statement indicating the test that is running. For example, in the bulkOpportunityTest add the following right after the call to Test.startTest.

```
DiagnosticsInstrumentation.debug('Performing bulkOpportunityTest');
```

Run the TestDiagnostics1.createTaskTest unit test with debug logs enabled (you may need to set the logging level to info to avoid exceeding the maximum debug log size). If you are using the developer console, open the raw debug log. You can scroll up from the end of the file to find a debug statement that looks something like this:

```
12:15:45.3 (1289631180)|USER_DEBUG|[41]|INFO|
    Diagnostic Log
Entering: handleTriggers TriggerObject: Opportunity Operation
BEFORE_INSERT
Entering: handleTriggers TriggerObject: Opportunity Operation
AFTER_INSERT
    Entering: DiagnosticsTriggers2.MainEntry
       Entering: DiagnosticsTriggers2.processStageUpdate
Performing createTaskTest
Entering: handleTriggers TriggerObject: Opportunity Operation
AFTER_UPDATE
    Entering: DiagnosticsTriggers1.MainEntry
       Entering:
DiagnosticsTriggers1.AfterUpdateOpportunityBetterQueries2
    Entering: DiagnosticsTriggers2.MainEntry
       Entering: DiagnosticsTriggers2.processStageUpdate
```

So what have we accomplished here?

You now have the ability to quickly find, near the end of the diagnostic log, a complete snapshot of the execution tree of your application. You can embed additional debug statements anywhere you wish, and view them without the clutter that is embedded in the debug logs. You can build on this concept further. For example, you could add a timestamp to each diagnostic entry, and add a System.Debug statement to the diagnostic debug function to make it easy to cross reference entries in the diagnostic log to the corresponding statements in the debug log.

Having all of the key information you need in one place that is easy to find can speed up the debugging process by reducing the time it takes to understand what happened during each test iteration.

But that's not all.

Did you notice how the Debug statement in the Pop function included a diagnostic level of info:

```
System.Debug(LoggingLevel.Info, 'Diagnostic Log\n' + CurrentLog()
```

This allows the debug statement to appear in the debug log even when the filter is set to Info – which captures less data than the default 'Debug' level, and far less data than the 'Finest' level used by default in the Developer Console. You could even set this level to Warning or Error to allow the debug information to appear at those levels as well.

This allows you to capture diagnostic data for tests that normally exceed the maximum debug log size, since choosing the lower level of data capture reduces the debug log size.

Faster debugging and avoiding debug log size limits are both incredibly useful, but are only the beginning. To see why, we first need to look at yet another benefit of the central trigger dispatching architecture described in Chapter 6.

Centralized Exception Handling

Whether you are a consultant or creating a managed package, the one thing you don't want to have happen is for your end users to be working in Salesforce.com and suddenly see Figure 10-2 ....

Or, in classic...

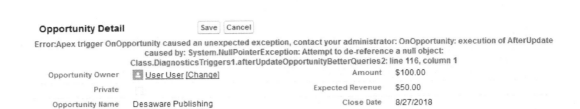

Figure 10-2 – User experience for unhandled Apex exceptions

Yes, it's the dreaded Apex exception. The ultimate bad user experience[4]. In this case, the exception was created in the afterUpdateBetterQueries2 function using the following code:

```
List<Task> newtasks;
// Comment out this line to fake a runtime error
//newtasks = new List<Task>();
```

Of course, this is an artificial example, but it represents a realistic scenario. Even with the best testing and QA, it is always possible that one of these will slip by. This is especially true on the Force.com platform because these kinds of errors can be created well after deployment of your application by the later addition of a required field, workflow or validation rule. Even the best developer can't anticipate every possible scenario that could cause an Apex exception.

You could wrap every single line of code and every method in its own exception handler. However, a centralized trigger dispatching architecture lends itself perfectly to centralized exception handling.

First, add the following method to the DiagnosticsInstrumentation class:

```
public static void debugException(Exception ex)
{
    String exceptionInfo = 'Exception occurred line ' +
        ex.getLineNumber() + ' - ' + ex.getMessage() +
```

---

4 It's curious that the Lightning message is friendlier, but considerably less useful when it comes to figuring out the problem

```
    ' stack: ' + ex.getStackTraceString();
  Debug(exceptionInfo);
}
```

Now the DiagnosticsMain.mainEntry method is modified to trap all exceptions.

```
public static void handleTriggers(TriggerOperation triggerType,
   List<SObject> newList, Map<ID, SObject> newMap,
   List<SObject> oldList, Map<ID,SObject> oldMap)
{

   try {
      SObject firstObject = (
         triggerType == TriggerOperation.AFTER_DELETE ||
         triggerType== TriggerOperation.BEFORE_DELETE)?
         oldList[0]: newList[0];

      DiagnosticsInstrumentation.push(
         'handleTriggers TriggerObject: ' +
         firstObject.getSObjectType() + ' Operation ' +
         triggerType + ' in progress: ' +
         string.valueOf(activeFunction!=null) +
         ' in DML: ' + string.valueOf(
         TriggerDMLSupport.updatingPendingObjects));
```

The standard dispatcher code comes next, followed by the end of the try/catch block. The exception handler records the exception details. It then pops all items from the stack – as there is no way of knowing how many levels deep the exception was. The finally block also has a pop statement. In normal operation, this matches the push statement at the start of the function and eliminates the need for separate pop statements for each return statement. If an exception occurs, the extra pop will do no harm, as the pop logic has validation to handle this situation.

```
   } catch (Exception ex ) {
      DiagnosticsInstrumentation.debugException(ex);
      DiagnosticsInstrumentation.popAll();
   } finally
   {
```

```
    DiagnosticsInstrumentation.pop();
  }
}
```

Now try updating the stage again. Be sure to set the enableDiagnostics field in the AppConfig__c default custom setting to true to see the diagnostic information. Now, if you look at the debug logs that result from this exception, you will see the following (slightly reformatted here to fit on the page):

```
12:50:53.0 (59063705)|USER_DEBUG|[49]|INFO|Diagnostic Log
Entering: handleTriggers TriggerObject: Opportunity Operation
AFTER_UPDATE in progress: false in DML: false
   Entering: DiagnosticsTriggers1.MainEntry
     Entering: DiagnosticsTriggers1.
        AfterUpdateOpportunityBetterQueries2
       Exception occurred line 116 -
          Attempt to de-reference a null object
   stack: Class.DiagnosticsTriggers1.
     afterUpdateOpportunityBetterQueries2:
     line 116, column 1
     Class.DiagnosticsTriggers1.mainEntry:
     line 42, column 1
     Class.DiagnosticsMain.invokeMainEntry:
     line 111, column 1
     Class.DiagnosticsMain.handleTriggers:
     line 87, column 1
     Trigger.OnOpportunity: line 30, column 1
```

Of course, centralized exception handling isn't a replacement for exception handling in individual functions where you actually need to perform specific processing based on the exception. But it's a great way to make sure that users rarely experience Apex exceptions, and a great way to capture exception information.

The risk of this approach is that you might fail to see errors that need to be addressed. In this example, the opportunity will be created successfully despite the exception – it is only our code that will fail. This brings us back to instrumentation, and to the real benefits of building a diagnostic system.

Instrumenting Apex – II

Displaying diagnostic data in the system debug log is fine when you're debugging, but because they only capture data for a specific user, and the number of debug logs that are stored is limited, debug logs are fairly useless for instrumentation.

The diagnostic system described here, on the other hand, is perfect for instrumentation. All you need is a place to store the data.

In this example, a custom object named "DebugInfo" that has a single long text custom field named "DebugData" is used to store the diagnostic information for Apex exceptions.

The DiagnosticsInstrumentation.DebugException method is modified as follows:

```
public static void debugException(Exception ex)
{
    String exceptionInfo = 'Exception occurred line ' +
        ex.getLineNumber() + ' - ' + ex.getMessage() +
        ' stack: ' + ex.getStackTraceString();
    Debug(exceptionInfo);
    DebugInfo__c dbg = new DebugInfo__c(DebugData__c = currentLog());
    exceptionTrace = ' Exception occurred line ' +
        ex.getLineNumber() + ' - ' + ex.getMessage();
    for(String st: stackTrace) exceptionTrace += ' | ' + st;
    exceptionTrace += ' |\n ';
    if(diagnosticsEnabled) insert dbg;
}
```

Now, when a user performs an operation that previously displayed the Apex error message, the operation will succeed (the centralized exception handler traps and ignores the error). A new DebugInfo record will be created with information about the exception as shown in Figure 10-3[5].

---

5 Remember, you will probably need to set the tab visibility settings in your profile for the DebugInfo tab to view these records.

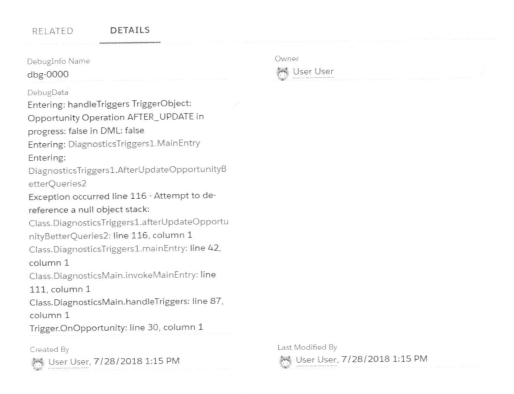

RELATED   **DETAILS**

DebugInfo Name
dbg-0000

Owner
User User

DebugData
Entering: handleTriggers TriggerObject:
Opportunity Operation AFTER_UPDATE in
progress: false in DML: false
Entering: DiagnosticsTriggers1.MainEntry
Entering:
DiagnosticsTriggers1.AfterUpdateOpportunityB
etterQueries2
Exception occurred line 116 - Attempt to de-
reference a null object stack:
Class.DiagnosticsTriggers1.afterUpdateOpportu
nityBetterQueries2: line 116, column 1
Class.DiagnosticsTriggers1.mainEntry: line 42,
column 1
Class.DiagnosticsMain.invokeMainEntry: line
111, column 1
Class.DiagnosticsMain.handleTriggers: line 87,
column 1
Trigger.OnOpportunity: line 30, column 1

Created By
User User, 7/28/2018 1:15 PM

Last Modified By
User User, 7/28/2018 1:15 PM

Figure 10-3 – DebugInfo objects hold diagnostic information

Let's take a moment and review what we have accomplished.

- You now have the ability to monitor your application for Apex errors 24x7 (as compared to debug logs that are only active when enabled).
- All users are monitored (as compared to debug logs that monitor a single user).
- You can capture and store large amounts of diagnostic data (as compared to debug logs where the number of logs stored is limited).
- You can effectively capture stack trace information even with managed packages (where the detailed stack trace information is hidden unless you are logged into a system via the subscriber system of the license management app). On those systems the final stack trace in the debug entry will be

missing, but you'll still have the stack trace information generated via the Push and Pop methods of the DiagnosticsInstrumentation class.

But that's not all.

The instrumentation system shown here is extremely simple. There are other features you may want to implement:

- Set up a scheduled Apex operation that periodically Emails to a support Email address all of the DebugInfo records that occurred during that period. In many cases, this can allow you to be proactive and address client or customer problems before they are even aware they exist. Note – you probably don't want to send an Email on each error that occurs so as to avoid exceeding Email limits.

- Instead of just storing a text string, consider capturing the data in XML or JSON. This not only allows you to capture more (or at least more structured) data, it makes it possible to perform automated processing of debug information, both on the deployed system and when handling incoming debug Emails.

- You can extend this concept to work with VisualForce and Lightning controllers, as long as you're careful to only save diagnostic records at times when DML operations are allowed.

- Remember to periodically delete old diagnostic data to avoid data bloat. This should be automated as well, perhaps during a scheduled Apex method where you delete all entries older than a specified period, or you can simply limit the number of records stored.

Instrumentation and Platform Events

Centralized exception handling can take care of detecting and reporting most exceptions. However, there are two situations where this approach fails.

- Any DebugInfo objects created by your code will be deleted if the overall execution context fails. In other words, if an exception occurs outside of your exception handler, say in another class or declarative operation, or if your code throws an exception, all database transactions that occur during the execution context are reverted – including any debug objects your code inserts.

- There are some limit exceptions, particularly the CPU time limit exception, that are not trappable by exception handlers. They cause the execution context to abort and the database to revert immediately.

These situations can potentially be addressed using platform events. Platform events are not part of the execution context transaction – once published, they are not reverted even if the execution context aborts.

The question is, how best to use them? You could publish every exception that occurs, but most exceptions can be handled by the approach described earlier.

How important is it to detect exceptions outside of your application that cause transactions to revert? Probably not very important. The more likely use case here is if it is your own code that is aborting the transaction and you wish to record the reason. In this case you might want to modify the main dispatcher exception handler to publish a platform event and then rethrow the exception or add an error to the record using the SObject or ID addError methods.

With regards to handling untrappable exceptions, the use case is less obvious. Once the exception occurs, it's too late to publish the event. If you always publish events you will not only fill the event queue with meaningless information, you run the risk of exceeding the number of events that are allowed during a 24-hour period. One can make an argument for implementing platform event-based monitoring that is intended to be used for diagnosing specific issues. The monitoring can then be controlled using configuration data.

Thinking about Debugging and Diagnostics

Debugging, diagnostics and instrumentation are closely related. While most debugging occurs (or should occur) during development, in reality it is not unusual to need to debug systems after deployment. This is particularly true with Force.com due to the enormous variability of organizations, and because the development system (be it a scratch org, developer org or sandbox) is never 100% identical to the production system. Even a full sandbox rarely has all of the production system apps enabled and fully functional. Even the best unit tests can't reproduce every scenario, especially in organizations with large amounts of data.

Building your own diagnostic infrastructure is a valuable supplement to the monitoring capabilities built into Force.com. It can provide critical information for debugging applications on production systems and in cases where unit tests are limited. It can provide ongoing monitoring to improve your ability to support your clients and customers.

For those of you creating managed packages, the value in building some kind of diagnostics and instrumentation system is clear and compelling.

The case is more difficult for consultants. In many organizations, Apex code is developed on an as-needed and ad-hoc basis. While any one trigger or class may be designed and coded properly, there is often no overriding architecture. It is difficult to justify building a diagnostics system for that "one simple trigger". It's only after that one simple trigger evolves into a dozen "simple" triggers that you begin to wish someone had built in and enforced instrumentation from the beginning.

However, all is not lost. Sooner or later most companies reach a point where, due to growth or changes in business process, they need to revisit their implementation and make substantial changes. That's a perfect time to review all of the existing code and invest in diagnostic infrastructure that will pay off in the long term.

11 – Unit Tests

Why Johnny Won't Test

The following is from the Apex language documentation.

Salesforce recommends that you write tests for the following:

Single action

Test to verify that a single record produces the correct, expected result.

Bulk actions

Any Apex code, whether a trigger, a class or an extension, may be invoked for 1 to 200 records. You must test not only the single record case, but the bulk cases as well.

Positive behavior

Test to verify that the expected behavior occurs through every expected permutation, that is, that the user filled out everything correctly and did not go past the limits.

Negative behavior

There are likely limits to your applications, such as not being able to add a future date, not being able to specify a negative amount, and so on. You must test for the negative case and verify that the error messages are correctly produced as well as for the positive, within the limits cases.

Restricted user

Test whether a user with restricted access to the sObjects used in your code sees the expected behavior. That is, whether they can run the code or receive error messages.

Doesn't that sound wonderful?

But how often do developers actually follow those recommendations? Very rarely – and then only for the most trivial examples.

In fact, the only consistent testing practice that I've seen is the development of unit tests needed to meet the 75% code coverage requirement for deployment.

Does this mean that most Apex developers are lazy and incompetent? Not at all.

The language documentation recommendations are great in principle but are actually somewhat simplistic – and they don't reflect the real-world priorities of developers.

Let's start by considering why most developers don't follow all of these recommendations.

Time and Money

Employees are often under enormous time pressure. Force.com developers are expensive, and most organizations are understaffed. Sometimes this results in code being written by beginners who don't really know how to write good test code. Sometimes developers just have so much to do that it's more important to meet a deadline or add a feature than add additional unit tests to code that seems to work correctly (and quite possibly does work correctly). Afterwards, it's hard to justify going back to build more test code.

Consultants face pressure both on bidding and on execution. Test code is expensive. It's not unusual for the amount of test code in an Apex application to exceed the amount of functional code, which some might interpret as doubling the cost of development. If a consultant's bid includes all of the recommended test code, they might lose the contract to someone who doesn't – the client probably will not know the difference. During implementation, whether the job was bid hourly or flat rate, any test code beyond the minimum potentially eats into profits, as even hourly consultants rarely have an open-ended budget. Test code that exceeds the original estimate requires a consultant to either go back for more money (which makes the consultant look bad and less likely to be trusted in the future), or absorb the cost.

Product developers, as you will see, have the most to gain from unit tests. But they too suffer pressure to meet release deadlines, and are also often understaffed.

As you can see, the pressure to cut corners on testing is enormous.

Perfect Testing Doesn't Exist

Programming today is a race between software engineers striving to build bigger and better idiot-proof programs, and the Universe trying to produce bigger and better idiots. So far, the Universe is winning. – Rick Cook

Testing for all positive and negative cases sounds good, but it's actually quite difficult (and in many cases theoretically impossible). This is especially true for the negative cases, where users have an infinite capability to come up with input that you never imagined.

Apex Applications Can be Complex

As the Salesforce platform has evolved, the platform limits have gradually been relaxed. This is in part due to customer demand, and in part because advances in hardware infrastructure makes it possible to support greater developer limits.

As those limits have been relaxed, the potential complexity of Apex applications has grown. In a complex application, it becomes increasingly difficult and costly (and eventually impossible) to test every code permutation. Moreover, testing individual units of code does not guarantee operation of the application as a whole – you need a completely different set of tests to validate functionality of the integrated system.

So while the Salesforce recommendations can work well for trivial code, more and more code on the platform is non-trivial.

Testing in the Real World

At this point it would be easy to say "I know testing is expensive and difficult, but you should do it anyway because..."

A. You are a software professional.

B. Salesforce says you should.

C. I say so.

Speaking as a software professional, these are all rather silly reasons. Test code is no different from any other code – you write it because it is cost effective to do so.

If we're really going to address the issue of testing beyond the required 75% code coverage, we need to start with the economic justification for those tests – because at some point, somebody has to pay for them.

So forget (for the moment) the recommendations from the Salesfore.com documentation, and let's view the problem from a completely different direction.

What are unit tests intended to accomplish?

As it turns out, we write tests for many different purposes. And each of those purposes can have a completely different cost justification, and require completely different design patterns.

Here are the most common reasons (in no particular order) for writing test code on the Salesforce platform:

- Meet the Salesforce 75% code coverage requirement.
- Validate the functionality of code (does it meet requirements or specifications).
- Bulk testing – can the code handle bulk operations?
- Debugging – reproducing errors during the development process.
- Regression testing – does a change you are making break existing code?
- Compatibility with target systems – will the application work on a production system after it is deployed?
- Configuration validation – is an organization configured correctly for the application?

Viewed this way, testing takes on a whole new level of complexity. Let's take a quick look at each of these in turn, after which we'll examine how they impact testing best practices.

Code Coverage

This is the one type of test that every Apex developer must build. It is also the last type of test you should write. Focus on implementing the other tests first. Then go back and add test code as needed to meet and maximize code coverage.

Some developers obsess over code coverage, taking pride over how close they can get to the nirvana of 100% coverage. You'll find articles, blog posts and conference sessions encouraging developers to reach for that as a goal. Clients and managers will sometimes look at the degree to which code coverage exceeds the 75% minimum as a measure of code quality.

This is complete and total nonsense.

The incremental cost to increase code coverage increases as you get closer to 100%, as scenarios can become more specific and harder to reproduce in unit tests. That represents money that is far better spent on functional or regression testing. Code coverage only measures that code was executed and has nothing to do with quality or even correctness.

While ideally every test you write will use Assert statements to validate functionality, there is a temptation to leave out validation when trying to meet code coverage requirements. It's alright to do so for trivial cases – for example, when writing tests for VisualForce controllers there may be cases where you will write code that reads property values in order to achieve code coverage on property Get statements, and completely ignores the resulting values.

Just remember that a unit test without an assert is not actually testing anything. It's just exercising code. It's not completely worthless, but comes close.

If you are creating a managed package, be sure to add at least one Assert statement to each test class, even if it is as simple as System.Assert(true). Failing to do so will generate warnings in the Force.com security source scanner that you may have to explain during security review.

Validating Functionality

This is perhaps the most important reason to write unit tests. Every project starts with a set of requirements. If you're lucky, they may even be written down somewhere. At some point, you have to validate if your code performs as specified.

You should always write test code to validate functionality. Even if you didn't have to write test code to meet code coverage requirements, it would still be worthwhile, as the cost of writing functional test code is more than offset by reduced debugging and QA costs.

Unit tests make it relatively easy to place an organization into a known state. And changes to the database made during unit tests are not persisted. This makes functional validation in unit tests dramatically faster than manual testing.

If you focus on functional testing, you'll often find that this is sufficient to meet code coverage requirements.

Bulk Testing

Bulk testing is an aspect of validating functionality. Though listed here separately, as you will see, unit test best practices dictate that all of your tests be written as bulk tests, even when running the test for single objects.

Debugging

Don't hesitate to write "throwaway" tests to help resolve bugs or to verify your understanding of Apex behavior. Just be careful to actually throw away tests that don't follow best practices (you'll read more about unit test best practices later in this chapter).

Regression Testing

Regression testing refers to the practice of verifying that changes in your code don't break existing functionality. On the Salesforce platform, regression testing takes on a greater significance, in that it is also used to verify that changes in the configuration of an organization don't cause errors in your application.

This latter factor makes automation of regression tests more critical than it is in other environments. Unlike other platforms, where you would normally perform regression testing only after making changes to your application, and can often limit your testing to those areas of the application impacted by changes, under Force.com it is advisable to perform regression testing after any changes to an organization. That includes everything from installation of new applications, to creation of workflows, validation rules or required fields.

The good news is that the unit tests you create to validate functionality are the same ones you will use for regression testing. The knowledge that they will be used for regression testing as well only serves to emphasize the importance of those tests, and to justify the investment needed to go beyond the minimal requirements to achieve code coverage.

Compatibility with Target Systems

This aspect of unit testing applies mostly to packages, as compatibility testing of an application written on a sandbox for a specific organization is inherent in the functional testing.

Aside from the code coverage requirement, installation unit tests can be valuable for validating that your application will run correctly on a target system – as you may not even have access to the system for manual testing.

Writing unit tests for deployment is a complex topic that will be covered later in this chapter.

Configuration Validation

Unit tests can be used to verify that an application or organization has been configured correctly after installation.

A good example of this kind of test is verifying that a user has configured lead field mapping of custom fields. You can't perform this test during installation, as it is not possible to configure lead field mapping during the installation itself – it has to be done manually after installation. But you can create unit tests to run after installation that validate that the manual lead field mapping configuration was done correctly.

Revisiting Recommendations

Looking at testing based on the goals described in the previous section makes it easier to develop a realistic test strategy.

Consultants working on a single organization should focus on validating functionality (both positive and negative tests), bulk testing and debugging.

For those of you who are coming to Salesforce from other platforms, or who are trying to learn and adopt best practices in software development, this is a form of blasphemy.

In most software development, the focus of testing is on true unit tests – a unit test being a set of tests that validate a particular unit of code. For example: each class or module would have its own set of tests. The idea behind unit tests is to ensure that developers don't change the behavior of individual software components. In theory, if the behavior of individual components is unchanged, the behavior of the entire system will remain consistent as well. So good unit tests, along with some integration tests (higher level tests that validate the behavior of the system), are an effective strategy. The integration tests can even be manual or semi-automated if the unit tests are good enough.

Attempting to apply this approach to Salesforce is a mistake. The reason is simple. Where on other platforms the greatest risk to software stability are changes to code by other developers, on Salesforce the greatest risk to software stability are changes to organization metadata that are made outside of the software development process. In other words – an administrator breaking your application through some declarative change.

Unit tests are generally not effective at catching those kinds of changes. Only integration tests – tests that validate overall application functionality, are able to do this.

So on Salesforce, your functional and integration tests come first. And if you only have time to build out one type of test, those are the tests you should build.

I'll go further into this subject in chapter 13 when we look at the challenges of maintaining Apex code.

Developers working on managed packages, especially on teams, should ideally implement both types of tests. Apex provides strong support for true unit tests, including support for mocking frameworks that make it easier to reduce interdependencies when testing individual classes. Though even there, functional and integration tests should be the priority.

Common Test Design Patterns

Now that you have a clear picture of the many roles that unit tests play, let's take a look at how those roles influence best practices in unit test development.

Centralize Object Initialization

It is very common to create test objects in a unit test. It is always advisable to test functionality against objects that you create rather than relying on existing objects in an organization. The default setting for the SeeAllData attribute on unit tests is false, meaning that unit tests by default can't even access most existing data in an organization. You should avoid creating tests with SeeAllData true except for very specific situations that will be covered later.

You should never create objects in the test function itself. You should, instead, create a single static method for creating each type of test object. For example, a typical function for creating opportunity objects would be as follows:

```
public static List<Opportunity> createOpportunities1
      (String baseName, Integer count)
{
   List<Opportunity> results = new List<Opportunity>();
   for(Integer x = 0; x< count; x++)
   {
      results.add(new Opportunity(Name = baseName +
                  String.valueOf(x) ));
   }
   return results;
}
```

An alternate version of this function can create an opportunity and at the same time initialize any default field values:

```
public static List<Opportunity> createOpportunities2
    (String baseName, Integer count)
{
   List<Opportunity> results = new List<Opportunity>();
   for(Integer x = 0; x< count; x++)
   {
      Opportunity op =
         (Opportunity)Opportunity.sObjectType.newSObject(
            null, true);
      op.Name = baseName + String.valueOf(x);
      results.add(op);
   }
   return results;
}
```

Note that the only difference between the two is when the default field values are set. Default field values will be set using the first approach when the object is inserted. In the second function, the default values will be available immediately to the test code, before the opportunities are inserted.

Later in this chapter you'll see another, more flexible approach for initializing default field values.

A unit test might use the initialization function as follows:

```
newopportunities = createOpportunities1(
    'optest_', numberOfOpportunities);
for(Opportunity op: newOpportunities)
{
   op.CloseDate = Date.Today().addDays(5);
   op.StageName = 'Prospecting';
}
// Insert the test opportunities
insert newOpportunities;
```

All of the test code in your application should share the same object initialization functions that set default field values that you specify. Your code should then modify any additional values as needed before actually inserting the object.

Object initialization functions should always have a parameter that specifies the number of objects to create. You'll see why this is important later in this chapter when we discuss bulk test patterns.

When inserting certain types of objects, such as leads and contacts, the similarities between algorithmically generated objects can lead Salesforce to think that you are attempting to insert duplicates (depending on the org configuration). This can result in object creation errors. To avoid this, use the DMLOptions DuplicateRuleHeader to disable duplicate management when inserting test data as shown here:

```
List<Lead> newLeads = createLeads('ldtest_', 10);
Database.DMLOptions dml = new Database.DMLOptions();
dml.DuplicateRuleHeader.allowSave = true;
dml.DuplicateRuleHeader.runAsCurrentUser = false;
database.insert(newLeads, dml);
```

Centralizing initialization has little immediate benefit, but serves to reduce the lifecycle costs of your application. That's because it is very possible that at some point in the future, someone will add a required field or validation rule to the object that will cause the object creation to fail during the test. If you centralize object creation, you will be able to add the required field to the initialization function, thus resolving the problem for all associated tests with a single edit, instead of having to track down every place in your code where that object is created, make the change and deploy the update.

Using Test.LoadData

The major limitation of generating records programmatically is that adding or changing field values in response to changing requirements or new required fields and validation rules requires a code change. Even if the change is simple, it still requires someone to modify code and deploy an update.

It is also possible to load test data from a static resource. Create a CSV file with the fields you wish to populate. For example:

```
FirstName,LastName,Company,Email
Jose,ldtest_1,ldtest,ldtest_1@test.com
Jose,ldtest_2,ldtest,ldtest_2@test.com
Jose,ldtest_3,ldtest,ldtest_3@test.com
Jose,ldtest_4,ldtest,ldtest_4@test.com
```

Create a static resource containing the file. Then use the Test.loadData function to insert records based on the file:

```
List<Lead> newLeads = Test.loadData(Lead.getSObjectType(), 'LeadData');
```

To insert related records, add an ID field and enter unique text values to match up records. For example: If you are adding accounts and contacts, you might put 'Account1' in the account ID field and the contact's AccountID field. Test.loadData will correctly associate the contact to the account with the matching ID.

One use case where this approach can be particularly valuable is for quality assurance. It allows a QA engineer to potentially test a wide variety of data sets without having to modify any code.

This approach also gives admins more flexibility – which can be both a good and bad thing. On one hand, they can add validation rules and fix the test data without modifying the code. On the other hand, they can modify test data in ways that break the unit tests without modifying the code.

From a developer perspective, using Test.loadData is potentially more effort. Programmatic data creation is easy, and the data is highly predictable. You don't have to create multiple static resources for each object (and you would need multiple static resources to handle a range of dataset sizes for bulk testing). You don't have to worry about someone modifying or deleting the data.

The programmatic design pattern you saw earlier has the added benefit of supporting centralized initialization of data, while still allowing individual tests to modify selected fields before the data is inserted. With the Test.loadData approach, the records defined in the static resource are inserted – there is no mechanism to change their values on the fly.

Both approaches are valid. For what it's worth, I almost always use the programmatic approach in my own development. Or rather, I use a hybrid approach that combines some of the best features of each.

Object Initialization Revisited

One way to make programmatic object initialization more resilient is to allow individual fields to be set based on a static resource.

Unlike most data, static resources are available to unit tests even when SeeAllData is false. Placing default field data in a static resource can allow developers or admins to set field values without having to modify code.

In our example, this is demonstrated through an opportunity validation rule named "Enforce Tracking Number" that has the following error condition:

```
ISBLANK(TrackingNumber__c )
```

TrackingNumber__c is a custom text field. If you have loaded the sample code, be aware that this validation rule is inactive in the sample code – you'll need to manually activate it if you are following along.

Running the CreateOpportunities1 unit test on a system where the validation rule is active results in the following error message:

```
FATAL_ERROR System.DmlException: Insert failed. First exception on row
0; first error: FIELD_CUSTOM_VALIDATION_EXCEPTION, Tracking number must
be set for opportunities: []
```

The DefaultFieldValues static resource has a line for each default field value to set. Each default value is specified by a line in the format:

```
objecttype:fieldname=value
```

To set the Tracking Number field on an opportunity, the entry could be:
```
Opportunity:TrackingNumber__c=somevalue
```

The SetDefaultFields function handles field initialization as follows:

```
public static Boolean setDefaultFields(
    String objectType, List<SObject> theObjects)
{
    List<StaticResource> resources = [Select Body from StaticResource
        where Name = 'DefaultFieldValues'];
    if(resources.size()==0) return false;
    String contents = resources[0].Body.ToString();
    if(contents==null) return false;
    List<String> lines = contents.split('\\n');
    for(String line:lines)
    {
        List<String> entries = line.split(':');
        try
        {
            if(entries[0]==objectType)
            {
                List<String> fieldinfo = entries[1].split('=');
                for(SObject obj: theObjects)
                {
                    // Implemented only for strings
                    obj.put(fieldinfo[0], fieldinfo[1]);
                }
            }
        }
        catch(Exception ex){}
    }
    return false;
}
```

This implementation is designed to handle any object type and batches of records, making it an efficient solution.

The current implementation only works with strings. A more robust approach would query describe information to obtain the correct data type and perform the necessary conversions. This is left as an exercise to the reader.

The current implementation ignores exceptions. At a minimum, you would probably want to add a system.debug statement within the exception handler to help diagnose problems.

Here is where the benefit of centralized object initialization really pays off. Instead of having to call SetDefaultFields throughout your test code, all you need to do is modify the CreateOpportunities function to the following:

```
public static List<Opportunity> createOpportunities1
    (String baseName, Integer count)
{
    List<Opportunity> results = new List<Opportunity>();
    for(Integer x = 0; x< count; x++)
    {
      results.add(new Opportunity(
          Name = baseName + String.valueOf(x) ));
    }

    setDefaultFields('Opportunity', results);
    return results;
}
```

This solution is not a perfect one. Validation rules can be complex, and it's possible that there is no one value that will work to allow your test code to create objects. In that case, you would have to disable that validation rule or make a code change to resolve the error. Still, this approach will work in a great many cases.

Organizing Tests into Classes

One of the dilemmas you will inevitably face is deciding how many test methods to include in a test class.

The nice thing about including multiple test methods in a class is that it helps organize test methods and makes it easier for them to share common code. So far in this chapter we've focused on sharing initialization code. Back in chapter 4, you saw how the validateOCRs function could be used by more than one unit test function to validate results.

While there used to be disadvantages to placing many unit tests in a single class, changes to the platform have largely eliminated them. Both the Developer Console and Salesforce DX can run individual unit tests in a class. Developers no longer have to waste time running tests they are not interested in, or struggle to seek out a specific test in a debug log (or worry about exceeding the debug log size because all of the unit tests in a class share the same debug log).

Keep in mind that having common code that is shared by test methods is not a strong reason for including multiple test methods in a test class. You can always place common code into a regular class, or into a public test class. Use a public test class if the common code is used only for tests. Use a regular class if the common code can also be used by your application.

My suggestion is that you combine tests in ways that make logical sense in your application. Place the tests that are related to each other in the same class. It is customary to name test classes based on the class or functionality they are testing.

For example: If you have a class named TriggerDispatcher, you would name the test class TestTriggerDispatcher or TriggerDispatcherTest. If you have a subsystem in your application that performs a quarterly financial analysis that is made up of multiple classes, you might have test classes for each of the functional classes, and another higher-level test class named TestQuarterlyFinancials that validates the overall functionality but is not related to a specific class.

Using the @testSetup annotation

The @testSetup annotation can be used on a method in a test class to initialize data for all of the test methods in a class. The data is reverted at the end of each test, so each test runs with the data defined by the @testSetup annotation. This annotation only works if the SeeAllData attribute is false for the class and all of its test methods.

While at first glance this is an extremely useful construct, it does have some cost in terms of flexibility, in that a generalized initialization function that is called each time by test methods can take parameters and return data. You can see an example of this in the initTestObjects function used in several of our test classes, where not only are various object counts passed as parameters, the newly created opportunities are populated into a list that is passed as a parameter, allowing the calling test methods to access the new objects directly.

If you do use the a common @testSetup initialization function, remember that it too can and should call out to your centralized object initialization methods rather than initializing objects directly.

Use Bulk Test Patterns

You may recall that in Chapter 4, I recommended that all of your code be built using bulk patterns. This applies to test code as well.

To understand why this is particularly important for unit tests, consider the reason for doing bulk testing in the first place. It is almost entirely related to validating functionality. It has little to do with code coverage or other testing goals.

If your bulk tests are a separate set of tests, you incur high costs for little added benefit. Not only is there the cost of building the tests, and running a second set of tests, but there is also a performance hit when doing a complete test run - bulk tests tend to run more slowly than single record tests.

Given the high cost and performance cost involved in creating a distinct set of bulk tests, along with the fact that they rarely add any code coverage over single object tests, there's a strong temptation to skip them, and in many cases that's exactly what happens.

However, if you write every unit test as a bulk test, the story changes. The incremental cost of writing a bulk test instead of a single object test is negligible – especially if you have focused on learning those patterns from the start.

You can use a static constant to define the number of objects to use during the test as shown here:

```
private static final Integer numberOfStageUpdateOpportunities = 5;

static testMethod void testTaskCount() {
    List<Opportunity> ops = createOpportunities(
        'optest_', numberOfStageUpdateOpportunities);
```

During development and debugging, use an object count of one or two. This will provide excellent performance. Using an object count of two will also validate your bulk handling in terms of functionality (though not against limits).

To perform bulk testing against limits, just increase the value of the object count constant.

The key thing to realize here is that you don't need to do bulk tests all the time. You do need to validate bulk handling at some point during development, but you can often avoid bulk tests during debugging and regression testing. If you are building an application for a specific organization, passing bulk tests on a full sandbox virtually guarantees that the bulk processing will work on the production organization. The same applies if you are deploying an AppExchange managed app, which has its own set of governor limits.

If you are deploying an unmanaged or unlocked package, or one that is not an AppExchange managed app, it can be a good strategy to test bulk handling on the target system. But that doesn't mean you need to do the testing during deployment. What you should do in that case is replace the object count constant with a field from a custom setting.

During deployment, when the custom setting is not yet defined, use a default object count of one or two to achieve a rapid deployment. After installation, set the custom setting value to a high number (typically 200), and use Apex test execution to validate that the application runs correctly.

If you build every unit test as a bulk test, and make the batch size configurable, you gain all of the benefits of bulk testing at almost no cost, making this a clear best practice for all Apex test development.

Other Limit Testing and SeeAllData

Bulk tests serve two purposes – they validate the functionality of your batch handling, and they ensure that you can perform your processing within the governor limits.

But bulk tests alone are not always sufficient to guarantee that your code will not exceed limits. There are a number of reasons for this:

- Test setup in unit tests also has governor limits, meaning there is a limit to the number of objects that you can insert into the database for testing.
- Triggers and web service calls are not the only sources of batch data. Queries and searches may return large numbers of records that can be difficult to process within limits. In fact, they can return larger numbers of records than you can generally create during your unit test setup.

The problems you will run into tend to fall into three categories:

- Queries or searches that have too broad a criterion, where the number of records returned exceeds limits.
- Queries or searches that return a large number of records, where the processing of the records causes you to exceed CPU limits.
- Queries that are not selective, and thus cannot be processed successfully on systems with very large numbers of records.

The best way to avoid these problems is through careful design. But as careful as you may be, it's always possible to miss something, so it's always a good idea to test as well. But these tests require large amounts of data that cannot be created during the test itself.

In the past, before the SeeAllData annotation existed, you would often catch these issues early because test code had access to all of an organization's data. In fact, test code queries would have to be written very carefully to filter out existing data so that your tests were only looking at objects created during the test.

The SeeAllData test attribute defaults to false, which hides most of an organization's data from a test. This does simplify test code, speed test execution and improve the stability of unit tests, but it also prevents unit tests from finding the kinds of limit errors that can happen on large organizations.

For this reason, it is often useful to create some unit tests with the SeeAllData attribute set to true for tests on code that performs queries or searches on objects other than those that are part of a trigger or API batch (including related objects). Even if you use criteria in your query to view only those records created during the test, the fact that there are a large number of records on the system will help expose any non-selective queries that may exceed limits.

Even setting the SeeAllData attribute to true is not sufficient to fully test an application against limits. Ultimately it requires testing on a large organization. A common approach is to set up a developer organization or enterprise sandbox specifically for these tests and use the Apex dataloader to import large amounts of data, and then perform manual testing of the application. A more sophisticated approach involves writing an external application, typically in Python, Java or .NET, that uses the API to populate data, perform operations, and validate the results – essentially building an external "unit test" that, through the use of multiple API calls, bypasses the limits of regular unit tests.

However, the cost of these kinds of tests on large organizations can usually only be justified by developers of managed packages. If you are developing a managed package for distribution, you absolutely need to perform those tests. If you are a consultant working on an individual organization, just be aware that these kinds of problems can occur. If possible, test your code on a full sandbox. If you only have a configuration sandbox available, allow extra time for launch and testing in case problems turn up during deployment.

Testing Exception Handlers

Good programming practice calls for generous use of exception handlers in your code, even for cases where you believe an exception is unlikely or even impossible. One of the unintended consequences of the 75% code coverage requirement is that it tends to discourage use of exception handlers because they are difficult to test, and the lack of those tests counts against the code coverage requirements.

The secret to testing exception handlers is actually quite simple: use a static variable to generate a fake exception.

The TestingApex.InsertOpportunities method is a simple function that inserts opportunities. If the insertion fails, it logs an error, though in a real application it would most likely perform a more complex operation to handle the error.

```
public static void InsertOpportunities(
    List<Opportunity> ops) {
```

```
    try {
        insert ops;
    } catch (Exception ex)
    {
        system.debug('Exception occurred ' + ex.getMessage());
    }
}
```

How do you test the exception handler? In this case one could do so by setting a field value that would cause a validation error or failing to set a required field. But this is not always possible, especially for higher level exception handlers or exceptions that are not easily reproduced. For example: it is impossible to create a DML lock error in a unit test.

One common approach is to use a static variable to "fake" an exception as shown here:

```
@testvisible
private static Boolean fakeException = false;

public static void InsertOpportunities(List<Opportunity> ops) {

    try {
        insert ops;
        if(test.isRunningTest() && fakeException)
            system.debug(ops[20000].id);
    } catch (Exception ex)
    {
        system.debug('Excepetion occurred ' + ex.getMessage());
    }
}
```

In the unit test, you set the fakeException static variable before calling the function as shown here:

```
@istest
public static void TestExceptionHandler()
{
    List<Opportunity> newopportunities =
        createOpportunities1('optest_', 10);
    for(Opportunity op: newOpportunities)
    {
        op.CloseDate = Date.Today().addDays(5);
        op.StageName = 'Prospecting';
    }
    TestingApex.fakeException = true;
    TestingApex.InsertOpportunities(newopportunities);
}
```

This will result in a list index out of bounds exception.

This pattern can be extended in a number of ways:

- You can explicitly throw custom exceptions instead of a more generic built-in exception. This can allow you to provide more information to the exception handling code to validate different scenarios.

- Exception handlers typically perform more complex operations than just outputting a debug statement. Your unit test can (and should) validate those operations using asserts.

- Instead of a static Boolean variable, you can define a number or text string in order to simulate many types of exceptions.

Depending on the exception and handler, it may be very difficult to reach 100% code coverage of exception handlers, or doing so may require a great deal of code that is specific to the unit tests. This is an excellent example of a case where pursuit of 100% code coverage makes little sense.

Testing, Static Variables and Test.isRunningTest

The previous example demonstrates a technique that actually has many applications. Just as static variables are a powerful tool for controlling execution of an application, they are a powerful tool for controlling testing. Some circumstances where you can also use them include:

- Testing exception handlers.
- Initializing configuration data (as you saw in chapter 9).
- Modifying query criteria. This is typically done when using the SeeAllData = true option to restrict queries to data you have created, or to limit the size of a query for a batch Apex test to ensure that only a single batch execution call takes place. In either case, you can use a static variable to select from two static SOQL queries, or to add a filter term to the WHERE clause of a dynamic SOQL query.

This is actually an area of some debate. In traditional unit testing it is considered poor practice to have any test related code outside of unit tests, or to have any behavior changes in non-test code based on whether or not it is being executed in a unit test. I've seen some Salesforce developers go through some significant gyrations to try to follow that philosophy.

To this I say, Salesforce is a different platform and Apex is a different language. Test.isRunningTest exists for a reason – and while I agree with the philosophy of minimizing test related constructs outside of test classes, one should feel free to do so where it is appropriate.

Testing Namespaced Code

In traditional Salesforce development, namespaces were only used by managed packages. However, development of managed packages would take place on developer orgs that did not have a namespace. This posed a challenge when it came to quality assurance, as namespaced code can behave differently than non-namespaced code in some ways.

For example: describe information includes namespaces in namespaced code, so any software that works with describe data must take that into account. As you learned in chapter 5, namespaced code has a greater risk of duplicate fields appearing in queries. Some of the markup in Lightning components includes the namespace, so the markup actually has to be changed when switching between namespaced and non-namespaced code.

Until recently these issues were only of concern to managed package developers – who are typically ISV partners. However, the newer unlocked packages, which will replace unmanaged packages, can be namespaced as well. So these issues will become common for all Apex developers.

Fortunately, Salesforce DX supports namespaced scratch orgs. Which means that going forward, the rule for namespaced development is easy:

If your code is going to be namespaced, all development and testing should be in a namespaced scratch org.

For those who are building managed packages and not yet switching over to Salesforce DX, keep in mind that it is very easy to import your package into a namespaced Salesforce DX project even if all you'll be doing is testing. So you can start to enjoy the benefits of this approach even if you are still developing using traditional developer orgs.

Testing and Fragile Code

Another problem that can occur with both custom settings and organization data has to do with interactions with existing code that relies on those settings or data being present. This is illustrated in figure 11-1:

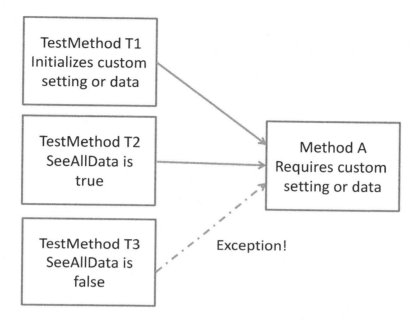

Figure 11-1 – Custom settings and SeeAllData

Let's say that method A is written to assume that organization data is present, and will raise an exception if it is missing. There are two ways that test methods can handle this situation. They can initialize the data as part of the test initialization. Or they can be defined with the SeeAllData=True attribute. Any test with SeeAllData=False that does not initialize the necessary data will fail.

This is easy enough to deal with inside of an organization, but what if TestMethod T3 is part of a managed package? Managed packages cannot access custom settings that are not part of the package, and are restricted on the types of organization data that they can access.

This leaves developers of managed packages with three options:

- Insist that customers fix their existing code so that it will fail gracefully (without exceptions) if data is missing (good luck with that).
- Insist that customers use custom metadata instead of custom settings, as custom metadata is visible when SeeAllData is false (a great idea, but you know they won't do that either).

- Use SeeAllData=True on any test that has the potential to run organization code.
- Don't run managed package tests on organizations where they are installed.

It goes without saying that all code should be written to fail gracefully when custom settings or data is missing. But the reality is that a great many Apex developers still write their code assuming custom settings will be initialized and data present – either they don't realize that this is an issue, or they are focused on doing what is easy and cheap to implement in the short term.

Testing in Packages

You already know that you need to have 75% code coverage in order to deploy code to a production organization. But what does that really mean?

When you deploy code to a production organization, the platform doesn't just check the code you are deploying, it by default runs all of the unit tests on the org to make sure that they pass, and collectively achieve 75% code coverage for all of the code on the system.

Well, not quiet all. There are mechanisms to run partial sets of tests when using changesets or the metadata API to deploy code. And managed package unit tests and code are not included. This is critically important. It is difficult, if not impossible to write a unit test that is guaranteed to run on every possible org – there are too many possible ways for metadata changes to cause failures. If managed package tests were included in code deployments, most large organizations would quickly reach a point where it was impossible to deploy new code. Turning off unit tests on installation would not be an option, and deploying managed packages would become much more difficult, and in some cases impossible.

Generally speaking, the only people who should ever care about failing unit tests in a manage package are those who work for the package vendor. The test failures, in and of themselves, have no impact on code or deployment outside of the package.

For this reason, by default managed package unit tests are not run when a managed package is installed. You can override this behavior using the onInstall attribute, but this is not recommended. If there are issues that you wish to test using unit tests, it's far easier to do so by running the tests manually as needed than during a deployment. Running tests manually allows you to capture debug logs (including debug logs of your own package if you are an ISV partner and it is an AppExchange package). It's also easier and more efficient to run individual tests than to wait for a deployment.

If there are tests that you feel must pass before your application is functional, it's still better to deploy the application and test than to run the tests during deployment. If your application was designed with an on/off switch (as it should be), the application should be safe to install and have no impact on the target org until it is turned on.

The OnInstall attribute does not apply to unmanaged and unlocked packages. Their unit tests must pass and meet the 75% code coverage requirement. When someone later decides to deploy code or a change set to an org, the unit tests from those packages are also run by default and the results incorporated into the code coverage calculations.

If someone makes a metadata change that causes a unit test to start failing, it has to be fixed – at least if you want to be able to deploy any more change sets or code. When you install an unmanaged or unlocked package, the code becomes yours, and you become obligated to maintain it.

When it comes to testing, packages pose unique challenges:

- Instead of targeting a single organization, your unit tests, like the rest of your code, have to take into account the virtually infinite possibilities of organization configuration and metadata – at least as much as possible.
- Managed packages protect your intellectual property by hiding your Apex code and other details relating to the operation of your application. This includes hiding stack trace information that can be crucial for debugging.
- Because of the high cost of supporting multiple versions of an application, your tests need to be able to adapt to a particular organization while still maintaining a single code base.

Meeting these challenges can be costly and have minimal benefit. For this reason, the most common strategy for unit tests in packages is as follows:

- Do not run managed package unit tests during installation (i.e. do not include onInstall=true for unit tests).

- Unlocked packages are ideal for enterprises as a mechanism to partition functionality. As these packages are designed for a specific org configuration, there is no need to worry about adapting them to multiple organizations – only to worry about someone changing the org configuration in ways that might break unit tests (a topic we'll return to in chapter 13).

- Unmanaged packages were only useful in the past as a way of distributing sample code. Since Salesforce DX provides an infinitely better way of accomplishing this task, Unmanaged packages should be retired and not used going forward.

Hiding Managed Package Tests

You've learned that you should avoid running managed package tests during deployments (onInstall=True). And you've learned that while there can be value for an ISV partner to be able to selectively run unit tests on a target system, in most cases this is unnecessary – that the effort to create unit tests that are adaptable to a wide variety of orgs is rarely worth the trouble. In the real world, managed package unit tests are run and must pass during the package upload, and only a small number of specific unit tests might have value and be intended to run on target systems.

However, there will be customers who will insist on running managed package tests on their orgs. Given that many of them will fail, you may find yourself in the awkward position of having to explain to your customer that no, those failures don't count against the overall code coverage of the org and no, those failures are generally occurring due to the inability of the unit test to create test data, and have nothing to do with the correct functioning of the package.

Wouldn't it be great if you could set up your unit tests so that they will run on all of your developer, packaging and QA orgs, but will abort quickly with a success status when run on an installed package? That way should a customer run the package unit tests, they'll see the tests all pass, and run very quickly.

Fortunately, this is easy to accomplish. You can find out if a package is installed by querying the PackageLicense object for the specified namespace.

```
public static Boolean isInstalledPackage()
{
    List<PackageLicense> packages = [Select Id, Status
        from PackageLicense where NamespacePrefix = 'your namespace'];
    return(packages.size()>0);
}
```

This should return true only if the package is actually installed in the org. Just add a call to this function at the start of every unit test, and exit immediately if it returns true. Note that at this time, this only applies to Packaging 1.0. As this book is being published, Packaging 2.0 is still in beta, and it's not year clear if this approach will be reliable. Watch for updates on AdvancedApex.com for more information.

What if you actually do want to run a unit test after installation? Simple – just create a configuration option using custom settings or custom metadata that defines which tests should run regardless.

12 – Designing for Packages

Whether you are a computer scientist or an experienced software developer, you tend to build a mental framework of how certain things are usually done. Part of the fun of learning a new language or platform are the surprises that you run into along the way – the innovations or unexpected decisions of the language or platform authors that challenge your preconceptions.

Sometimes those surprises don't make any sense at first. More than one Apex developer I know was puzzled initially by the unusual approach that Force.com takes with static variables. Yet, after becoming familiar with the framework, it becomes obvious that the Force.com creators knew what they were doing, and it's hard to imagine static variables working any other way.

Like most Apex developers, I started out doing consulting work on specific organizations. It was only when I started designing my first managed package that I ran into what was, for me, the greatest surprise of all. I came to realize that in many cases the best practices for developing a package are completely different from the best practices when developing for a single organization.

I've been both consulting, and writing production commercial code on other platforms, for a long time. There is always a difference between the two – turning specialized code into production code is always a big effort. But aside from the obvious need to generalize functionality, that effort usually consists of polish – improved exception handling, instrumentation, and support code or application metadata.

This was the first case I recall where writing code for a redistributable package called for completely different design patterns.

You already saw this in the last chapter. The ability to selectively enable tests has absolutely no value when you are deploying organization specific code using unlocked packages or changesets to deploy from a sandbox to a production organization.

Many, if not most of the design patterns that you've already learned in this book, are heavily influenced by packaging best practices that turn out to also be advantageous for organization specific code. In this chapter you'll not only learn a number of common (or useful but uncommon) approaches to use when developing Force.com packages, you'll also see a number of other cases where the best practices for packaging should actually be avoided when developing code for single organizations.

Dynamic SOQL and Dynamic Apex

Dynamic SOQL allows you to use Apex code to define a SOQL query string at runtime. Static SOQL is hard-coded and validated at compile time.

If you are building an application for a specific organization, you should almost always use static SOQL for two reasons:

- Compile time validation reduces the chance of runtime errors and speeds the debugging process, as all syntax and most semantic errors are caught during compilation.
- Static SOQL is not vulnerable to SOQL injection attacks, where a user provided parameter can change the meaning of the query to expose more data than intended.

In fact, it's rare that you'll ever need to use dynamic SOQL when building code for a single organization, as most user specified criteria can be incorporated into a query using variables. In cases where query terms vary depending on user input, you can often use conditional code to select among several static queries rather than building a dynamic query.

For managed packages, the exact opposite is the case – dynamic SOQL is often preferred over static SOQL. There are three reasons for this:

- Your application may need to reference fields that do not necessarily exist on target systems.
- Your application may need to adapt to features that may or may not be available on target systems.
- Using dynamic SOQL, you can use a central list of fields to query for specific objects across multiple queries. If you add a new field to a later version of

the application, you can add it in one location instead of editing multiple queries. In complex applications, this reduces the chance that you will fail to query for a required field.

Let's look at the first two of these in detail.

Organization Dependent Fields

Let's say your application has some functionality in which processing is influenced by the RecordType of an object. When writing code for a single organization, you wouldn't think twice about querying the code like this:

```
List<Lead> rtypes = [Select ID, RecordTypeID from Lead Limit 1];
```

In a package, this approach is deadly. That's because this code will fail to install on any organization that does not have record types defined for leads. You see, on the Force.com platform, if no record type is defined for an object, the RecordTypeID field doesn't even exist – so any query that tries to use it will fail.

The correct way to use record types in a package is as follows:

```
Boolean leadHasRecordType =
    Schema.Sobjecttype.Lead.Fields.getMap().containskey(
    'recordtypeid');

String fieldString = 'ID ';
if(leadHasRecordType) fieldString += ', RecordTypeID ';
List<Lead> rtypes = Database.Query('Select ' + fieldstring +
                ' from Lead Limit 1');
```

First use Apex describe functionality to find out if the desired field (in this case RecordTypeID) exists on the object. If so, add it to the query string.

There are numerous other objects and fields where this situation arises, enough so that it is a rare application where using dynamic SOQL in this manner is unnecessary.

It is important to note that this code presents no risk of SOQL injection – all of the data used in the query is generated programmatically.

Organization Dependent Features

When you upload a package, Salesforce.com calculates a set of requirements for the target system. Figure 12-1 shows the package requirements for the sample code used in the various chapters of this book until this point.

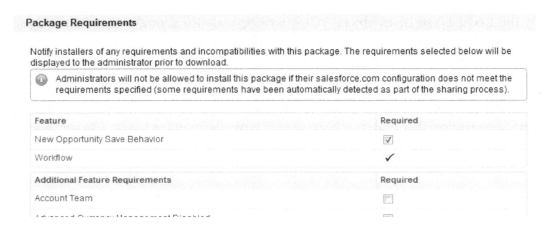

Figure 12-1 – Sample package requirements

So far the only requirements relate to opportunities (which is the main object used in the examples), and workflow – and that only because the sample workflow used earlier to demonstrate errors is currently part of the application.

Let's say you add a feature to your application that can optionally display information about the products related to an opportunity. At some point you might have a query on the Product2 object, of which the following is a trivial example:

```
List<Product2> aproduct = [Select ID from Product2 Limit 1];
```

One side effect of this code is that you've now added a package dependency. If you upload the package now, you'll see the requirements specified in Figure 12-2.

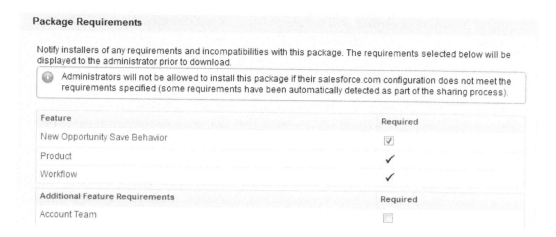

Figure 12-2 – Package requirements now has Product2

Every time you add a requirement to your package, you potentially reduce the number of systems on which your package can install, and thus the number of potential customers.

For large functional components, it might make sense to use a base package and create an extension package to support this kind of flexibility – where the extension package has its own, more restrictive, set of requirements.

But for optional features – where your application adapts to the existing configuration of the system, dynamic SOQL allows you to avoid adding requirements to your package. Because the Apex compiler is not aware that you are using a feature, it won't impose that feature as a requirement.

Remember though, that you must check if a feature is available on a target system before using it, or implement good exception handling – as any attempt to access an object or field that is not present on the system will result in an exception. This includes test code.

At this time, the mechanism for understanding feature dependencies on packaging 2.0 is as yet unclear. What is certain is that for managed packages you should not enable any features on your main development scratch orgs that you do not wish to have as dependencies for your package. This will help ensure that you do not add any static references that will create feature dependencies. You can, however, create QA scratch orgs with different feature sets – more on this later.

Dynamic SOQL and Security Reviews

Use of dynamic SOQL is one of the red flags checked for during the AppExchange security review. You should include in your submission an explanation that you are using dynamic SOQL in order to allow your application to process fields that may or may not exist on a target system, and that the queries are generated programmatically and are not dependent on user input (assuming, of course, that this is accurate). Also note that you are taking SOQL injection precautions including escaping strings (the escapeSingleQuotes string method) on user input, and are validating any user specified field names if those apply to your application. Most of the security reviewers understand the tradeoffs involved, and will not raise this as an issue once they are confident that you are using dynamic SOQL correctly, and for the right reasons.

Dynamic Apex

Dynamic Apex refers to the ability to set and retrieve the values of object fields by specifying the name of the field at runtime.

Here is an example that combines dynamic SOQL and dynamic Apex to solve a common problem: how do you support currency conversion when multiple currency support is only available on some organizations?

In this example, the getCurrencyConversionMap function returns a map of conversion values for each ISO code, where the value can be used to convert a specified currency to the current corporate currency (this differs from using the convertCurrency SOQL option that converts values to the user's currency).

The cachedCurrencyConversionMap map holds the cached value of the conversion map. The corporateCurrency property can be used to retrieve the corporate currency (note the call to getCurrencyConversionMap to make sure the backing property m_CorporateCurrency is set.

```
private static Map<String,double> cachedCurrencyConversionMap = null;

private static string m_CorporateCurrency = null;

public static string corporateCurrency {
    get {
        getCurrencyConversionMap();
        return corporateCurrency;
    }
}
```

The getCurrencyConversionMap function has to address the fact that the CurrencyType object does not exist on single currency organizations. All access to the object and its fields must be dynamic for the code to compile on a single currency organization.

```
public static Map<String, double> getCurrencyConversionMap()
{
    Boolean currencyTestMode = false;

    if(cachedCurrencyConversionMap!=null)
        return cachedCurrencyConversionMap;

    if(Test.isRunningTest() && !userinfo.isMultiCurrencyOrganization())
        currencyTestMode = true;
    if(!userinfo.isMultiCurrencyOrganization() &&!currencyTestMode)
        return null;

    List <SObject> ctypes = null;
    if(!currencyTestMode) ctypes  = database.query(
        'Select conversionrate, isocode, iscorporate from currencytype');

    Map<String, double> isoMap = new Map<String, double>();
    if(!currencyTestMode)
    {
        for(SObject ct: ctypes)
        {
            string ctCode = string.ValueOf(ct.get('isocode'));
```

```
            if(Boolean.valueOf(ct.get('iscorporate')))
            {
                m_CorporateCurrency = ctCode;
            }
            double conversionRate =
                double.valueOf(ct.get('conversionrate'));
            if(conversionRate!=0)
                isoMap.put(ctcode, 1/conversionRate);
        }
    }
    cachedCurrencyConversionMap = (currencyTestMode)? null: isoMap;
    return cachedCurrencyConversionMap;
}
```

The currencyTestMode variable is used to obtain at least some code coverage over the function on single currency organizations.

This example raises an interesting question. How would you build and test the multi-currency code while not adding an installation dependency?

The answer is to use two developer orgs. Your main developer org should not have the multi-currency feature enabled. Your second developer org will have the multi-currency feature enabled. You then develop and test on both. As long as your code compiles and unit tests pass on both, you can be confident that you will not inadvertently add the multi-currency features as a requirement for your package to install.

In the past, working on two orgs and keeping their code in sync was painful, to say the least. Fortunately, this kind of work is trivial on Salesforce DX.

In Salesforce DX, the code is the source of truth. It's absolutely trivial to configure two different scratch orgs, one with multi-currency, and one without. You can then work on the code in your editor, periodically pushing it out to the different orgs to verify compilation, and for testing and debugging.

You can do this even if you are not yet using Salesforce DX for your main developer efforts! Just retrieve the metadata for your package from your main developer org and convert it into Salesforce DX format. Work on that part of the project using scratch orgs until you are satisfied, and then deploy or copy that code back to your developer org.

There are a variety of algorithms that benefit from dynamic Apex that are not related to packaging. As far as packaging design patterns go, the issues that apply to dynamic SOQL are the same ones that apply to dynamic Apex – you should always use dynamic Apex to access fields or objects that may not be present on a target system, and to avoid fields that, if referenced, impose an undesired requirement for package installation.

Person Accounts

If you create an application that references contacts, you need to be aware of a curious entity called a "person account". Person accounts only exist on organizations for which they are specifically enabled. They are not enabled by default, and in order to enable them you have to file a case, and convince Salesforce.com support that you really know what you are doing and that you understand that the conversion can't be reversed. Once the person accounts feature is enabled on an organization, it can never be disabled.

Of course, the easiest way to enable person accounts during development is to specify it as a feature on a newly created scratch org.

A person account is differentiated from a regular account by the account record type. Person accounts have the following characteristics with regards to Apex programming:

- Each person account has a "shadow" contact object. The ID of that object can be retrieved using the PersonContactID field on the account object.
- You can access standard contact fields for person accounts two ways – by querying the underlying contact and accessing the field as you would a normal contact field, or by accessing the field on the account using a special name that typically consists of the contact field name preceded by the word "Person". Thus, the contact Email field can be retrieved on the account using the field name PersonEmail. The contact fields FirstName, LastName and Salutation do not have this prefix.

- You can access custom contact fields for the person account object two ways – by querying the underlying contact and accessing the field as you would a normal contact field, or by accessing the field on the account using a special name that consists of the contact field name ending with the suffix __pc instead of __c.
- Contact triggers do not fire on person accounts. Only account triggers fire on these accounts, even if you change a field on the underlying Contact object.

If the package you are developing does not reference the contact object, you can probably ignore person accounts. Otherwise, you should design your code with them in mind, as packages that use contacts probably won't work correctly with person accounts without additional work.

Your first step in supporting person accounts will be to create a scratch org with the PersonAccounts feature specified in its configuration file, or create a separate developer org and request that it have person accounts enabled.

Next, you can implement a couple of helpful functions to work with person accounts. The first is a static function to let your application determine if it is running on an organization with person accounts enabled.

```
private static Set<string> accountFields = null;

public static Boolean isPersonAccountOrg()
{
   if(accountFields==null) accountFields =
      Schema.Sobjecttype.Account.fields.getMap().keyset();
   return AccountFields.contains('personcontactid');
}
```

The isPersonAccountOrg field caches the set of account fields so that you can efficiently verify person account fields.

Another function that can prove useful maps contact field names to their equivalent person account name:

```
// Map from contact field to account field
public static String getPersonAccountAlias(String fieldName)
{
    fieldName = fieldname.toLowerCase();// Case insensitive

    // Unchanged - FirstName, LastName, etc.
    if(accountFields.contains(fieldName)) return fieldName;

    // Replace aliased __c with __pc
    fieldName = fieldName.replace('__c', '__pc');
    if(accountFields.contains(fieldName)) return fieldname;

    if(accountFields.contains('person' + fieldName))
        return ('person' + fieldName);

    return null;
}
```

You should always access person account fields using dynamic Apex, and should only access them on account objects where the PersonAccountID field is true.

Person Account Triggers

To see the challenges you can face when working with person accounts, consider the following very simple example – a Contact trigger that sets the Level2__c field based on the LeadSource field as described in the following pseudocode:

```
If the LeadSource is 'Web' or 'Phone Inquiry',
    set Level2__c to 'Primary'
Otherwise set Level2__c to 'Secondary'.
```

If you were not concerned about person accounts, you would probably implement this as follows[6]:

---

[6] This particular sample code is located in class PersonAccountSupport because it is related to this section of the book. Despite the name of the class, the sample code at this point only applies to contacts.

```
trigger OnContact1 on Contact (before update, before insert)
{
   PersonAccountSupport.processContactTrigger(
      trigger.isBefore, trigger.new, trigger.oldMap);
}
```

and in a class (in this case class PersonAccountSupport):

```
public static void processContactTrigger(Boolean isBefore,
   List<Contact> newList, Map<ID, Contact> oldMap)
{
   for(Contact ct: newList)
   {
      if(ct.LeadSource=='Web' || ct.LeadSource=='Phone Inquiry')
         ct.Level2__c = 'Primary';
      else ct.Level2__c = 'Secondary';
   }
}
```

The test code for this class might be as follows (see class TestPersonAccount in the sample code):

```
static testMethod void testWithContacts()
{
   List<Contact> contacts =
      TestDiagnostics2.createContacts('patst', 3);
   contacts[0].LeadSource='Web';
   contacts[1].LeadSource='Phone Inquiry';
   contacts[2].LeadSource='Other';
   Test.StartTest();
   insert contacts;
   Test.StopTest();
   // On query we'll get the same 3 contacts
   Map<ID, Contact> contactMap = new Map<ID, Contact>(
      [Select ID, Level2__c from Contact]);
   system.assertEquals(
      contactMap.get(contacts[0].id).Level2__c,'Primary');
   system.assertEquals(
      contactMap.get(contacts[1].id).Level2__c,'Primary');
```

```
system.assertEquals(
    contactMap.get(contacts[2].id).Level2__c,'Secondary');
}
```

How do we extend this to support a person account organization? There are a number of challenges:

- Not every account on a person account organization is, in fact, a person account. They are distinguished by record type.
- When creating or updating a person account, only the account trigger fires.

Your first thought might be to use a before trigger and to update the fields on the person account. For testing purposes we'll use an account trigger that processes both before and after triggers, though we'll only look at the before functionality for the moment.

```
trigger OnAccount1 on Account (after insert, after update,
    before insert, before update)
{

    PersonAccountSupport.processAccountTrigger(
        trigger.isBefore, trigger.new, trigger.oldMap);
}
```

Let's look at how the processAccountTrigger handles the before trigger case.

```
public static void processAccountTrigger(Boolean isBefore,
    List<Account> newList, Map<ID, Account> oldMap)
{
    if(!isPersonAccountOrg()) return;

    if(isBefore)
    {
        // Using before approach
        String leadSourceAlias = getPersonAccountAlias('LeadSource');
        String levelAlias = getPersonAccountAlias('Level2__c');
        for(Account act: newList)
        {
```

```
        if(leadSourceAlias!=null && levelAlias!=null &&
           (Boolean)act.get('IsPersonAccount'))
        {   // Will only be valid on person accounts
           if(act.get(leadSourceAlias)=='Web' ||
              act.get(leadSourceAlias)=='Phone Inquiry')
              act.put(levelAlias,'Primary');
              else act.put(levelAlias,'Secondary');
        }
      }
    }
}
```

This approach suffers from two problems. First, it duplicates the functionality in the processContactTrigger code. That means that you have to support and maintain the same exact functionality in two different places, taking care to update both if any changes are required.

That may not mean much on a simple example like this, but for a complex example, this type of support or maintenance can result in significant costs over the lifetime of the software.

The second problem is more serious. Remember – this is a package, and your development and deployment organizations will almost certainly not be person account organizations. That means your code must meet code coverage requirements on a non-person account organization in order to be uploaded as a package. As it stands, the code coverage provided on the PersonAccountSupport class by the TestPersonAccount unit tests stands at 42%.

Figure 12-3 illustrates the current architecture.

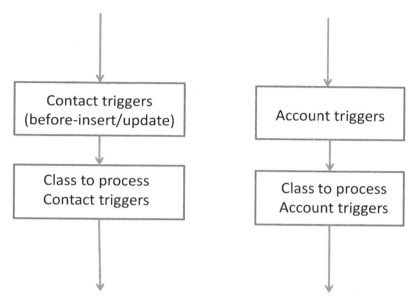

Figure 12-3 – Separate person account code is hard to
maintain and test

The first problem is quite easy to solve, and demonstrates yet another reason why you should always implement your trigger code in a class.

Remember that every person account has a shadow contact object. Why not update that object directly?

You can't do this during a before trigger, but you can do it during an after trigger. The approach is as follows:

- Use an after-insert/update trigger on the Account object.
- If it is a person account organization, build a list of any accounts that have a PersonContactID value (these are the person accounts).
- Query for these contacts.
- Call the class method used to process contact triggers.
- Update the contacts (being careful not to process the resulting account trigger).

This approach is illustrated in Figure 12-4.

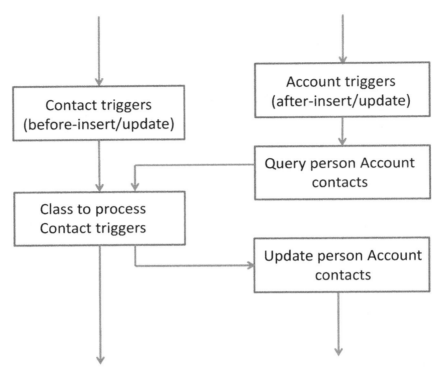

Figure 12-4 – Leveraging contact functionality when using
person accounts

The way to address the code coverage issue is to use static variables to allow most of your code to run even on a non-person account organization.

Here's what the resulting processAccountTrigger function looks like with both of these solutions implemented.

```
@TestVisible public static Boolean fakePersonAccountDuringTest = false;

public static List<ID> fakePersonContactIDs = null;

private static Boolean updatingPersonContact = false;

public static void processAccountTrigger(
    Boolean isBefore, List<Account> newList, Map<ID, Account> oldMap)
{
```

```
if(!isPersonAccountOrg() && !fakePersonAccountDuringTest ||
    updatingPersonContact) return;

if(!isBefore)
{
    // Better approach can work on after trigger
    Set<ID> personContactIds = new Set<ID>();
    for(Integer x = 0; x<newList.size(); x++)
    {
        if(fakePersonAccountDuringTest ||
            newlist[x].get('PersonContactID')!=null )
            personContactIds.add(
                (fakePersonAccountDuringTest)? fakePersonContactIDs[x]:
                (ID)newList[x].get('PersonContactID') );
    }
    if(personContactIds.size()==0) return;
    Map<ID, Contact> personContacts = new Map<ID, Contact>(
            [Select ID, LeadSource, Level2__c
            from Contact where ID in :personContactIds]);
    processContactTrigger(true, personcontacts.values(),
        personcontacts);
    updatingPersonContact = true;
    update personcontacts.values();
    updatingPersonContact = false;
}
}
```

There are a number of subtle issues to note in this code. First, the fakePersonAccountDuringTest constant is tested before the check for the personContactID field. Apex processes conditionals in left to right order, so testing fakePersonAccountDuringTest first prevents the test for the personContactID field (which would cause a missing field error) when testing.

Remember to gate the entire function with code that validates that you are even running on a person account org, and exit if not (except when testing). Never forget that non-person accounts will also raise this trigger.

The updatePersonContact flag is used to prevent the function from being processed again when it is retriggered by the update to the underlying Contact object. If you were using the centralized trigger model described in Chapter 6, you wouldn't need to do this – as the resulting trigger would be dispatched to the inProgressEntry method of the currently executing class instead of the mainEntry method – thus would be ignored by default.

The personContactIds set is used by the test code to provide fake shadow contacts in order to obtain code coverage.

To conclude, let's look at the test code:

```
static testMethod void testWithAccounts() {
    List<Contact> contacts = createContacts('patst', 3);
    List<Account> accounts = createAccounts('patest', 3);
    contacts[0].LeadSource='Web';
    contacts[1].LeadSource='Phone Inquiry';
    contacts[2].LeadSource='Other';
    insert contacts;
    String leadSourceAlias = PersonAccountSupport.
        getPersonAccountAlias('LeadSource');
    String levelAlias = PersonAccountSupport.
        getPersonAccountAlias('Level2__c');
    if(PersonAccountSupport.isPersonAccountOrg())
    {
        accounts[0].put(leadSourceAlias,'Web');
        accounts[1].put(leadSourceAlias,'Phone Inquiry');
        accounts[2].put(leadSourceAlias,'Other');
    }
    else {
        PersonAccountSupport.fakePersonContactIDs = new List<ID>();
        PersonAccountSupport.fakePersonAccountDuringTest = true;
        for(Contact ct: contacts)
            PersonAccountSupport.fakePersonContactIDs.add(ct.id);
    }
    Test.StartTest();
    insert accounts;
    Test.StopTest();
```

```
// We'll get the same 3 contacts
Map<ID, Contact> contactMap = new Map<ID, Contact>(
    [Select ID, Level2__c from Contact]);
system.assertEquals('Primary',
    contactMap.get(contacts[0].id).Level2__c);
system.assertEquals('Primary',
    contactMap.get(contacts[1].id).Level2__c);
system.assertEquals('Secondary',contactMap.get(
    contacts[2].id).Level2__c);
if(PersonAccountSupport.isPersonAccountOrg())
{

    Map<ID, Account> accountMap = new Map<ID, Account>(
        (List<Account>)Database.query('Select ID, ' +
        levelAlias +' from Account'));
    system.assertEquals('Primary', accountMap.get(
        accounts[0].id).get(levelAlias));
    system.assertEquals('Primary', ccountMap.get(
        accounts[1].id).get(levelAlias));
    system.assertEquals('Secondary',accountMap.get(
        accounts[2].id).get(levelAlias));
}
}
```

The unit test does create person accounts if possible, so it actually does validate functionality on person account orgs.

But the real magic in this approach is that it resolves our code coverage issues on non-person account orgs, bringing the code coverage up to 93% from the previous 42%. That means that it can be successfully deployed on non-person account orgs.

Other Best Practices

There are a number of other best practices to consider when developing packages. Some of these recommendations apply only to managed packages, and some to unmanaged packages as well.

On/off switch

Your application should have an "on/off" switch – a configuration setting that globally enables or disables your application. When your application is disabled all triggers should return immediately and most other functionality should be disabled. The only code that should work is your configuration code.

There are a number of reasons for doing this:

- It allows you to configure your application completely before making it active on a client system.
- In case of errors in the organization, it allows you to easily disable your application so that you can quickly determine if it is your application that is causing the problem, or prove that it is not.

Fun with Namespaces

Apex is fairly clever when it comes to understanding namespaces. Consider the Level2__c contact field from the previous example. What would happen if you dropped that code into an org whose namespace was aapex? The field would immediately become aapex__Level2__c. However, you would not need to add the namespace to field references – Apex understands that when you reference classes, objects and other entities from code that exists within the same namespace, you do not need to specify the namespace for those entities.

This means that if you wish to create code that can be used under multiple namespaces, you never want to include the namespace in the code. If you leave the namespace off, you can drop it in to any namespaced org and it will just work.

However, it is sometimes necessary for code to be aware of the namespace under which it is running. You saw a good example of that in chapter 5, where knowing the current namespace was an essential part of reliably removing duplicate fields from a SOQL query.

Fortunately, this is very easy to do. The getNamespacePrefix function shown here starts by retrieving the describe information for a custom field in the org – in this example it uses the Level2__c field defined earlier. It then looks at the full name and local name of the field. If they are the same, the org has no namespace, so the storedPrefix field is set to the empty string. If they are different, the prefix is stripped off the field name and stored. The storedPrefix static variable is used to cache the namespace for efficiency sake, as this function may be called frequently.

```
private static string storedPrefix = null;

public static String getNamespacePrefix()
{
    if(storedPrefix!=null) return storedPrefix;
    Schema.DescribeFieldResult testField =
        Schema.sObjectType.Contact.fields.Level2__c;
    Integer theposition =
        testField.getName().length() - testField.getLocalName().length();
    if(theposition==0)
    {
        storedPrefix = ''; return storedPrefix;
    }
    // Subtract another 2 for the __ after the prefix
    storedprefix = testField.getName().substring(0, theposition-2);
    return storedPrefix;
}
```

The need for this particular function is likely to decrease going forward. In the past it was absolutely necessary for managed package development, as developer and QA orgs typically did not have a namespace. Building a beta package and testing with a namespace was one of the last steps in package development – so it was essential that all code be written to function correctly both with and without a namespace.

Not only that, but if you were creating more than one managed package, each one would have its own namespace – so creating code that could be reused between packages without having to modify the namespace was essential.

In truth, this is still the case at the time this book is being published.

However, two things have changed.

First, Salesforce DX makes it easy to develop in namespaced orgs. You'll read more about this in the next chapter. Since all developer and QA orgs can share the same namespace, there is less incentive to build non-namespaced code.

With packaging 2.0 (currently in beta), it becomes possible for multiple packages to share the same namespace. Thus, sharing namespaced code between packages will become easy as well.

In fact, it is likely we will see a complete reversal of the current situation. Instead of having large amounts of non-namespaced code and having to worry about testing it with namespaces, the challenge will be to remember to intentionally create and test code without namespaces in order to ensure that it can be easily reused and shared.

Avoid External ID and Rollup summary Fields on Standard Objects

There is an organization limit of no more than three external ID fields and ten rollup summary fields on an object. If you include these fields, and installing your application would cause these limits to be exceeded, your application will fail to install. So it's best to avoid these field types if possible.

If you do use an external ID field, be sure to mark it as unique before you release your managed package. Once your package is released it is no longer possible to add the unique attribute. Records that have a non-unique external ID field can only be upserted by system administrators – a restriction that you do not want to impose through your package.

Use a Single Code Base

You will almost inevitably run into a situation where you will want to implement some functionality in your application that is unique to a specific customer, and that cannot be implemented outside of the application through workflows or other Apex code.

This is easy enough to do using configuration once an application is installed, but you may also need to define unique behavior during installation.

For both of these cases, keep in mind the approach described in Chapter 11 for setting the initial values of object fields during tests by using information stored in static resources. This approach can easily be extended for other configuration purposes.

Doing so allows you virtually infinite flexibility within a single code base. This is important because the cost of supporting multiple code bases can be substantial.

Managing Organizations – Without Salesforce DX

Not ready to use Salesforce DX yet?

You're going to accumulate developer organizations and sandbox organizations as time goes on. Don't try to do everything on a single org. Here are some of the organizations you will have, and some tips on using them.

- Code development org – This is the organization where each developer builds and tests code that they are working on. Most developers use an IDE for development, though the Developer Console is reaching the point of being reasonable for smaller projects. Keep in mind that you can have multiple projects in an IDE workspace. You may want one for development, and a separate project that defines metadata to deploy.

- Package test org – This is an org that will contain the full source code and both an unmanaged and managed package that uses a test namespace. You'll use this for package testing outside of the main package versioning. In particular, it will help you resolve problems with code that doesn't work correctly with a namespace assigned, and it will allow you to deploy an unmanaged package to get code quickly onto another developer organization or sandbox so that you can debug code[7].

- QA orgs - One or more organizations for those doing quality assurance and testing. Outside QA will typically be done using an installed package. But inside QA, where you don't mind testers seeing the code, will at least part of the time be done on an org that contains the source. That makes it possible for your developers to log into the QA org to see problems and try fixes

---

[7] The IDE and ANT also make it easy to push code quickly into another organization, but a package also makes it easy to remove the code when you are finished.

on the org itself – something that is not possible with a managed package. You'll need a set of orgs for each type of organization you are targeting – group, professional, enterprise, etc.

- Deployment org – The main org from which the managed package is deployed. Never test on this org (other than running unit tests), and don't create any objects or fields on this org that are not part of the package. All code on this org should have passed QA and be checked in if using source control.

- Patch orgs – Supported for managed applications on the AppExchange, these are used for point releases.

- Security Review org – A separate developer org on which you have installed your managed package for the AppExchange security review.

- Two person-account orgs – If you are supporting person accounts you will need one person account org that contains the source code for testing and debugging, and another on which to install the managed package for testing and QA.

- Other feature specific orgs – You will need at least one and sometimes two orgs to test specific features, such as multiple currency support. In some cases, you can combine features to reduce the number of organizations.

- Limit test org – This will probably be a full enterprise sandbox if you are an ISV partner, though in some cases you can get by with a developer org. This is a QA org on which you load large amounts of data to test your application's readiness to deploy to larger organizations. Try to have at least a few hundred thousand records of each type that your application works with – over a million is better.

- Bug sharing org – See the section on Using Salesforce.com support in chapter 13.

Managing Organizations – With Salesforce DX

Ready to use Salesforce DX?

Your life has just become a lot easier.

With Salesforce DX the source of truth is the source code repository, typically a git repository. Instead of accumulating large numbers of orgs, you will spin up scratch orgs as needed.

- Code development org – Each developer will work on their code using an editor and one or more scratch orgs. Changes made using the editor get pushed to the scratch org. Changes made in the scratch org get pulled in to the editor. Each developer pushes their changes to a common source code repository.

- QA orgs - One or more organizations for those doing quality assurance and testing. These will generally be scratch orgs created as needed and loaded with the source code to be tested. QA orgs should be created for different features that are used by the application.

- Packaging/Namespace org – For packaging 1.0, this is the main org from which the managed package is deployed. Never test on this org (other than running unit tests), and don't create any objects or fields on this org that are not part of the package. All code on this org should have passed QA. When using packaging 2.0, this is the org where the package namespace is defined. It serves no other purpose.

- Patch orgs – Supported for packaging 1.0 managed applications on the AppExchange, these are used for point releases.

- Security Review org – A separate developer org on which you have installed your managed package for the AppExchange security review.

- Limit test org – This will probably be a full enterprise sandbox if you are an ISV partner, though in some cases you can get by with a developer org. This is a QA org on which you load large amounts of data to test your application's readiness to deploy to larger organizations. Try to have at least a few hundred thousand records of each type that your application works with – over a million is better.

- Bug sharing org – See the section on Using Salesforce.com support in chapter 13.

With Sharing

Use the "with sharing" setting on all Lightning and VisualForce controllers. If you need to bypass sharing rules, call into another class that is defined "without sharing".

This applies primarily to Lightning and VisualForce controllers.

This will help you pass security review.

If you specify the Without Sharing setting in other classes, be prepared to justify your choice.

Watch for Older Software When Deploying

Some of the organizations that you deploy to may have applications that have not been updated in a while. This can potentially lead to unexpected interactions with your software.

One classic example relates to custom settings. It is not uncommon to use custom settings to save application information. However, on API version 17 and earlier, any attempt to perform a regular DML operation after modifying a custom setting can lead to a MIXED_DML_OPERATION error. That means that if you have a trigger that modifies a custom setting, and it is followed by a trigger in another application running on API version 17 or earlier that performs a DML operation, you can see this error.

Given that API version 17 dates back to 2009, it's not unreasonable to require customers to update older software. It's just something to be aware of.

13 – Maintaining Apex

These days everybody talks about learning to code. And the Salesforce platform is a great place to learn to code. Not only is it a flexible and powerful programming environment with vast amounts of training material available, but it is still largely neglected by the "serious" software development community. Which means that even beginning and self-taught Apex developers get to enjoy a booming job market without too much competition from those highly trained computer scientists, who are more interested in using and building complex JavaScript frameworks and big data analytic systems.

There is one thing, however, that many of those highly trained computer scientists know – at least the ones with experience know (many of the highly trained beginners don't really understand this). It's the dirty little secret of professional software development.

It's called the software lifecycle.

You see, coding – actually writing code – represents a very small fraction of the cost of a software project. By most estimates, maybe 10%.

Coding, and quality of code, is rarely the reason software projects fail – and the percentage of software projects that fail is staggering – over 50% by some measures.

So where is the true cost of software? A fair amount is at the start – in gathering requirements and doing design work. Testing and documentation play a part as well, though it is often neglected and put off as long as possible.

But all of these together typically represent perhaps half of the total cost of software. The big cost – the never-ending cost – is in maintenance. Every time someone has to fix a bug, modify a unit test, or add a feature without which the application will fail to serve its original purpose, it costs time and money. And it adds up, because software almost always lives on long past anyone's expectation.

The cost to fix problems increases as you go farther along the software lifecycle. The cheapest time to solve problems is during the requirements and design stage.

Next is coding. Then testing and acceptance testing. Once code has been deployed, costs escalate wildly. Bugs, when found, may need to be addressed on an emergency basis (expensive!). Plus you may have to clean up or recover corrupted data. And there are the costs not measured in money – the damage to your reputation and loss of confidence in the application that may require additional training expense.

When it comes to maintaining software, the Salesforce platform has significant differences when compared to traditional software development.

In traditional development, there is a loose linkage between the platform and application. If the operating system and web server work, the application will as well. The main risks to the application come from the programmers – someone making a modification to the application that is not reviewed or tested properly and that unintentionally breaks some functionality. Secondary risks include changes to the underlying system, but those risks can be controlled – you can usually test a system, server or framework update with your application before deploying it.

On the Salesforce platform, the greatest risk to your application is not updates by your programmers, even though that risk does exist. The greatest risk comes from metadata changes that are outside of the control of your application – the workflows, validation rules, flows and lightning processes that can change the behavior of an organization. Another risk comes from platform changes that occur three times a year. Yes, Salesforce does a great job of testing and versioning upgrades, but they aren't perfect, and when they deploy an update, it's deployed – there's nothing you can do to stop it.

As developers who are interested in writing code, we tend to focus on how to code more quickly and efficiently. But that's the wrong approach. The right approach is to ask yourself where you can spend extra time writing code that can reduce your maintenance costs – because that's where the real payoff lies.

Looking back, I suspect you can think of more than one example of a design pattern in this book that does just that – demonstrates how writing more code can create a pattern or framework that can result in reduced maintenance costs. Whether it is centralized exception handling, or defensive programming that is resilient to changes in system metadata, or diagnostics that can help monitor your application, this book has always focused far more on design and the long-term consequences of design than on mere coding.

The existence of limits and dynamic metadata has a huge impact on Apex best practices and design patterns, and you can see aspects of that in virtually every example in this book.

But in most cases your job doesn't stop when the code is delivered and deployed. You, or someone else, will have to maintain it. And that is the subject of the rest of this chapter.

The Nightmare Scenario

Every production organization has the ability to create a sandbox – a copy of that org that has the exact same metadata and varying amounts of data, ranging from little or no data on a development sandbox, to a copy of all of the organization's data on a full sandbox.

While you cannot edit code directly on a production org, you can modify its metadata, adding validation rules, workflows and other elements.

Which leads to the following extremely common scenario:

A company hires a consultant to build some functionality in Apex. They deliver it and deploy it, and everyone is happy.

Over the next few months, administrators continue to make various changes in the organization.

One day the company hires another consultant to build some new functionality. They do so and their tests pass. However, they can't deploy the code because other tests are not passing.

The system administrator responsible for this can't understand why those old unit tests are now failing. After all, they couldn't have been deployed if they hadn't passed, right? Something must have been changed on the system. But which change was it? Who do you blame? The first consultant for not anticipating a metadata change? The administrator who unknowingly broke the tests without realizing it? The new consultant who didn't notice the problem and offer to fix the other code for free?

Typically, the first consultant gets blamed. After all, they aren't around anymore to defend themselves.

And the fun has only just begun, because next they discover that not only are the earlier tests failing, but the application wasn't working at all for the past couple of months, so they've lost data or have inconsistent or corrupt data in their org which will cost time and money to fix (assuming it's even possible). And they still have to hire someone to fix the original tests and code if they want to deploy the new functionality.

This kind of nightmare happens all the time.

So whose fault is it really?

It's not the first consultant. I don't care how good you are – you cannot anticipate and code for every metadata change.

It's not the second consultant – they were hired to build new functionality, not validate all of the tests and processes in the org.

It's not even necessarily the system administrator who modified the org's metadata – as in many cases their job is to implement requests for functionality, not monitor the integrity of all of the processes implemented in the organization.

The fault lies with the company – for failing to implement and enforce sound maintenance processes in their organization.

Maintenance is all about process. It's about the discipline to require everyone with metadata access in an organization to follow those processes without exception. Writing defensive code as you've learned to do in this book will help enormously, because you will see fewer problems over time and be able to resolve them more quickly, but it is not and cannot be enough. You have to have maintenance processes in place.

Let's take a look at some of the processes that every organization should follow.

The Perfect Scenario

Until recently there really were no clear best practices on how to address the challenge of managing metadata. Organizations took a variety of approaches with mixed success. The nightmare scenario occurred, and continues to occur, far too often.

This has changed.

Salesforce DX, or SFDX, is the new developer experience. It is a fundamental change in the way we look at metadata. Before SFDX, the source of truth – the place you would go to determine the actual and correct metadata of an org or application, was always an org. With Salesforce DX, the source of truth can and should be source code – that is, text files that can and should be stored in a source control system.

Instead of building metadata on orgs, trying to keep them in sync and occasionally pulling metadata from an org and storing it in a source control system, the source control system becomes the source of truth, and from there metadata can be deployed anywhere.

It is finally possible to build a "perfect" or at least near perfect metadata management system.

And it's remarkably easy.

All you need to do is ensure that everyone who is making any code or metadata changes does so in their own scratch orgs. That includes not just code, but database schema changes such as new objects and fields, and declarative changes such as workflows and processes. When they've made their changes, they push the changes to the common repository. In some cases, there will be an approval step here – where someone reviews the change request and allows or disallows it.

At that point some automation takes over and creates some test scratch orgs. Unit tests run automatically – if there are any failures, the process stops and the person who made the change is notified so that they can fix whatever they broke.

There may or may not be some manual testing and further approval. In either case, once this QA step has passed, the change is automatically deployed to production, and possibly sandboxes as well.

Everyone else working on the application or org can retrieve the latest changes at any time and will generally do so before making any changes of their own.

The important thing is that every metadata change is tracked – you know what changed and who changed it. Most of the updating and deployment process can be completely automated. If a mistake occurs, you can quickly undo the change and restore the application or org to its previous state.

All you need to do is convince every single admin or person with the ability to modify metadata to work in Salesforce DX and only make metadata changes through this process.

Now I know that any of you who have been working on the platform for any amount of time realize, as I do, one key thing about this scenario.

It's not going to happen.

Not now. Now soon. Maybe never.

Oh sure, one company among thousands may be prepared to enforce this level of governance on their Salesforce org. But it's going to be a very long time before this approach becomes widely adopted.

That doesn't mean that there aren't a lot of good things about Salesforce DX and that it can't be used to improve metadata maintainability. But it will not magically resolve the challenges that organizations face in the real world when it comes to managing and maintaining their orgs.

So, let's reluctantly leave our utopian ideals behind, and look at the real world of maintaining Apex.

Salesforce DX in the Real World

While the perfect scenario may remain elusive, in the world of software development it is possible to come very close. The challenge is, how to get there? As with many things related to Salesforce development, it depends to a degree on whether you are an ISV partner building a managed package, or working on a single org.

As this book is published, Salesforce DX is still very new, and packaging 2.0 and unlocked packages are still in beta. So consider what follows preliminary suggestions. Best practices are still evolving.

Salesforce for the Enterprise

If you are building software for a single org, most of your development work probably takes place on one or more sandboxes that match the schema of the production org.

In the long run, what you'll want to do is divide the software in your orgs into independent applications, each of which can be worked on, tested, and deployed individually. Each can then be an individual SFDX project. The primary means of deploying those applications can become unlocked packages.

The problem is that dividing your software into independent applications can be very hard – especially on complex orgs. Without that, it's often necessary to develop on orgs that, like sandboxes, match the production org exactly.

Fortunately, there is nothing about Salesforce DX that prevents you from creating scratch orgs that match the schema of your production org or sandbox. You can import all of that metadata into your code repository and use it during scratch org creation. This can solve the problem of making sure that your code is developed based on the schema of the production org.

Except, of course, that the production org may be changing. How do you ensure that any changes made there are pulled into the repository so that developers are working on the latest? Without strong governance, the production org, sandboxes and repository can quickly become inconsistent.

One solution is to mimic the way sandboxes are handled. Divide your metadata into two parts – Apex code, and everything else. Use two distinct source control branches, one for the code, and one for the declarative constructs and database schema.

This allows your software team to treat the code repository as the source of truth for Apex, but continue to use the production org as the source of truth for everything else. You can pull in the latest metadata into the repository any time (just as you would refresh a Sandbox).

This does not prevent the nightmare scenario, but it does make it possible for developers to take full advantage of Salesforce DX while remaining confident that their code will work in production.

It goes without saying that any code developed this way should be tested on an up to date sandbox before being deployed to production.

Salesforce DX for Managed Packages

The SFDX story for managed packages is very different. As a package vendor, you deal with the nightmare scenario primarily by building resiliency and instrumentation into your code to deal with metadata changes after deployment. But you don't have to deal with it during the development process – all developers should be working on the same base schema that reflects the minimal set of features required by the application.

The only real challenge for package developers to transition to Salesforce DX is to learn it, and the fact that your existing source repository likely uses the standard metadata format, which is different from the SFDX source format. To truly transition to Salesforce DX, you ultimately have to bite the bullet and switch to what is effectively a new repository. On a busy development team with multiple developers, this requires some serious coordination. One day people are using standard metadata – the next, Salesforce DX.

Fortunately, as a package vendor, you don't have to make this switch to start gaining the benefits of Salesforce DX. Individual developers can start using it right away by importing metadata into SFDX format, working on it, and exporting it.

As long as you're modifying code, this works very well. Try to avoid exporting other metadata – it will work, but minor formatting changes can lead to extraneous and meaningless changes in the repository, mostly related to formatting.

You can gain immediate benefits by using Salesforce DX as part of your QA process. The ability to quickly spin up orgs with different features sets makes it ideal for testing. You can also start taking advantage of SFDX's support for automation – more on this later.

Fun with Sandboxes

If Salesforce DX does not magically prevent the nightmare scenario, is there any hope? There is. Good sandbox management can help.

Every production org should maintain an up-to-date staging sandbox. Its purpose is to stage and test metadata changes before deploying them to production.

Every metadata change should be built on the staging sandbox and tested before it is deployed to production. After each metadata change, all of the org's unit tests (excluding those of managed packages) should be run. If any failures occur, they should be fixed, or the metadata change corrected before the changes are deployed.

An org can have multiple sandboxes, and it's fine to develop or test code on a different sandbox. In fact, it's often preferable. However, the code should still be deployed and tested on the staging sandbox before being deployed to production.

Managed packages should be deployed to the staging sandbox and the org unit tests (not the package unit tests) run before the package is deployed to production to ensure that the package does not interfere with existing tests or code. If you experience test failures you should reach out to the application vendor before installing that package to production.

If this process is followed religiously, the nightmare scenario from the previous section will almost never happen. In fact, theoretically you will never need to refresh your staging sandbox, because it will always be in sync with production (though you should do so periodically just in case).

Unfortunately, many organizations have not, and probably will never adopt even this level of discipline. It's just too easy to make changes in production orgs, and people are frequently under time pressure – the kind of process described here takes time. If you told most system administrators that they had to make each change on a sandbox, run all of its unit tests (which can take hours on a large org), and deploy the change through a change set for every validation rule or workflow, they'd probably either laugh at you, or politely agree and then ignore you, depending on your level of authority in the company.

But there are steps you can take even in the real world – processes that you may be able to get adopted to some degree.

You can and should enforce a test and deployment process on your developers and any consultants. Use Salesforce DX if you can, otherwise larger projects should go in their own sandbox if possible. Before deploying to production, the code should be tested on a newly updated sandbox – a full one if possible, and they should run all unmanaged unit tests, not just the ones they wrote. If the nightmare scenario has occurred and you have failing unit tests, take the time to resolve them. Don't just comment out asserts to bypass the errors in order to get the new code deployed – you'll just be digging yourself into a deeper hole.

Implement an ongoing test policy on your production org to watch for problems. This is one aspect of a methodology called continuous integration.

Continuous Integration

Continuous integration is a software practice that involves developers frequently integrating their code with that of the rest of their team, and relying on automated build tools to verify the code by compiling it, running unit tests to make sure they still pass, and ultimately deploying the code to production. It defines a pipeline – a series of automated and semi-automated steps that take place from the time a developer commits their code to a source repository until it is released.

Organizations have taken all kinds of approaches to implementing continuous integration on Salesforce. All of them were a bit cobbled together, with endless challenges - keeping developer orgs in sync with the source repository, then using ant to transfer metadata to and from the repository and various QA orgs.

Salesforce DX is a true game changer with regards to continuous integration. With a fully scriptable CLI, it is able to quickly and automatically create scratch orgs, deploy metadata, run tests, and then tear down the scratch orgs and report the results. It integrates beautifully with external development orchestration systems such as Heroku pipelines and similar services. It works well with Jenkins and similar CI tools.

You don't even need to migrate all your developers to SFDX or use the SFDX metadata format in your repository. The Salesforce DX CLI is perfectly capable of automatically converting your repositories metadata into SFDX formatted metadata.

There is no doubt in my mind that Salesforce DX will simplify and drive the adoption of continuous integration methodologies by Salesforce development teams.

The only downside is that doing so may provide a false sense of security.

Remember our nightmare scenario? Where declarative developers make changes to an org that breaks existing applications?

Continuous Integration with Salesforce DX will not help prevent those scenarios unless your organization governance treats declarative developers the same way as coders – requiring them to ensure that all metadata changes go through the source code repository.

Salesforce DX is great at detecting declarative change in an org and pulling them into source – but that only works on scratch orgs. Which means that your declarative developers would have to work on scratch orgs instead of sandboxes and production.

And we've already realized that this is rarely going to happen.

So yes, you should implement continuous integration with Salesforce DX. But it is not enough.

Even if you can't prevent the nightmare scenario, you can at least detect it early. Running your organization's unit tests at least once a day will do this. This is especially true if you followed the practices described in chapter 11 and made sure that all of your unit tests are functional tests.

How do you do this? There are a number of possibilities:

- Someone in the company (such as a system administrator) can be assigned to run unit tests daily and follow a defined process to address any failures that occur.

- You can set up a Jenkins server that automatically runs unit tests and notifies someone of any failures via Email

Or...

It turns out that you can run unit tests using Apex code and later retrieve the results. The process is remarkably simple.

You can retrieve a list of test classes as shown here:

```
// Get a list of all presumed Apex test classes
// (See AdvancedApex book for discussion)
public static Map<ID, ApexClass> getApexTestClasses(String namespace)
{
    if(namespace=='default') namespace = null;
    Map<ID, ApexClass> results = new Map<ID, ApexClass>(
        [Select ID, Name, NameSpacePrefix from ApexClass
        where Status='Active'
        And NameSpacePrefix = :namespace
        And Name Like '%test%' ]);
    return results;
}
```

Now this approach isn't perfect. There is no requirement that an Apex test class contain the word "Test". However, it is very much an industry convention – now that unit tests have to be in a test class, I can't think of a case of a unit test class name that does not include the word "test". However, you could extend this code to handle that situation by creating configuration data that contains the names of additional test classes. You could automate detection of those classes by iterating through all classes, reading the class body and searching for the @isTest term to identify test classes that are not named Test. But honestly, it's probably easier to just change the name of the test class.

False positives – classes that are have names that include "test" but are not test classes, are not a problem. When you queue them to run, you'll get a result that no tests were found.

Queueing the test to run is easy, though doing so properly is not quite as simple as is shown in the Apex language reference. Here is an example:

```
public static void queueTests(Set<ID> testClassIds)
{
    // Are any currently running?
    List<String> runningStatus = new List<String>{
            'Holiding','Queued','Preparing','Processing'};
    List<ApexTestQueueItem> currentItems =
        [Select ApexClassId from ApexTestQueueItem
        where Status in :runningStatus ];

    // Don't request run of any test current running or scheduled
    for(ApexTestQueueItem runningItem: currentItems)
    {
        testClassIds.remove(runningItem.ApexClassId);
    }
    // Nothing left to run
    if(testClassIds.size()==0) return;

    List<ApexTestQueueItem> queueItems = new List<ApexTestQueueItem>();
    for (ID classId: testClassIds)
    {
        queueItems.add(new ApexTestQueueItem(ApexClassId = classID));
    }
    // Can't schedule tests during a test
    if(!Test.isRunningTest()) insert queueItems;
}
```

The code first determines if any of the proposed test classes are currently running – it makes no sense to queue up a test class that is currently scheduled or executing. It then simply creates and inserts an ApexTestQueueItem object to schedule the test.

The entire class runs in test mode except for the final insertion into the queue. That ensures that you can obtain test coverage for the class, so you can package it or deploy it.

You can use this code as a basis for an application that is scheduled to run tests periodically – say every 24 hours or more often if desired. If you want to get really fancy, you would store the results of tests in an object and look only for failures either on initial deployment, or test classes that are failing that previously passed. That way you only notify administrators of changes that they should be concerned about, instead of flooding them with information of which tests passed or failed. Naturally, the failure results should also be stored in the database so that they can be reviewed at any time.

You could write an application like that...

Or you can use the one I wrote. It's available both as source code and a private managed package which you are welcome to use (see the open source license on the site).

Visit www.AdvancedApex.com/testtracker for more details[8].

By the way, did you notice that the getApexTestClasses function takes a namespace as a parameter? The software is written so that managed package authors can incorporate it into their software and configure it to run their package test classes and notify them directly should one or more of their tests suddenly start failing.

---

[8] The sample code shown above is not included in the sample code for the book – refer to the AdvancedApex.com/testtracker for a link to the repository for the Test Tracker sample code.

Salesforce.com Updates

Salesforce updates their software three times a year. Actually, that's not quite accurate – the platform is updated with minor bug fixes much more often, but those changes are unpredictable and rarely cause a problem.

In theory, the behavior of your application will remain unchanged as long as you keep the API version the same. In practice, that doesn't always work. With so many possible sets of software features, organization metadata, system configurations, and third-party applications running different API versions, it's almost miraculous that anything works at all.

Be sure to have at least one sandbox ready to be updated to the next release preview as soon as it is available. Sign up for pre-release preview orgs on those releases where they are available. Deploy your code on the preview sandbox as soon as possible and verify that all unit tests pass. Perform a manual or automated test of all Lightning components and VisualForce pages. If your tests pass and the pages function correctly, you can breathe a sigh of relief – chances are good your application will work on the next release. Until then, continue to do QA in preparation for the release.

If you are developing a package, do not change the API version of your software during this preview period other than perhaps to do initial experiments on a separate preview organization. Do not change the API version of the software on your deployment org until after everyone has been upgraded to the next release. Otherwise you risk running into a situation where you cannot deploy urgent updates.

Change API versions of your software between Salesforce.com releases if you wish. Don't feel you have to stay in sync with Salesforce. Update the API version of your application when Force.com incorporates new features that you want to use. Be sure to perform a full QA cycle when you update the API version of your application – that is where you are more likely to see behavior changes in your application (as compared to platform updates where your software stays on the same API version).

Using Salesforce.com Support

The Salesforce platform is large and complex, which means that it, like any large and complex software platform, has bugs. The day may come where you will find one.

Your first step should be to search Google, the appropriate section of the Force.com forums, and salesforce.stackexchange.com to see if anyone else has run into the same problem and has a work-around. Most of the time, this will be the case.

You can speed the search process using SearchTheForce.com, which implements a Google custom search engine across numerous Salesforce related sites[9].

Check the Salesforce known issues site (currently at http://success.salesforce.com/issues_index but you can always just search for "Salesforce known issues") to see if it is a known platform bug.

If you don't find any helpful information (which is more likely if you are using a newer or less frequently used feature on the platform), try the following:

- Find a way to reproduce the issue, preferably on a clean or relatively clean developer org that is dedicated to demonstrating bugs. An SFDX scratch org can work for this as well.
- Document in the simplest possible terms a set of step by step instructions to reproduce the bug. Use screenshots where possible.
- Submit a case. Include the org ID and specify that you have granted Salesforce login access to the developer org where you have reproduced the problem.
- Once again, provide the org ID and specify that you have granted login access, in response to the request for this information that will inevitably come from the person assigned to your case. Don't think about why you are being asked for this again when you included it in the original request, it will just cause you more stress.

---

[9] For the record: SearchTheForce.com is a site that I built and maintain as a service to the community

- Depending on who you are, you may get a response indicating that they really aren't interested in hearing about platform bugs unless you purchase premium support. Whether this is because only people who purchase premium support are capable of finding platform bugs, or due to some other reason, is unknown.

- If you are lucky, you will quickly receive an explanation of an error that you made in your code, and you will somewhat sheepishly thank the support agent and the case will be closed.

- Otherwise, you will wait for a period of time (hours? Days?) and possibly several exchanges while the agent reproduces and comes to understand the problem and is convinced that yes, it is a real problem that should be referred to tier 3 support.

- You will receive a message that your case has been forwarded to tier 3 support and that you will be notified as soon as there is additional information.

- You will receive a message that your case has been forwarded to tier 3 support and that you will be notified as soon as there is additional information.

- You will receive a message that your case has been forwarded to tier 3 support and that you will be notified as soon as there is additional information.

- You will be notified either that the bug you found is either "by design" and is thus a feature, or that it is a bug that they are aware of, so the case will be closed, and you will be notified if it is ever fixed.

- If you are lucky, a known issue will appear. At which time you may as well allow them to close the case, as they've done all they can.

- If you subscribe to the known issue, you will be notified when it is resolved. Otherwise, you will never be notified, even if the bug if fixed.

Ok, I'm being just a little bit mean here. The support agents are actually a very nice group of people. The problem is, they spend a lot of their time answering beginner's issues, and it takes a while for them to sort out tougher problems. That filtering is part of their job, for all that it can be frustrating.

Sometimes, especially if you've identified a bug during the release preview period, you'll get a lot of quick action on a case – as that's the period when they really are trying to track down and solve any breaking changes on the platform.

Sometimes your case will land on the desk of a support agent who is really, really good, who will reproduce the problem in no time and know how to get it to the right people quickly. This is more likely if you have purchased premier support, but can happen even if you haven't.

Keep in mind that this sequence is subject to change at any time, as Salesforce.com support policies do change. If you're curious what kind of support you qualify for, you can always submit a case and find out...

Here's a hint. If you think you've found a real platform bug, at the same time as you submit the case, post a question to the relevant Force.com forum, success community group, and on salesforce.stackexchange.com. Note that you think it may be a platform bug.

If you are lucky, your post will be noticed by someone from Salesforce.com – a number of them monitor the forums. If so, you will have the pleasure of communicating directly with someone who will understand what you are saying, be able to look at and understand your steps to reproduce the problem, and work directly with the people responsible for solving the problem (in fact, he or she may be the person responsible for solving the problem). In that case, not only may you get a forecast for when the problem will be fixed, you may even be notified when it has been fixed and asked to verify if the fix works.

Finally, don't wait for them to solve your problem. It's almost always possible to come up with a workaround.

Conclusion

At the start of this book I made a promise – that it would not be a rehash of the Force.com documentation. I think I've kept that promise. It is my hope that developers at all levels will find this book a good companion to the other developer resources that are available. I know that it is not a replacement for those resources, and that is by intent.

This book contains all of the things that I wish I had known many years ago when I began the transition from part-time Apex consultant to full time Apex application developer. But, like you, I'm still learning. And the platform continues to change. Fortunately, thanks to modern publishing technology, this book can change as well. Many of the things I learned over the past few years have been incorporated into this fourth edition. I have no doubt there will be a fifth someday.

So here is my invitation to you – I would love to hear your view of what topics or contents should go in future editions of the book. I'd also be glad to hear of additional best-practices and design patterns, or even places where you disagree with my conclusions. After all, the term "best practices" only means that set of practices that are, in the opinion of experienced developers, the best ways to solve certain problems.

Contact me via Email at dan@desawarepublishing.com

Or follow me on twitter at @danappleman

Remember you can view any corrections to the book at www.advancedApex.com and download the sample code at www.advancedApex.com/samplecode

Acknowledgements and Dedication

The genesis of this book started in late 2010 in a conversation with George Hu, who was at the time EVP of Platform and Marketing at Salesforce.com, in which one of the topics we discussed was why many developers had a difficult time with limits and what could be done to help them. I wasn't ready to do anything about it at the time, but I never forgot the conversation, and I knew, even then, that when I did have the time and sufficient expertise, that would be the first subject I would want to tackle. Thanks, George.

Others currently or previously at Salesforce.com who helped include Adam Seligman, Steve Bobrowski and Mario Korf, whose enthusiastic support and comments encouraged me to push forward on the way towards publication. Thanks to Michael Floyd for his support on the previous editions. Thanks to Erica Kuhl, Holly Fireston, Mallory Leggere and the entire Salesforce MVP community for your ongoing support and friendship – it is a privilege to be part of the Ohana.

I'm deeply grateful to Don Robins, Adam Purkiss, David Watson, David Claiborne and Jon Kilburn who offered great technical and general feedback.

This book is dedicated to the team at Full Circle Insights. They continue to tolerate me taking time to work on this book while I could have been developing more product features. That said, I do think there is some value in that when people look at our product, our sales people will be able to hold up this book and say: "this is how we built it", and hopefully convey a sense of the effort and technology we put into developing a world-class application. And, if you have moment, point your marketing team to www.fullcircleinsights.com. I think they'll like what they see.

About the cover

Funny story. The first edition cover featured a sign "Caution, Software Ahead" that was a riff on the Salesforce "No Software" logo. What I didn't realize at the time is that when Salesforce said "No Software" they didn't mean no software development (in the sense of you can do your development entirely in the user interface), but no software in the sense of not having to install and maintain software on your machine. Which goes to show that the way marketing messages are interpreted really does depend on the audience. With the Salesforce platform's evolution into a software development platform, that logo, and the first edition cover, were both good candidates for retirement.

The second and third edition used a Penrose triangle, representing something that is very real, but not quite what it seems at first glance – a description that can certainly be applied to Apex as well.

For this edition I'd like to extend my thanks to Maya Peterson, for her interpretation of code in the cloud.

Index

Online Courses by Dan Appleman

Dan Appleman has also published a variety of courses online at Pluralsight.com. These include:

Career Strategies and Opportunities for Salesforce Platform Developers

Force.com and Apex Fundamentals for Developers

Getting Started with JavaScript in Salesforce

Formula Fundamentals in Salesforce

The Future of Technology Careers

The Dark Side of Technology Careers

Keep up with Technology

Career and Survival Strategies for Software Developers

Introduction to Leadership and Management for Developers

So You Want to be an Entrepreneur?

Data Visualization for Developers

Pluralsight also offers many additional Salesforce courses by well-known experts in the field including David Liu, Sara Morgan Nettles, Chuck Liddell, Scott Wells, Bonny Hinners, Phil Weinmeister, Scott Lee, Mike Topalovich, Jeff Susich, Matthew Morris, Steve Drucker, Peter Tempfli, Matt Kaufman, Richard Seroter, Adam olshansky, Carl Brundage, Don Robins and more.

PLURALSIGHT

Visit Pluralsight.com for more information and to obtain a free trial subscription.

Impress a marketing friend today!
Tell a marketer about
Full Circle Insights
and be their hero.

Recommend Full Circle Insights, a best-in-class
Apex application that extends marketing
campaign visibility in Salesforce.

With Full Circle Insights you can know which
marketing campaigns really work because the
data can finally make sense.

Drive more revenue. Plan with confidence.
- Closed-loop Funnel Visibility and Metrics
- Multi-touch Campaign Attribution
- Response Lifecycle Management

Share this link with a marketer and they will thank you:
www.FullCircleInsights.com/Apex

Also from Desaware Publishing:

In addition to developing software, Dan Appleman has spent over 25 years volunteering with a youth leadership program. If you have teens, work with them, or even manage a software development team, you'll learn valuable leadership skills and how to teach them with this unique book.

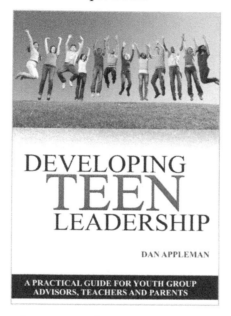

Not long ago, all it took to have a comfortable career was to do well in high school, get a college degree, and find a nice stable job. But today, good grades are not enough.

But there remain endless opportunities for those with real leadership skills - regardless of career choice.

Developing Teen Leadership covers virtually every topic today's parents, teachers and youth advisors need to help teens gain the leadership skills they will need in today's rapidly changing world.

www.teenleadershipbook.com

Made in the USA
Columbia, SC
16 September 2020